D1542229

Christ

teaches us

today

Mark J. Link, S.J.

LOYOLA UNIVERSITY PRESS
Chicago 60657

Imprimi potest John R. Connery, S.J., Provincial of the Chicago
Province, February 4, 1964. Nihil obstat John B. Amberg, S.J.,
censor deputatus, February 7, 1964. Imprimatur Most Reverend
Cletus F. O'Donnell, J.C.D., Vicar General, Archdiocese of
Chicago, February 10, 1964. The nihil obstat and imprimatur
are official declarations that a book or pamphlet is free of doctrinal or moral error. No implication is contained therein that
those who have granted the nihil obstat and imprimatur agree
with the contents, opinions, or statements expressed.

PREFACE

Christ Teaches Us Today has four goals. First, it aims at preparing the student to meet Christ in the proclamation of the Holy Scriptures at Mass. ". . . it is he [Christ] himself who speaks when the Holy Scriptures are read in the Church." (Second Vatican Council). Christ Teaches Us Today is a handbook to God's textbook, the Bible. It must never become more than that. It seeks to prepare the student to understand, appreciate, and respond in mature faith to God's self revelation, especially, in Jesus Christ.

Second, this book aims at preparing the student to meet Christ in the liturgy. Through the liturgy "we come in contact with Christ and receive from Him living vitality as do branches from the tree and members from the head." (Mystici Corporis). Toward this end Christ Teaches Us Today introduces the student to the liturgy through a presentation that is both gradual and in prayerful harmony with the liturgical seasons.

Third, this book aims at preparing the student to live Christ in daily life. Toward this end it encourages a maximum of guided class discussion and personal student reflection on the implications and implementations of Christ's teaching in daily life.

Finally, this book aims at leading the student to a deeper appreciation of doctrinal points that now begin to emerge in his study of Christ's teaching. They are taken up gradually and as they naturally emerge from the unfolding of God's plan of love for his people.

Christ Teaches Us Today is still experimental in format and content. It is hoped that wider experimentation, facilitated by this publication, will develop it into a dynamic instrument for bringing Christ to young men and women. Toward this end the author invites a pooling of teacher insights and suggestions.

Book II, We Live in Christ, is in preparation and scheduled for wider experimental release in the summer of 1965.

Special attention is called to the table of visual aids. A procedure of interrogation accompanies many of the aids as they occur in the text. Further information will be found in the teacher's manual.

Special attention is called to the Study Index in the back of the book. It has been designed to help the student to review and to guide the teacher in presenting, discussing, and reviewing biblical, liturgical, and doctrinal themes. As such, it becomes an invaluable aid to both student and teacher.

Resurrection of our Lord   M.J.L.
March 29, 1964

table of contents

Table of visual aids

Acknowledgments

Confraternity of Christian Doctrine, Washington, D.C., for
    quotations from the Old Testament
Bruce Publishing Company, Milwaukee, Wisconsin, for quota-
    tions from the Kleist-Lilly translation of the New Testament
The publisher is grateful to Helicon Press, Inc., Baltimore,
    Maryland, for permission to use Mass prayers from the
    Layman's Missal, Prayer Book and Ritual.

Photo credits

E. Lettau, Farmingdale, New York, frontispiece and page 174
Brebeuf Preparatory School, Indianapolis, Indiana, page 2
St. Gregory High School, Chicago, Illinois, pages 17, 136, 262
Union Pacific Railroad, page 41
St. Ignatius High School, Chicago, Illinois, page 154
Hartford Catholic Transcript, page 184
Algimantas Kezys, S.J., pages 208, 234
Notre Dame University, Notre Dame, Indiana, page 253

O Lord . . .
guide me in your truth
and teach me
for you are God
my savior. Psalm 24:4-5

Christ wants to speak to you

The key event of your life happened, perhaps, without your knowing it. This was the coming of Christ into your soul at baptism. Later, you discovered Christ for the first time--probably while listening to a story from the Bible. From that time on, Christ was someone important in your life.

When you grew older you began to go to church. One day as you knelt before the Blessed Sacrament, a fascinating idea formed in your mind: Christ is extraordinarily different from other people. Christ is God.

When you grew still older you discovered something else about Christ. Though he is completely different from other people, he is not far away from you. He is someone friendly and close--closer than even your best friend. Christ is someone you can talk to and be with always.

Now that you are becoming an adult you are going to make even richer discoveries about Christ. These will come at unpredictable times and in unpredictable places. They may come when you are in the midst of a cheering crowd, when you are alone by yourself, or when you are prayerfully attending Mass. There is no rule.

Christ wants to speak to you. He will speak to you. He has a message for you and a role that he wants you to begin playing in the spread of his kingdom. You are on the brink of a new adventure with Christ.

1

Look to him
that you may be
radiant with joy.
Psalm 33:6

1

CHRIST TODAY

1 Christ attracts men today

Every high-school student knows what a hero or leader is. He is a person everyone likes and wants to be like. He is someone who dares to be different and to stand up for what he thinks is right when everyone else is afraid to.

Contrary to what people think, heroes and leaders are not born; they are made. Every high-school student has a capacity for heroism and leadership. It is just a question of developing it.

What makes a person a hero or a leader? How does a high-school student develop his or her powers of heroism and leadership? These are questions we now explore.

Christ is the greatest hero

Of all the world's heroes and leaders, none has ever measured up to Christ. Christ stood head and shoulders above the men of his time--even his enemies, the Pharisees, admitted this. Let us read in the Bible where this is taught us.

The next day, the common people
who had come to celebrate the feast,
on hearing that Jesus was coming to Jerusalem,
provided themselves with branches
from the palm trees nearby,
and went out to meet him, shouting:
    "Hosanna! A blessing on him
    who is coming in the name of the Lord,
    who is also Israel's King!" . . .
    The Pharisees then said among themselves . . .
"Look, the whole world is running after him!" John 12:12-13, 19

Christ still attracts men

Today Christ still attracts men. His message is translated
into hundreds of languages. Christ himself is the world's most
written-about man. His life is the subject of countless books.
He is loved the world over as no other man is loved.

In an article called "The Three Greatest Men," historian
H. G. Wells says, "Now it is interesting and significant that
. . . a historian like myself, who doesn't even call himself a
Christian," should name Christ as history's greatest man.

Speaking about Christ's teaching, Wells says, "He spoke with
a knowledge and authority that baffled the wise." His message
triggered "one of the most revolutionary changes of outlook that
has ever stirred and changed human thought."

What makes Jesus Christ different from all other men in
history? Why does he still have such an impact upon the minds
and hearts of men, even today?

The answer is clear. Christ is no mere man; he is the Son of
God. He is the Redeemer promised by God who brought salvation
to the world by his life, death, and resurrection.

Christ has a twofold impact on men

Because Christ is God, his impact on people surpasses that
of all other leaders. Other human leaders and heroes can only
stir men's hearts; they cannot enter men's souls. Christ can do
both. By the example of his heroic life, Christ can stir men's
hearts. By the power of his divine life (grace), Christ can enter
men's souls and plant in them the seeds of his own life and power.

Because he is God, Christ can transform men and lead them
to heights of heroism and greatness they never dreamed possible.

4

BIBLE MESSAGE

Christ today.   Imagine that you are part of the crowd going to meet Jesus on the first Palm Sunday. A group of Pharisees grab you and ask you why you are a follower of Christ.

1 What would you say? 2 How does Christ's impact on men today surpass that of other leaders?

LITURGY & LIFE

1 Christ is king.   When Christ came riding into Jerusalem, the people shouted, "Hosanna! A blessing on him who is coming in the name of the Lord, who is also Israel's king!"

What Mass prayer is similar to this shout? What would we say today in place of "Hosanna"?

2 Christ is leader.   The Duke of Wellington once said that Napoleon's personal presence on the battlefield was equal to 40,000 men.

Discuss: a) the meaning of Wellington's statement, b) the qualities that make up a good leader, c) how Christ has these qualities, d) how a high-school student can learn about leadership and heroism from Christ.

3 Christ is friend.   A recent book about Christ has an interesting title. It is called A Most Perfect Friend.

Discuss: a) the qualities that go to make up a good friend, b) how Christ has these qualities, c) how a high-school student can learn about true friendship from Christ.

4 Talk to Christ.   Contacting Christ need not be a solemn affair. In fact, at times, it is better if it isn't. Here is how one writer suggests going about it.

Go into church and make yourself comfortable. You are with your best friend. Then begin to tell him about your life. For example, tell him about your interests, the friends you have, what you and your friends do and talk about. Tell him how much time you spend helping others, how much time you give to your studies, how much time you give to him. After that ask him, "Lord, what do you think of my life?" Then just listen.

What is prayer? Does Christ "talk" to us in prayer? Write out a prayer talk to Christ. Center it around one point. For example, you might thank Christ for something special, ask him for help with a problem, express sorrow for failing to be as loyal to him as you could be, or just tell him what you think of him as a divine friend and leader.

5 Christ is God.   To show that Christ is both human and divine, ancient artists sometimes drew Christ larger than normal men. Recently a modern artist returned to this practice when he painted "The Baptism of Jesus" for a church in Germany.

Why do you think the artist returned to this ancient practice for this particular painting? Read John 3:30. Discuss the size of the dove. What do the white rays behind Christ stand for? Read Matthew 3:16. Discuss ways you have seen Christ depicted in art or the movies. Why is it hard to depict Christ.

Of him there must be more and more;
there must be less and less of me.   John 3:30

DOCTRINAL POINTS

Jesus Christ is God and man

Christ is God from eternity. He is man, however, only from the time of his Incarnation in the womb of the Virgin Mary. Christ as man is like us in all things except sin. Hebrews 4:15. That is, he has a human body, a human soul, a human will, and whatever else pertains to man.

Christ has two natures

Because Christ is truly God and truly man, he has two natures: a divine nature and a human nature. These two natures are not mixed into one, but remain distinct. Christ also has two wills: a divine will and a human will. In the agony in the garden he prayed to his Father, "May your will, not mine, be done!" Luke 22:42. Christ thus showed he had a human will. It was, however, always conformed to his divine will.

Christ also had a twofold knowledge: human and divine. As God he knew all things. As man he had the ordinary human knowledge obtained by experience and study. In addition, he had the Beatific Vision and infused knowledge. Though Christ had the Beatific Vision, it was suspended so that he could suffer. Thus he felt the pangs of hunger, grew thirsty, and got tired. He even was subject to painful wounds and death.

In his soul Christ felt joy, sadness, fear, and anger; but he could not sin. He loved his friends with a human as well as a divine love; he wept over the fate of Jerusalem and at the tomb of Lazarus. He appreciated favors and felt the sting of unkindness.

Christ is only one person

Though Christ has two separate natures, he is only one person: the only-begotten Son of God. He is a divine person. We can get a faint inkling of the mystery of the union of Christ's two natures in one divine person by recalling that we ourselves have a mixed nature. That is, we have a body and a soul, and so are partly corporal and partly spiritual. We perform spiritual actions like thinking up ideas; we perform corporal actions like building rockets. And yet we are not two persons but only one. But here the comparison stops because we have only one composite nature and not two--as Christ has.

7

We adore the whole Christ

Because Christ is a divine person, we adore him. We adore
not just a portion of Christ, but the whole Christ. This includes
Christ's human nature and his human body, which are inseparably
united to his divinity. Since Christ's body is worthy of adoration,
so also is his heart, which is a part of his body and united to his
divinity. There is a special reason, too, why we should worship
the Sacred Heart of Jesus. It is a symbol of his divine and human
love for us.

Study questions

"Know Christ well and it matters not if you know nothing besides," said St. Peter Canisius. 1 What did he mean? 2 Discuss
Christ's: a) Incarnation, b) two natures, c) divine personality,
and d) Sacred Heart as a symbol of his love for us.

2 Christ remains on earth today

In our opening lesson we caught a glimpse of Christ's magnetic
personality. We saw that after 2,000 years he still attracts men.
We learned that one of the reasons for this is that Christ is not
only man but also God. But there is still another reason for
Christ's continued influence over men. It is this. Christ is still
on earth today.

In order that we may better understand how Christ remains
on earth today, let us go back and review how Christ lived on
earth in gospel times.

Christ lived on earth with a human body

Christ lived on earth in gospel times with a human body. People saw his sun-tanned face, heard his clear voice, and felt the
warmth of his strong hands. St. Matthew sums all this up in a
passage in his Gospel.

And so Jesus toured the whole of Galilee,
instructing the people in their synagogues
and preaching the Good News of the kingdom,
besides healing every disease
and every infirmity found among his countrymen.
The result was that the report about him spread. Matthew 4:23-24

Today Christ remains on earth by his mystical body

Today Christ is still on earth. Moreover, he is present in a
way that is as real as when he lived in Galilee 2,000 years ago.

Before ascending to his Father, Jesus promised his followers
that, although he was now going to the Father, he would, nevertheless, always remain with them. When Jesus promised this no
one understood what he meant. Only later, when his followers
were suffering persecution, did the meaning become clear. It
happened like this.

One of the leaders of the persecution, a man named Saul, was
on his way to Damascus when "suddenly a light from the sky flashed round about him, and falling to the ground, he heard a voice
saying to him, 'Saoul, Saoul, why do you persecute me?' 'Who
are you, Lord?' he asked. Jesus replied, 'I am Jesus whom you
are persecuting.'" Acts 9:4-5.

Saul didn't understand. As far as he was concerned, he had
never persecuted Jesus; he had only persecuted his followers.
What did the mysterious voice mean?

Christ and his followers form one body

The answer to Saul's question came after his conversion. En-
lightened by the Holy Spirit, Saul slowly began to see that Christ
and his followers form one body. They are united much as the
parts of the human body are united into one being. Romans 12:4-5.
We call this body Christ's mystical body, the Church.

Christ is the head of the body

Christ is the head of the body formed by him and his followers.
It is he who forms the members into one body, directs them, and
makes them live. "He is the head of his body, the Church." Colossians 1:18.

Thus it is clear how Christ remains on earth today. He remains on earth in and through his mystical body, the Church.

Christ is the vine; we are the branches

How is it possible for Christ and the members of his Church to form one body? We do not know. But Christ may have given us a hint when he said, "I am the vine, you are the branches." John 15:5. Somewhat as branches are separate but yet united into one plant by the vine, so all Christians are separate but united into one body by Christ.

The same Christ

The Christ who remains on earth today in his mystical body and the Christ who lived 2,000 years ago in Galilee are not two different persons. They are the same. Christ so willed it, says Pope Pius XII, that the same life which he began in his "mortal body should continue without intermission down the ages in his mystical body." The Church is Christ remaining on earth until the end of time.

BIBLE MESSAGE

Christ remains on earth today.   The Bible refers to the union between Christ and the members of his mystical body by using several vivid comparisons. This union is like: 1) the union between members of a family (Romans 8:16); 2) a vine and its branches (John 15:4-5); 3) parts of the same body (Romans 12:4-5); 4) a body and life in the body (John 6:56-58); 5) building stones and the building they make up (Ephesians 2:20-22); 6) the persons of the Holy Trinity (John 17:21).
    1 Show how each of these biblical images is similar to but different from the union that exists between Christ and his followers. 2 What is Christ's role in this union?

LITURGY & LIFE

1 Christ's mystical body.   The author of a book on the mystical body says, "That Christ is on earth in the Holy Eucharist the Catholic believes. But that he is on earth in another way we do not always realize."
    If you polled the Catholics of your parish about Christ's presence on earth today, what answer do you think they would give?

How would you go about explaining to them how Christ is also present through his mystical body?

2 Our union with Christ.   We know by faith that when we go to Holy Communion we enter into closer union with Christ and the other members of his mystical body. Someone has suggested that the act of receiving Holy Communion is an apt symbol of our union with Christ, while the act of receiving Holy Communion in a group is an apt symbol of our union with the other members of the mystical body.

What is a symbol? How are the two acts mentioned above symbolic of our closer union with: a) Christ, and b) the other members of the mystical body?

3 Picturing Christ's mystical body.   To picture Christ's mystical body, some artists show Christ's head joined to a body made up of many little people. Some people make up Christ's arms, others his feet, and so on.

List and discuss the advantages and disadvantages of showing Christ's mystical body this way. How else might artists picture the mystical body of Christ?

DOCTRINAL POINTS

The Church is Christ's mystical body

By his death and resurrection Christ merited for us a treasury of grace. Christ could have given us all of this grace directly, but he decided otherwise. "He willed to do this by means of a visible Church in which men would be united, and through which they would cooperate with Him in distributing the divine fruits of Redemption." So wrote Pope Pius XII in his encyclical, Mystici Corporis.

The Church is a visible body

The pope continues. "That the Church is a body we find asserted again and again in the Sacred Scriptures . . . Now if the Church is a body it must be something one and undivided . . . it must also be something concrete and visible." Like its head, who has both an invisible divine nature and a visible human nature, the Church has both an invisible inner life and a visible external structure. All members profess the same faith, share the same sacrifice and sacraments, keep the same laws, and recognize the same head.

The members of Christ's body have different functions. "Just as in nature a body does not consist of an indiscriminate heap of members, but must be provided with organs," each of which performs its own service, so it is with the mystical body. The pope continues, quoting St. Paul, "'As in one body we have many members, but all the members have not the same office; so we, being many, are one body in Christ; and every one members of one another.'" Romans 12:4.

Christ's members help one another

"But a body requires a number of members so connected that they help one another. And, in fact, as in our mortal organism when one member suffers the others suffer with it, and the healthy members come to the assistance of those that are ailing, so in the Church individual members do not live only for themselves but also help their fellow members, all cooperating with one another for their mutual support."

Finally, just as the human body "has its own means for fostering life, health, and growth of itself and each of its members," so "the Savior of the human race in His infinite goodness has in like manner admirably equipped His mystical body by endowing it with the Sacraments." These sacraments make "available for its members a progressive series of graces to sustain them from the cradle to their last breath." Moreover, they provide "also for the social needs of the whole body."

The name, mystical body

The name mystical body does not appear in the Bible. It appears for the first time in the fourth-century writings of St. John Chrysostom. Oddly enough, the saint uses the term to refer to the Blessed Sacrament. Not until the thirteenth century is the expression used to designate the one body formed by Christ and the members of his Church.

The term mystical body serves several useful purposes. First of all, it reminds us that the Church is totally different from any other organization we know. For example, it is not like a political party or labor union. In fact, it is not an organization at all. It is an organism: something that lives as one being. It is the body of Christ

The expression also keeps us from confusing Christ's mystical body with the Eucharistic Body of Christ, which we receive in Holy Communion. Finally, the expression keeps us from confusing Christ's mystical body with his glorious (flesh and blood) body in heaven.

Christ's human body was born on the first Christmas. On that day he became like us to redeem us. Christ's Eucharistic Body was instituted at the Last Supper. At that moment he became our food. Christ's mystical body was perfected and manifested for the first time on Pentecost. On that day he became our head.

Study questions

On the backs of United States coins is written "E Pluribus Unum" (One from Many). 1 How is this also true of the Church? 2 What difference is there between the United States and Christ's mystical body? 3 Can we see Christ's mystical body? 4 Do all members have the same office? 5 Do members live only for themselves? 6 How are the members, individually and collectively, preserved in life and health? 7 What useful purposes does the term mystical body serve?

3 Christ acts in men's lives today

In our last lesson we saw that Christ is still on earth today. We saw that he remains on earth not through his human body but through his mystical body. In this lesson we will see that Christ also acts in men's lives today. To understand how Christ does this, it will help to go back and review how Christ acted in men's lives in gospel times.

How Christ acted in gospel times

Christ acted in gospel times through the members of his human body. With the touch of his own hand, he healed the sick.

13

With the words of his own voice, he forgave men and taught them the meaning of Sacred Scripture. Let us read how the Gospel records this.

On the Sabbath, he went . . . to the synagogue
and stood up to read.
A scroll of the prophet Isaias was handed him,
and, after unrolling the scroll,
he came upon the place
where the following text occurs:
  "The Spirit of the Lord rests upon me,
because he has anointed me.
He has appointed me a messenger
to bring the Good News to the humble;
to announce release to captives,
and recovery of sight to the blind;
to set the oppressed at liberty;
to proclaim a year of grace
ordained by the Lord."
  He then rolled up the scroll and . . . sat down.
The eyes of everyone in the synagogue
were fixed upon him,
and he proceeded to speak to them:
  "Today the Scripture text you have just heard
has been fulfilled."
  Everyone . . . was charmed by the winning words
that fell from his lips . . ." Luke 4:16-22

Christ acts today, especially in the liturgy

Today Christ still acts in men's lives. He does this every day and in different ways. There are, however, times when Christ acts in men's lives in a way that surpasses all others.

The first of these is at Mass. At Mass not only the priest but the whole congregation is a sign of Christ's special presence and action. For each member of the congregation is a member of Christ's mystical body and, therefore, united to and sharing in the offering of Christ their head. Christ acts, however, in a special way through the priest. For the priest alone is ordained to act as Christ's official representative.

Secondly, Christ acts in men's lives in a special way in the sacraments. Thus, when the priest absolves in confession, it is really Christ acting through the priest who forgives. John 20:21-23.

14

Finally, Christ acts in a special way during the celebration of the Divine Office: The Divine Office is the official prayer of the mystical body. It is made in the name of the whole Church by specially designated members.

Because Christ acts in a special way in the celebration of the Mass, the sacraments, and the Divine Office, we give these actions a special name. We call them liturgical actions or the liturgy.

Christ's action in the liturgy is twofold

By the liturgical actions of his mystical body, Christ continues the twofold work that he began in gospel times: 1) he sanctifies men, and 2) he glorifies his Father.

We may draw this parallel. As Christ acted in a visible manner in gospel times by the personal actions of his human body, so Christ acts today in a visible manner by the liturgical actions of his mystical body.

As members of Christ's mystical body, we can share in the action of our head. Through the Mass and the sacraments we can join Christ in his work of sanctifying men and glorifying the Father.

We may define the liturgy as those privileged actions of the mystical body, head and members, wherein Christ continues today to sanctify men and to glorify his Father.

BIBLE MESSAGE

Christ acts today. "He then rolled up the scroll and . . . sat down." Luke 4:20. 1 Why didn't Jesus read from a book? 2 When and how does Christ act, in a special way, in men's lives today? 3 What name do we give to these actions? 4 What twofold work does Christ continue in these actions? 5 Why and how can we share in Christ's twofold work?

LITURGY & LIFE

1 Christ teaches at Mass. In the gospel passage cited, St. Luke describes Christ as, first, reading a passage from Holy Scripture and, then, explaining the meaning of the passage to the people.

Of what part of the Mass does this remind you? Compare Christ's actions then to what the priest does today.

2 Christ offers himself at Mass.   A World War II soldier wrote this memorable experience in his diary:

When I jumped from the landing barge the sea was already frothing with blood, oil, and debris. I waded through the water and I hit the beach. Inch by inch, I wormed my way inland.

Later--forty long hours! Still on the alert! How much can a guy take? My ears feel like a drum.

Later--Finally! A relief squad! Someone reminds me that it is Sunday. (I had forgotten.) He says Mass will be said two miles down the road. Through the mud and rain I slog. I get there just as Father Fabian bends down to say the Confiteor.

Mass goes on. My foggy mind clears a bit. Then Father Fabian comes to the Consecration. As he bends over the altar something flashes inside me. I realize something tremendous--it isn't just Father Fabian up at the altar who is offering this great sacrifice. It is Christ acting through Father Fabian.

Why do you think the soldier went to Mass during the precious time he had off? Why do you think men in the battlefield begin to realize for the first time truths they have held all their lives? What does it mean to realize something?

3 We offer ourselves with Christ.   A British priest said, "The dialogue Mass is not a device to keep us busy or to help us follow the Mass. It is to make us conscious of what we really are at Mass: Christ's mystical body, offering ourselves with Christ to the Father."

How does the dialogue Mass help us realize what we are at Mass? Why is it difficult to realize what we are at Mass?

4 Prayer of the mystical body.   Twenty miles outside Cedar Rapids, Iowa, a pickup truck pulled off the road and parked. "O.K., fellows," yelled a voice to twenty boy scouts in the back, "get out your rosaries. I have to finish my Office."

Minutes later Father F. Joyce was seated on the front bumper under one of the headlights saying Vespers. At the end of the first psalm a diesel pulled alongside. "Having trouble, neighbor," came a voice from the cab. "No, nothing wrong," replied the priest. The truck driver eyed him suspiciously. "Whatcha doin' then?" "Just reading," said the priest. There was a grunt and a crashing of gears as the diesel pulled away. The priest smiled at the driver's parting remark, "Must be a darn good book!"

Why is the priest's breviary a darn good book? Of what kind of prayers is the breviary largely composed?

The Church's liturgical year

Whether you are at Mass or in class, whether you are watching TV or a lab experiment, Christ is interested in what you are doing. Because you are a member of his mystical body, you are intimately united to him every moment of the day. He is ever-present and ever-acting in your life.

Yet there is one time during the day when Christ wishes to act in your life in a special way. This is in the Mass.

The Mass is the "memorial of the Lord"

When Christ took bread and wine at the Last Supper and changed them into his body and his blood, he told his apostles, "Do this as my memorial." Luke 22:17. Since then the members of Christ's mystical body have joyfully carried out this sacred act which we call the Mass.

Because the Mass is a sacred act, we surround it with prayer and reverence. It would be possible to celebrate Mass--"the memorial of the Lord"--always in the same way and with the same prayers. But "memorial of the Lord" is so rich that it is impossible for our finite minds to grasp it all at once. Thus, guided by the Holy Spirit, the Church has adopted the practice of focusing on one aspect of the "memorial of the Lord" in each Mass. Thus each feast day Mass, while recalling the entire memory of the Lord, highlights in particular one special mystery in Christ's life. Out of this practice has grown the Church's liturgical year.

The liturgical year is composed of sacred seasons: Advent, Christmastide, Time after Epiphany, Septuagesima, Lent, Eastertide, and the Time after Pentecost.

Each season recalls a different aspect of the memory of the Lord. Thus by recalling the different mysteries, the Church enables us to take part in them and to offer them in worship to almighty God at Mass.

The liturgical year brings us into contact with Christ

But the liturgical year is not just a celebration of past events. At Mass we really come in contact with the mysteries of Christ and receive from them special graces corresponding to our needs and to the feasts being celebrated. Said Pope Pius XII: "The liturgical year . . . is not a cold lifeless representation of the events of the past . . . It is rather Christ Himself who is ever living in His Church . . . Each mystery brings its own special grace for our salvation.

"Through the liturgical year," continues Pope Pius XII, "we come in contact with Christ and receive from Him living vitality as branches do from the tree and members from the head."

We may define the liturgical year as the systematic, sacramental reliving and reoffering of the mysteries of salvation by Christ and the members of his mystical body.

Study questions

Explain the statement that "A liturgical feast cannot be anything that is not already contained in the Mass." Show how "the Mass has been like the grain of mustard seed from which has sprung the whole liturgy of the Church." Construct a liturgical calendar; list on it the major events of the school year.

Christ teaches today

In Christ's time every Jewish town had a synagogue. It was a place of instruction presided over by a rabbi (teacher). The synagogue service consisted of hymns, prayers, readings from the Bible, and a commentary on the Bible readings.

Today Jews have basically the same synagogue service. Many modern Protestant services are also patterned on the synagogue service: hymns, prayers, Bible reading, and a sermon. The Catholic Church, too, has retained certain features of the synagogue service. This is evident in the first part of the Mass, called the Liturgy of the Word or the Mass of the Catechumens. In the early Church, catechumens were permitted to attend the Mass of the Catechumens, to learn the faith, but they were not allowed to remain for the sacrifice. They had to leave at the beginning of the Offertory.

The Liturgy of the Word is the school of Christ

In attending Mass we should keep in mind the importance of the first part of the Mass. It has been rightly called the "school of Christ," for during this part of the Mass Christ, through his mystical body, continues to teach us.

St. Augustine said, "Let us listen to the Gospel as if the Lord Himself stood before us." More recently a theologian of our time said, "It is the living Christ Himself who speaks to us when the Scriptures are read and the homily is preached, even though He uses the voice of ministers." Both of these men are echoing Christ's words to his disciples, ". . . who listens to you listens to me . . ." Luke 10:16.

This is why we listen to the Gospel and Epistle being read at Mass in a way entirely different from the way we listen to a TV talk or to a classroom lecture. In a TV talk or lecture, only a man--regardless of how intelligent he is--talks to us. In the Mass it is Christ who speaks to us through his representative.

How to listen to the Gospel and Epistle at Mass

Because it is Christ himself who speaks to us when the Holy Scripture is read at Mass, we listen to it with a special openness of heart. This openness implies a humble recognition that the priest is, at that moment, Christ's divinely appointed spokesman. It, also, implies a generous willingness to follow whatever inspiration the Holy Spirit might plant in our hearts at this time.

Study questions

Discuss: a) the Jewish synagogue service, b) the Liturgy of the Word as the "school of Christ," c) how we should listen to Holy Scripture being read at Mass.

". . . it is he [Christ]
himself who speaks
when the Holy Scriptures
are read in the Church."
Second Vatican Council

2

CHRIST TEACHES US ABOUT GOD'S PLAN

1 Christ teaches us today through the Bible

In the last chapter we saw that Christ still attracts men after
2,000 years. We saw the reasons for this: 1) Christ is God,
2) Christ is still on earth, and 3) Christ still acts in men's lives.
    Among the ways Christ still acts in men's lives today is to
teach them about his Father. Christ does this not through the
voice of his human body but through the voice of his mystical
body, the Church.
    In this chapter we will begin to make a study of the textbook
that Christ uses to teach men today. This textbook is the Bible.
Let us read how St. Paul describes the Bible in a letter to Timothy.

> . . . from your infancy you have known the Sacred Writings.
> They can instruct you for salvation through the faith
> which is in Christ Jesus. All Scripture is inspired by God
> and useful for teaching, for reproving,
> for correcting, for instructing in holiness,
> that the man of God may be perfect,
> fully equipped for every good deed. 2 Timothy 3:15-17

The Bible is different

The Bible is the record of God's dealings with men. Because the Bible records God's dealings with men, it is sometimes called sacred history.

Unlike other books relating real events, the Bible's purpose is not so much to tell what happened many years ago as to tell what God wanted to teach by these happenings. John 12:14-17. Since God's activity always has in mind man's salvation, the Bible is also called salvation history.

The Bible is divinely inspired

Because the Bible is different from other books, it is not surprising to learn that it was written in a different way. It was written under God's inspiration. This means that God guided the biblical writers in such a way that they wrote down all and only what he wanted them to write. Since every page of the Bible was written entirely under God's inspiration, he is its principal author; and the Bible is truly God's Word.

The Bible is humanly expressed

When God moved the sacred writers to write, he did so in a way that left them free to use their own language, style, and idiom. Thus we find some authors writing in Greek, some in Hebrew, and others in Aramaic.

In the same way we find the sacred writers using different literary forms to record God's Word. For example, some used hymns (Luke 1:68-70), prayers (Luke 11:2-4), and parables (Luke 15:11 ff.). Some used sermons (Matthew 5) and family trees (Matthew 1:1-16). Others used letters (St. Paul). Some even used pagan sayings (Proverbs 22:17-24:22).

Since the sacred writers were free to use their own language, style, and idiom, they are also true authors of the Bible, but not in the primary sense that God is.

The Bible is sometimes hard to understand

Because many authors helped to record God's Word, the 72 books of the Bible sometimes appear to be a hodge-podge of overlapping facts and stories. This is only on the surface. Actually the books of the Bible fit together into a unified whole. Each contributes in some special way to the revelation of the mystery of God's love for man. It is our job to discover how they do this.

This job is not always easy. Nor is this surprising when we recall the unfamiliar expressions the writers used, the strange cultures from which they came, and the times in which they wrote. Occasionally not even scholars can agree completely on the exact purpose or meaning of certain parts of the Bible.

The Holy Spirit helps us

To guide us in such cases, Christ gave to the teaching members of his mystical body the promise of guidance by the Holy Spirit. John 14:26. This does not mean that the Holy Spirit immediately reveals to them the true meaning. On the contrary, Christ's teaching members must laboriously study and weigh the findings of biblical experts, language professors, archeologists, and other scholars. Then when they come to make the final decision, they have Christ's promise that the Holy Spirit will keep them from error if it regards faith or morals.

God guides his Church today somewhat as he guided the sacred writers centuries ago. Though he gives them special graces to protect them from errors in matters of faith and morals, he calls upon them to use all the natural helps at their disposal. God does not destroy nature, he builds on it.

BIBLE MESSAGE

Christ teaches us today. In its pronouncement on the sacred liturgy, the Second Vatican Council said, ". . . it is he [Christ] himself who speaks when the Holy Scriptures are read in the Church."

1 Explain how Christ still teaches men today. 2 What is the Bible? 3 Make a diagram to show how the following fit together: Old Testament, New Testament, Gospels, Acts of the Apostles, Epistles, and the Apocalypse. 4 How does the Bible's purpose differ from other books dealing with real events? 5 What do you mean when you say the Bible is inspired? 6 Why is God the principal author? 7 How are men also the authors of the Bible? 8 List some literary forms they used. 9 By whom and from what kind of errors is the Church safeguarded in interpreting the Bible? 10 Compare the guidance God gives his Church in interpreting the Bible to that given the sacred writers in recording it.

1 Christ teaches through the Bible.   In your missal check
the prayer that the priest says before he reads the Gospel. In it
he asks God to cleanse his heart and his lips with a live coal,
just as the angel did the lips of the prophet Isaia. Isaia 6:6.
   Why do you think the priest says this prayer at that moment?
How does the server's response before and after the Gospel at-
test to the Church's faith that it is Christ who speaks to us when
the Bible is read at Mass?

2 Honoring the Bible.   The Bible is honored in many ways
during the celebration of the liturgy. This is especially true
during a solemn high Mass. With the aid of your missal, list the
ways the Church honors the Bible at liturgical functions.
   How is the Bible frequently honored at civic functions?

3 Reading the Bible.   Just before his martyrdom in Rome, St.
Peter got the word that false teachers were undermining the faith
of Christians in Asia Minor. They were doing this by twisting the
meaning of Christ's teaching in the letters (Epistles) of St. Paul.
St. Peter immediately wrote the Christians a letter of warning.
A part of it reads, "In his [St. Paul's] letters there are some passages hard to understand. The unlearned and unsteady twist the
meaning of these to their own destruction, as they do also the
other Scriptures." 2 Peter 3:16.
   Explain St. Peter's statement. List reasons why the Bible is
sometimes hard to understand.

4 Literary forms in the Bible.   A good example of a literary
form is the parable. It has been well described by Life magazine
as an "earthly story with a heavenly meaning." Perhaps the one
who made the best use of this way of teaching was Christ, himself.
Reread the parable of the Prodigal Son. Luke 15:11 ff.
   Put in your own words the "earthly story" that Christ tells here.
What is the "heavenly meaning" of Christ's story? Do you think
this story actually happened, or do you think that Christ just
made it up to teach a truth about his Father? Compose a "modern"
parable of your own to teach this same truth.

5 Salvation history in the Bible.   Recently a writer pointed
out that there are "many ways of writing history, and all of them
valid." Take a historical event like the Civil War. A historian

who is writing the church history of the United States will give
this event much less prominence than a historian writing the
political history of the United States.

Now in the same way the Bible historian is mainly interested
not in political events but salvation events. Moreover, he will
describe these events so as to bring out this aspect. Thus in
recording the Hebrew exodus from Egypt, the sacred writer was
not interested in Egyptian politics or the name of Pharao. He
was mainly interested in the fact that God freed the Hebrews.
Everything else was incidental.

Why is the Bible called salvation history? Explain the writer's
statement that there are "many ways of writing history, and all of
them valid." Illustrate with an example of your own.

DOCTRINAL POINTS

Inspiration and revelation

God inspired the Bible. St. Paul tells us this in 2 Timothy 3:
16-17. "All Scripture is inspired by God and useful for teaching,
for reproving, for correcting, for instructing in holiness, that the
man of God may be perfect, fully equipped for every good deed."

Divine inspiration

For Jews the word inspired meant "breathed by God." For
them, both God's own life and his giving of life were symbolized
by his breath. "For the spirit of God has made me, the breath
of the Almighty keeps me alive." Job 33:4. Thus to say that the
Scriptures were inspired was to say that they were composed by
someone under God's life-giving power.

Pope Leo XIII sums this up saying, "By His supernatural
power God excited and moved the human authors to write, and
assisted them in the writing with the result that they conceived
rightly in their mind, and willed faithfully to write down, and
actually did express with infallible truth everything and only
those things which He commanded."

Divine revelation

It is most important not to confuse the notion of divine inspiration with that of divine revelation. Whereas inspiration is

God's <u>making</u> <u>use</u> <u>of</u> <u>someone</u> to say something, revelation is God's <u>making</u> <u>known</u> <u>something</u> to someone. These two notions are totally different and can exist distinct from the other. For example, in the Psalms we have prayers which are inspired but which contain no revelation. On the other hand, in the revelations of the Sacred Heart to St. Margaret Mary, we have revelation, but not in the inspired sense that the Bible is. We call such revelation <u>private</u> revelation, as opposed to the Bible which is called <u>public</u> revelation. We are not obliged to assent to private revelation.

What books belong to the Bible?

How do we know which books belong to the Bible and which do not? This information comes to us through tradition: the handing on of God's revelation by word of mouth. It is important to realize that Christ commanded his apostles to <u>preach</u> to all nations. The Gospels were preached long before they were written.

The Church, as a whole, has never at any time rejected any one of the inspired books. As early as the second century the books of the New Testament had all been gathered together. In A.D. 397 the pope approved a list of the true books of the Bible drawn up by a group of bishops. Not until the Council of Trent, however, did the Church authoritatively define which books were inspired.

Deposit of faith

The sum of revealed doctrines given into the keeping of the Church is sometimes called the deposit of faith. This deposit was completed at the death of the last apostle.

Study questions

Jews of Christ's time often wore tiny leather pouches strapped to their foreheads and arms. These pouches (called phylacteries) were worn during the daily prayer and contained passages from the Old Testament.

1 Why did the Jews hold the Old Testament in such high regard?
2 Where are we taught that God inspired the Bible? 3 Distinguish between revelation and inspiration. 4 Distinguish between private revelation and public revelation. 5 How do we know which books of the Bible are inspired? 6 When was the deposit of faith completed?

```
God's
Word
          ┌Old
          │Testament
          │
          │        ┌Law Books      ┌Genesis
          │        │(Torah)        │Exodus
          │        │               │Leviticus
          │        │               │Numbers
          │        │               └Deuteronomy
          │        │
          │        │               ┌Josue          Kings, 1-4
          │        │               │Judges         Paralipomenon, 1-2
          │        │               │Ruth           Esdras, 1-2
          │        │Historical     │
          │        │Books          │   Special Books
          │        │               │
          │        │               │Tobias
          │        │               │Judith
          │        │               │Esther
          │        │               │
          │        │               └Machabees, 1-2
          │        │
          │        │Wisdom         ┌Job            Canticle of Canticles
          │        │Books          │Psalms         Wisdom
          │        │               │Proverbs       Sirach
          │        │               └Ecclesiastes
          │        │
          │        │               ┌   Major Prophets
          │        │               │
          │        │               │Isaia          Baruch
          │        │               │Jeremia        Ezechiel
          │        │               │Lamentations   Daniel
          │        │Prophetic      │
          │        │Books          │   Minor Prophets
          │        └               │
          │                        │Osee           Nahum
          │                        │Joel           Habacuc
          │                        │Amos           Sophonia
          │                        │Abdia          Aggai
          │                        │Jona           Zacharia
          │                        └Michea         Malachia
          │
          │        ┌Gospels        ┌Matthew        Luke
          │        │               └Mark           John
          │        │
          │        │               ┌Acts of the Apostles
          │        │
          │New     │               ┌Romans         Thessalonians, 1-2
          └Testament               │Corinthians, 1-2 Timothy, 1-2
                   │               │Galatians      Titus
                   │               │Ephesians      Philemon
                   │Epistles       │Philippians    Hebrews
                   └               │Colossians
                                   │
                                   │James          John, 1-3
                                   └Peter, 1-2      Jude
                                   
                                   ┌The Apocalypse
```

2 The Bible reveals God's plan of love for us

In the preceding lessons we learned that Christ still teaches us today. He does this through the voice of his mystical body, the Church. We also learned that the textbook that Christ uses to teach us is the Bible. It is the record of God's dealings with men, and it contains the story of God's love for us.

In this lesson we begin to study God's love as it is revealed in the Bible.

When St. Paul began teaching about God's love for men, he started by giving an overall view of the Bible story. Beginning with the first book of the Old Testament, he traced God's actions right down to the present day. Let us read one of the passages in the Acts of the Apostles where this is described for us.

Then Paul rose, and motioning with his hand for silence said,
"Israelites and you who fear God, hearken.
The God of this people of Israel chose our fathers
and made our people great
when they were sojourners in the land of Egypt.
With great might he led them forth from there, and . . .
After destroying seven nations in the land of Canaan,
he divided their territory among the Israelites by lot.
This period covers about four hundred years.
     After that he provided them with judges,
until the time of Samuel the prophet.
Then . . . God raised up David to be their king . . .
From his offspring God according to promise
brought to Israel a Savior, Jesus. . . .
     We now bring you the Good News
that God has fulfilled the promises
made to our forefathers for us . . ." Acts 13:16-33

Overall view of salvation history

The area where the early chapters of salvation history take
place is about the size of Vermont. As we look down on this area
after Adam's sin, we see nothing that looks like the paradise
that God created in the beginning. In fact, as St. Paul says,
"There is not one just man . . . there is none that seeks after
God. All have gone astray together." Romans 3:10-12.

God calls Abraham

But just as we are about to turn away in disgust, we catch
sight of a man in bright colored clothes and a waterskin slung
over his back. This is Abraham. In response to a voice from
heaven he left his pagan city in Haran to search for an unknown
land that God has promised to show him. In God's plan Abraham
is to be the mustard seed from which the kingdom of God will
grow. From Abraham's descendants will spring the Savior, who
will repair the damage of Adam's sin. The time is about 1850 B.C.
     Soon Abraham disappears into the midst of history, but before
he does he passes the torch of faith to his son, Isaac. In turn
Isaac passes it to his son, Jacob.
     With Jacob and his twelve sons we travel to the land of the
pyramids. Here Abraham's descendants are enslaved about
1600 B.C. and condemned to years of hard labor under the

scorching sun of Egypt. But the torch of faith stays burning. Patiently they await deliverance.

God calls Moses

Then one day a man with a staff in his hand emerges from the desert. This is Moses. In response to a voice coming from a burning bush, he has come to bargain for the release of the Israelites. With God's aid Moses is successful. Soon we are surrounded by a mob of shouting, singing ex-slaves passing over the Red Sea to freedom. The time is about 1250 B.C.

God chooses the Israelites

Next we find ourselves at the foot of Mt. Sinai. Here in the mysterious silence of the hot desert, we hear God speak to all the Israelites through Moses, their leader. "You have seen for yourselves how I treated the Egyptians . . . and brought you here to myself. Therefore, if you hearken to my voice and keep my covenant, you shall be my special possession, dearer to me than all other people . . . You shall be to me a kingdom of priests, a holy nation." Exodus 19:4-6. This is Israel's greatest hour. It will be remembered forever.

God gives Israel a home

Next, around 1225 B.C., we find ourselves standing on a plateau in Moab with Josue, Moses' successor. Before our eyes stretches the promised land. Some day it will be called the Holy Land. But for the time being it is to be the home of Israel. It will also be the classroom in which God schools his people.

After Josue leads the Israelites into this new land, the torch of faith passes to a series of leaders, called Judges. In spite of the leadership of these men, the Israelites begin to drift away from God. Punishment comes swiftly, as the promised land falls into the hands of a pagan army of Philistines. The scar of this still remains, for the name by which the Holy Land is known today--Palestine--comes from their name.

God gives the Israelites a king

When all seems lost, God raises up a heroic, young Israelite, named David. Under his dynamic kingship the tribes of Israel unite into a single kingdom. The Philistines are routed and disappear into the shadows of history. David makes Jerusalem the capital of the new kingdom, and he brings to it the Ark containing the tablet of the law of the Sinai covenant. God once again reigns in the hearts of his people. The time is about 1000 B.C.

David passes the torch of faith to his son, Solomon. Under Solomon's reign the new kingdom prospers. But at the close of his life the sword of sin descends upon the kingdom, cleaving it into two pieces. The northern tribes (retaining the name Israel) revolt from the southern tribes who take the name Juda.

Juda survives

The story of Israel and Juda is a continual cycle of sin, punishment, repentance, and forgiveness. In the north, prophets like Elias, Amos, and Osee try to draw the people from their sinful ways but to no avail. Then in 721 B.C. the Assyrian army sweeps down upon the northern kingdom and leads its people into slavery and obscurity.

Juda now holds the torch of faith. But she, too, is far from the holy nation God had in mind. In her midst, however, is a great prophet, Isaia. This noble figure warns Juda of her impending doom unless she repents. At the same time, however, he assures the faithful that though God should level Juda as a woodsman might fell an oak, still in her stump would remain a "holy seed." Isaia 6:13. God will save the faithful few and from them will come the Savior and the future kingdom.

Juda is exiled

Next we find ourselves in a long line of Judean prisoners being led off in exile to Babylon. Behind us the night sky glows in red and orange. Babylonian soldiers have set fire to Jerusalem. Among the exiles, however, is a man who still clutches the torch of faith, Ezechiel, the prophet. The time is about 587 B.C.

In the years that follow, Ezechiel and another prophet, called the Second Isaia, preach a message of hope and consolation. They point out that God is using this hour of sorrow to teach Juda an important lesson. Up until now she has looked upon God's promises in a material way: she has dreamed of a great earthly king and kingdom. Now Juda begins to realize that God has another kind of king and kingdom in mind. The kingdom God has in mind is not a political or earthly one.

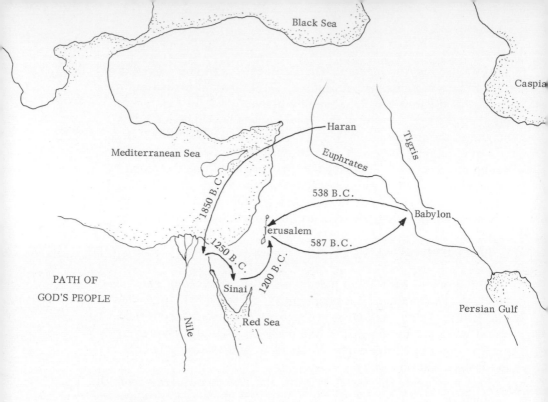

Black Sea

Caspia

Mediterranean Sea

Haran

Euphrates

Tigris

538 B.C.

Babylon

1850 B.C.

Jerusalem

587 B.C.

1250 B.C.

1200 B.C.

PATH OF
GOD'S PEOPLE

Sinai

Nile

Red Sea

Persian Gulf

Juda is freed

Finally in 538 B.C. the day arrives when Persians under Cyrus invade Babylon and free the exiled Jews. Amid prayers of thanks and shouts of joy, a faithful remnant pack their meager belongings and set out for Jerusalem.

Once in Jerusalem they rebuild the city and the temple and renew their Sinai covenant with God. But the Hebrews never do regain the full independence they once enjoyed. God purifies them even more by persecution at the hands of invaders. Around 165 B.C., under the gallant leadership of Judas Machabeus, the Jews finally gain their freedom. But in 63 B.C. the Romans move in, and Juda once again falls under the yoke of an outside power. Now they realize as never before that their sole hope lies in God.

Christ comes

At last Juda's night runs its course, and we see on the horizon a great morning star. In Bethlehem of Juda is born to a virgin a child named Jesus.

With the birth of Christ a new day dawns for the world. Christ the "sun of justice," comes to dispel the darkness of sin and error. He is the promised Messia and the one who will redeem man and establish God's kingdom on earth.

The Holy Spirit comes

After his death and resurrection, Christ ascends gloriously to his Father. On Pentecost morning the Holy Spirit, promised by Christ, descends in tongues of fire on the followers of Christ. From this moment on they are the reality and sign of God's kingdom on earth. They are the descendants of Abraham. They are God's "priestly kingdom and holy nation." But they are even more. By the action of the Holy Spirit, Christ and his followers form one body: the mystical body of Christ, the Church.

The Bible story continues

Through the members of Christ's mystical body, God still speaks to us today, just as he did to Abraham and the Israelites. By the liturgical actions of Christ's mystical body, God continues to save men and to invite them into his kingdom. The story begun in the Bible continues. We belong to it. We are as much part of it as the Israelites who fled from Egypt and the apostles who talked with Christ. We merely appear in a later chapter of the story. According to God's plan, men will continue to be invited into his kingdom until the time he has appointed. Then the kingdom will be complete and Christ will return gloriously to lead it to his Father. 1 Corinthians 15:24.

BIBLE MESSAGE

At a press conference Bishop Henri Jenny of France told reporters, "The liturgy is the Bible still in progress." Imagine a reporter, writing up the story for a daily paper, asks you to explain to him the bishop's remark. 1 What do you say? 2 Identify: Abraham, Isaac, Jacob, Moses, Josue, David, Solomon, Elias, Amos, Osee, Isaia, Ezechiel, Second Isaia, Cyrus, Machabeus. 3 Identify: Haran, Red Sea, Palestine, Jerusalem, Juda, Babylon. 4 Identify the following dates: 1850 B.C., 1600 B.C., 1250 B.C., 1225 B.C., 1000 B.C., 721 B.C., 587 B.C., 538 B.C., 165 B.C., 63 B.C. 5 Identify: Egyptians, Philistines, Assyrians, Babylonians, Romans.

1 Salvation history continues.   "We must begin to realize
that we are a part of salvation history. The story begun in the
Bible is not yet finished. We are actors in it, just as truly as
were the Israelites who fled from Pharao and as were the apostles
who walked with Christ. The only difference is that we appear
in a later chapter of the story." Clifford Howell, S.J.

Why isn't the story begun in the Bible finished yet? How does
God still act in a modern high-school student's life, just as he
did in the lives of the Israelites and the apostles?

2 Salvation history and us.   "We must begin to think of ourselves as the people of God. The chosen people of the Old Testament
were bearers of God's truth and holiness. Each Israelite bore witness to God's truth, justice, and holiness.

"Now we are the people of God. Each Christian by his incorporation into Christ's mystical body, the Church, has the high dignity of being a personal witness to God's truth and holiness in the
modern world." Anselme Robeyns, O.S.B.

What does the author mean by saying that the chosen people
were the bearers of God's truth and holiness? Why are we now
God's people? How can a high-school student give personal
witness to God in daily life?

3 Picturing salvation history.   On a piece of paper draw
with a yellow crayon or pencil a dotted horizontal line about an
inch long. Continue this line in solid green. At the beginning of
the yellow line draw a yellow triangle with an eye in it. Where
the yellow line joins the green line, draw two small people. The
triangle represents the Holy Trinity; the dotted line, eternity;
the two people, creation; the green line, time.

Along the first half of the green line place dates and symbols,
showing the important events by which God prepared for the
coming of Christ. At the center of the line place something
special to indicate Christ's birth. Along the last half of the line
place dates and symbols of important events after Christ's
birth. Be sure to include your own baptism. At the end of the
line place something to show that salvation history will continue
until Christ's final coming at the end of time.

Why is Christ placed in a special way at the center of all
salvation history? Why is it better to show on the line your day
of baptism rather than your day of birth?

DOCTRINAL POINTS

God's kingdom plan

"Kingdom of God"--this is an expression we see frequently in the Gospels. To understand its meaning, we must go back to the plan that was in God's mind before the creation of the world.

God's plan was this. In his infinite love God willed to create men and to share with them his own love and divine life. In other words, he planned to have a heavenly kingdom: a happy union of mankind with himself.

Christ fully explained and established God's kingdom

God prepared for the kingdom when he created the world. He fully explained and set up his kingdom by the work of his Son, Jesus Christ. Today, God's kingdom among men is the Church, Christ's mystical body. The kingdom is now building up and will do so until the end of time. Then Christ the King will return gloriously to lead the kingdom to his Father. 1 Corinthians 15:24.

St. Paul wrote beautifully of God's kingdom and Christ's role in it in a letter to Christians at Ephesus.

Blessed be the God and Father
of our Lord Jesus Christ,
who in Christ has blessed us
with every manner of spiritual blessing . . .
in Christ before the foundation of the world . . .
Out of love he predestined us for himself
to become through Jesus Christ his adopted children . . .
he decreed . . . to gather all creation
both in heaven and on earth
under one head, Christ.
. . . to me, the very least of all the saints,
this grace was given to announce among the Gentiles
the Good News of the unfathomable riches of Christ,
and to enlighten all men
as to what is the wonderful plan, that mystery
which has been hidden from eternity in God . . .
    I, therefore, the prisoner in the Lord,
exhort you to conduct yourselves
in a manner worthy of the calling
to which you have been called . . . Ephesians 1:3--4:1

Christ is the key figure in God's kingdom plan

Christ is the key figure in God's kingdom plan. For this reason he stands at the central point of all history. Before Christ, everything prepared for his coming and the setting up of God's kingdom. After Christ, everything builds on Christ and looks ahead to the completion of the kingdom. Christ gives meaning and direction to history. He is the "light of the world." Who follows him "will not walk in the dark, but have the light of life." John 8:12.

Study questions

Speaking to 20,000 people in St. Peter's square on the feast of Christ the King, Pope Paul VI said, "The feast of Christ the King makes us think of the centralness of Christ in world history." 1 Explain what the pope meant. 2 What plan was in God's mind when he created the world? 3 By whom was God's kingdom fully revealed and set up? 4 Define kingdom. 5 Where is God's kingdom today?

3

GOD'S KINGDOM PLAN UNFOLDS IN HISTORY

1 God prepares for his kingdom

In the last chapter we studied the overall view of God's kingdom plan for men. In this chapter we will begin a closer study of that plan. We will start by reading how God set in motion his plan. He created the world. Let us see how the Bible records this.

In the beginning . . .
the earth was waste and void; darkness covered the abyss,
and the spirit of God was stirring above the waters.
God said, "Let there be light," and there was light. . . .
Then God said,
"Let there be a firmament . . . to divide the waters. . . .
Let the waters below the heavens be gathered into one place
and let the dry land appear. . . ."
God called the dry land Earth
and the assembled waters Seas. . . .
Then God said,
"Let the earth bring forth vegetation . . .
Let there be lights in the firmament of the heavens . . ."

the greater light to rule the day
and the smaller one to rule the night,
and he made the stars. . . .
Then God said,
"Let the waters abound with life . . .
let winged creatures fly
below the firmament of the heavens. . . .
Let the earth bring forth all kinds of . . . animals."
And so it was. . . .
And God saw that it was good. Genesis 1:1-25

God reveals three important truths

These opening lines of the Bible come from the hand of an Israelite who lived over 2,500 years ago. The inspired message that they contain, however, comes from the heart of God. It is a loving message of how God began preparing for his kingdom.

In the first chapter of the Bible God reveals to us three important truths about the world.

First, he teaches us that before the world came into being, he alone existed. There were no other beings. "In the beginning . . . the earth was waste and void; darkness covered the abyss, and the spirit of God was stirring above the waters."

Second, God teaches us that the world happened not by an accident or chance, but according to his plan and through his almighty command. "God said, 'Let there be light,' and there was light."

Third, God teaches us that everything he created was good. "And God saw that it was good." The world was a beautiful and holy place. Its mountains, whirling planets, and vast expanse of outer space were faint reflections of God's own power, wisdom, and infinity. Commenting on this St. Paul says, "Since the creation of the world, his [God's] invisible attributes are clearly seen . . . through the things that are made." Romans 1:20. The world, like the Bible, teaches us about the Creator.

BIBLE MESSAGE

Christ teaches us today. Some people think that God dictated the account of creation to the sacred writer as a businessman dictates a letter to his secretary. 1 What do you say about this? 2 What three truths does God teach us in the first chapter of Genesis?

Some important biblical background

After God made the Israelites his chosen people at Mt. Sinai, he began to teach them more about himself. For centuries these inspired truths were never recorded but merely handed down vocally. Exodus 12:26 ff. It was only later that the Hebrews began to write down God's teaching. Thus, sometime around the year 538 B.C., God's revelation about creation was recorded as we have it today.

The Book of Genesis is a book of beginnings

The book in which the creation account occurs is called Genesis. The Jews did not call this book Genesis at first. They called it Beresheeth (Hebrew for "In the beginning"). Like the Holy Father, the Jews named their writings after the first few opening words. Later, when the Jews of Alexandria, Egypt translated the Bible from Hebrew into Greek, the book got the name Genesis, or "beginning." This is an excellent name. For the Book of Genesis is truly a book of "beginnings." It tells about the beginning of the universe, the beginning of nations, and the beginning of God's people.

Genesis reveals revolutionary truths

For us today the religious truths in Genesis seem elementary, but to the Hebrews they were revolutionary. For example, almost all the nations of the day practiced polytheism: the worship of many gods. Moreover, these gods were often things of nature, like the sun, moon, stars, and even animals and trees.

The inspired writer had all this in mind when he recorded what God had revealed about himself and creation. In fact, it seems that God's revelation was deliberately passed on in the form of poetic argument. The Genesis writer seems to say to the pagan world, "No, the sun and the moon are not gods. Neither are the stars, nor animals and trees. The one true God created all those things that you worship in your ignorance."

The idea that the world was made according to a divine plan was also revolutionary. The Babylonians, for example, believed that the world was a kind of afterthought, the by-product of a war between angry gods. To these the sacred writer is saying, "No, you are wrong, too! God has revealed to our forefathers that the world is not the product of blind chance. On the contrary, it is the result of God's free will and his eternal plan."

Finally, the idea that the world was good was a great revelation.

Many of Israel's pagan neighbors believed that material things were the evil handiwork of an evil god. To these the sacred writer says, "You, too, are wrong. The world is not evil. Everything in the world is good, for the one, true God made it that way."

Study questions

Some people think the Hebrews wrote down God's Word at the very moment when it was revealed. 1 What do you say about this? 2 When approximately was the creation account written out as we now have it? 3 How did most ancients look upon the sun, moon, stars, and so forth? 4 How did they explain the existence of the universe? 5 How did many of Israel's pagan neighbors look upon material things?

LITURGY & LIFE

1 An astronaut's prayer about creation.   On the seventeenth orbit of his flight Astronaut Cooper, aboard space capsule Faith 7, spoke this prayer into his tape recorder: "Father, thank you, especially, for letting me fly this flight. Thank you for the privilege of being able to be in this position, to be up in this wondrous place, seeing all these startling wonderful things that you have created."

Do you think Cooper found this prayer in a book or did he just make it up? What were some features of God's creation seen by Cooper which most people have never seen?

2 A scientist speaks about creation.   A famous scientist, Arthur H. Compton, said, "The probability of life originating from accident is comparable to the probability of the unabridged dictionary resulting from an explosion in a printing shop."

What is his point? Do you think this is an apt comparison? Can you think of any other comparisons?

3 A soldier finds God in creation.   One of the most popular pieces written in the last war was called Conversion. You found it everywhere. It was tacked to trees in the jungles. In England a copy was found in the hand of an unconscious turret gunner as he was pulled from a shot-up plane. On D-Day a chaplain found it clutched in the hands of a dying soldier on Normandy Beach. Read it and tell why you think soldiers liked it.

The heavens declare the glory of God, and
the firmament proclaims his handiwork.   Psalm 18:2

Look, God, I have never spoken to you--
But now--I want to say, "How do you do."
You see, God, they told me you didn't exist--
And like a fool--I believed all of this.
Last night from a shell-hole I saw your sky--
I figured right then they had told me a lie.
Had I taken the time to see the things you made,
I'd have known they weren't calling a spade a spade.
I wonder, God, if you'd shake my hand.
Somehow I feel that you will understand.
Funny--I had to come to this hellish place
Before I had time to see your face.
    Well, I guess there isn't much more to say,
But I'm glad, God, I met you today.
I guess the zero hour will soon be here,
But I'm not afraid since I know you're near.
The signal! Well, God, I'll have to go.
I like you lots--that I want you to know.
Look, now--this will be a horrible fight--
Who knows--I may come to your house tonight--
Though I wasn't friendly with you before,
I wonder, God, if you'd wait at your door.
Look, I'm crying, me shedding tears!
I wish I had known you these many years--
Well, I will have to go now, God--goodbye.
Strange--since I met you--I'm not afraid to die.

Frances Angermayer

How and what does God's creation teach about its creator?
Why do you think soldiers like the poem so much? How does
looking at God's creation help you to pray? Is it good to pray in
your own words? Compose a prayer like the one above. It can be
any length but make it relate to something in creation that speaks
to you best about God.

4 The Mass and God the creator.　From memory or with the
help of your missal, list the various places in the Mass where we
explicitly refer to God as the creator of heaven and earth.

How many times do we do this? Discuss the context of the Mass
in which each reference occurs.

5 Creation project.　Ancient Hebrews had a completely different idea of the world from that which we have. They thought of
the earth as a plate floating on waters of endless depth. Above the

earth was the "firmament," an inverted shell, thrown up over the earth to separate the waters above from the waters below. Small gates in the firmament occasionally let water fall. From the firmament were suspended the sun, moon, and stars.

With the help of this description and your Bible, draw a picture of the ancient Hebrew's idea of the world.

6 The psalmist sings about creation:

How manifold are your works, O Lord!
In wisdom you have wrought them all--
the earth is full of your creatures . . .
I will sing to the Lord all my life;
I will sing praise to my God
while I live. Psalm 103:24,33

DOCTRINAL POINTS

How to read the Bible

At times God's message can be hard to understand. This is particularly true of parts of the Old Testament. A knowledge of how the Church, under the guidance of the Holy Spirit, goes about determining the meaning of these parts will help us in our own reading of the Bible. The method the Church uses is simple in principle. She seeks to determine what the sacred writer intended to say. Though this principle is relatively simple, its application is somewhat more complicated. It involves four steps.

First step: learn the historical background

The first step is to study the background of the author, the time in which he lived, and the people for whom he wrote. Archeologists and historians are a big help here. The importance of this first step is illustrated in the Book of Genesis. For example, unless we know that the Genesis author wrote for a less developed people in an agricultural society where idolatry and polytheism flourished, we risk missing both the significance and the meaning of this book. This is why Pope Pius XII insisted, "The interpreter must endeavor to determine the personal traits and background of the sacred writer, the age in which he lived, the oral or written sources which he used, and his ways of expressing himself."

43

We may now formulate our first rule for reading the Bible: Find out about the author, his time, and the people for whom he wrote.

Second step: determine the literary form

The problem of literary form is next in importance. Sometimes the sacred author says something that, at first glance, seems false. Further study, however, shows that he is merely using a literary form that was known and understood by his audience. Commenting on this point the Holy Father said, "Quite often when the sacred writers have been accused of a historical error or an inaccuracy in what they have recorded, a closer examination has shown that they were only expressing themselves in a conventional form of narration that was normal to the everyday life of those ancient times and sanctioned by common usage."

An example is the "stopping of the sun" mentioned in the Book of Josue 10:12 ff. This expression is from the poetic Book of Jasphar. It is, therefore, to be understood in the same spirit as the poetic exaggeration in Psalm 28, where the psalmist speaks of Mt. Lebanon as "leaping."

Another example is the creation account in the Book of Genesis. In it the sacred writer presents God's message within the artificial framework of six twenty-four-hour days. This clever arrangement makes an excellent memory aid for his unlettered audience. It also provides a natural framework for refuting, in order, each of the false "nature" Gods. Finally, it gives him an ideal opportunity for teaching the divine origin of Israel's Sabbath obligation.

We may now formulate our second rule for reading the Bible: Find out the kind of writing used by the author to communicate God's message; i.e., identify the literary form.

Third step: determine the author's purpose

The third step to keep in mind in reading the Bible is the author's purpose in writing. In the past some people have worried that the inspired authors of the Bible have taught errors. For example, they point to the Book of Genesis where the inspired writer gives a description of the world that is scientifically inaccurate.

Does this mean that the inspired author is guilty of teaching error? Far from it. All experts agree that the inspired writer of Genesis had no intention of teaching anything about the physical or chemical composition of the world. His purpose was not to give a scientific explanation of the world. His purpose was a religious one.

We may now formulate our third rule for reading the Bible: Find out the sacred author's purpose in writing.

Fourth step: discover the religious truths

The fourth step is the most important of all. It is to determine the religious truths God and the sacred author wish to teach us. In the creation account this becomes perfectly clear once we have correctly taken the first three steps. In the first chapter of Genesis, God teaches us: 1) that he alone existed before the world came into being, 2) that the world came into being not by accident but according to his plan and his almighty command, and 3) that everything he created was good.

The fourth rule for reading the Bible is as follows: Find out the religious truth that God wishes to teach us.

In brief, the four rules for discovering the meaning of more difficult passages in the Bible are:

1 Learn the historical background.
2 Determine the literary form.
3 Determine the author's purpose in writing.
4 Discover the religious truth God wishes to teach.

Men are God's partners

One final point might be cleared up. Why did God allow his word to be recorded in a way that is sometimes not perfectly clear to us today? The answer is that God works through human instruments. He accepts men as they are. In the case of the sacred writers, he merely inspired them to write. He left them free to use their own language, style, and words. He respected their intellects and free wills.

God acts the same way today with his bishops, priests, and lay leaders. They are all human beings with different personalities and intellects. God does not change all this when he calls them. He respects these differences and uses them. God treats men not as slaves and machines, but as partners and friends. This is just another part of God's great mystery of love for men.

Study questions

Writing over 1500 years ago, St. Jerome said, "You cannot make your way in the Bible without having someone go before you to show you the road."

In saying this, he was merely repeating what the Bible itself teaches. Read 2 Peter 3:16, Acts 8:30, and Luke 24:25 ff.

1 Restate and explain in your own words the four rules the Church follows in discovering the meaning of the more difficult passages in the Bible. 2 Why did God permit the Bible to be recorded in a way that is not always perfectly clear to us today?

What is God like?

Anyone who scans the star-flecked sky on a clear night knows that it had a creator. Moreover, this creator had to be infinitely powerful. We know, for example, that the constellation Andromeda is so far away that if the light from it suddenly burned out, it would take 900,000 years before we would know it. The last light beam from Andromeda would continue racing toward earth at the rate of 186,000 miles per second for 900,000 years. That's how far away it is.

But the universe shows us only a fraction of God's greatness. Let us look at other facts about God.

God is self-existent

God is self-existent. This means God exists because of his very nature. He did not need anyone to make him exist. On the other hand, everything else exists because it had a creator.

God is almighty

God is almighty. This means God can do all things by the mere act of his will. There is no limit to his power. God could, if he wished, begin today to create a universe a week, each larger than the one before, and each more beautiful. God is infinitely powerful.

God created everything

God created all things. To create means to make from nothing. When we say "from nothing" we mean that neither was the thing itself in existence nor anything from which it was made. When our nation's top engineers build a space ship, they use existing materials; they do not make it from nothing. Before God created a single thing--whether angels, men, or the universe--there was nothing in existence but himself.

God conserves everything

God holds all things in existence. As long as we see light gleaming on an instrument panel, we know power is reaching it. In a similar way, everything that exists--plants, animals, men, angels-- depends upon the constant action of God. If that action were withdrawn, the things would drop into nothingness. God is constantly "conserving all things by his mighty command." Hebrews 1:3.

God governs everything

God governs all things. He is all-knowing. Nothing ever happens unless God either wills or permits it. But how does God govern the world? He governs it first of all by physical laws. He made things according to certain laws. We call these the laws of nature. Because of these laws, things in nature act in a constant manner. For example, we know exactly when the sun will rise on a given day a century from now. The entire visible universe continues year after year to act in the way God made it to act.

Secondly, God governs the world by moral laws. It is a moral law, for example, that we should not lie. God made these moral laws, and he gave us minds capable of knowing right from wrong. Our conscience tells us that we should do certain things and avoid others. Conscience is an act of our intellect enabling us to judge whether certain actions are morally good or morally bad. We are obliged to follow its dictates. Men can, if they wish, ignore the moral laws and go against God's plan of love. God permits this, having given man a free will. But in the end God always draws good from evil.

Finally, God governs the world by revelations, miracles, and grace. This is particularly evident in the case of the Old Testament Jews and the Catholic Church. God chose the Jews to be the race from which the Redeemer came. The entire Old Testament is an example of how God governs the world. So, too, today God preserves the Catholic Church from corruption from within and without; and he will continue to preserve it until the end of time. God shows his greatness and his power by governing the world as he does.

Study questions

"If all the world were full of books, and if every creature were a writer, and if all the water in the seas were changed into ink, the books would be filled, the writers exhausted, and the sea dried up, before a single one of his [God's] perfections could be expressed."

1 Do you think this statement of St. Augustine is an exaggeration?
2 What do we mean when we say God is: self-existent, almighty,
creator, conservor, governor? 3 List and explain the three ways
God governs the world.

2 God creates Adam and extends an invitation to him

God's second step in realizing his plan was to create Adam and
Eve. God created them in his image and likeness. He gave them a
share in his divine life and invited them to collaborate with him in
bringing about the kingdom of God. Let us read the Bible to see how
God teaches us these truths.

God said, "Let us make mankind in our image and likeness;
and" . . . God created man in his image. . . .
Male and female he created them.
Then God blessed them and said to them,
"Be fruitful and multiply; fill the earth and subdue it.
Have dominion over the fish of the sea, the birds of the air,
the cattle, and all the animals . . ." Genesis 1:26-28

Thus the heavens and the earth were finished . . .
And he [God] rested on the seventh day
from all the work he had done.
God blessed the seventh day and made it holy . . . Genesis 2:1-3

God reveals three important truths

In this second part of the creation account God reveals to us
three important truths. First, he teaches us that he created man.
"God said, 'Let us make mankind in our image and likeness.'"
God formed man into a person and blessed him far above all other
earthly things. He gave him an intellect, a will, and a share in his
own life and power.

48

Second, God teaches us that after creating man, he invited him to cooperate with him in bringing about the kingdom of God on earth. "Then God blessed them and said to them, 'Be fruitful and multiply; fill the earth and subdue it. Have dominion over the fish of the sea, the birds of the air, the cattle, and all the animals . . .'"

Third, God teaches us to keep holy the seventh day. "God blessed the seventh day and made it holy."

BIBLE MESSAGE

Christ teaches us today. Christ said: "Do not five sparrows sell for two pennies? And yet, in the providence of God, not one of them is a poor, forgotten creature! . . . Have no fear; you are more precious than whole flocks of sparrows." Luke 12:6-7.

1 Why is man more precious than whole flocks of sparrows?
2 Using your Bible, point out the three truths about man that God teaches us in the second part of the creation account.

Some important biblical background

In the second chapter of Genesis the sacred writer describes God as making Eve from Adam's rib. The sacred writer's purpose here is not to give a scientific explanation of women's origin. What he is trying to teach his readers is that woman, who was often debased by oriental society, is to be honored and respected. She is to be man's helpmate, and together they are to collaborate with God in bringing about God's kingdom. Genesis 2:18, 21-22.

LITURGY & LIFE

1 Man is created in God's image. "Planets, mountains, and stars," says an author, "reveal God; they are his work. But man makes him better known, for he is his image."

How do planets, mountains, and stars reveal God? Explain the difference between a mineral, a plant, a brute animal, and a human being. Make a diagram of your findings.

2 Man is the masterpiece of God's creation. Speaking to a youth group from Milan, Italy, the Holy Father said, "The human body is, in itself, the masterpiece of God in the order of visible creation."

Why is the body a masterpiece? How can a healthy body aid in spreading God's kingdom? How does this fact make sports not only enjoyable but also meritorious?

3 Man is God's partner in creation. "Men think of creation as a wonderful work of God and stand in awe and admiration of it. It does not occur to them that creation is a continuing process and that they are called upon to participate in it." Walter J. Handren, S.J.

What does the author mean? Does man truly "create"? What part does God himself play in the process? How does this show that sex is a beautiful and even holy thing?

4 The psalmist sings about man:

O Lord, our Lord . . .
what is man that you should be mindful of him . . .?
You have made him little less than the angels,
and crowned him with glory and honor.
You have given him rule over the works of your hands,
putting all things under his feet . . .
O Lord, our Lord, how glorious is your name
over all the earth! Psalm 8

DOCTRINAL POINTS

God's reason for creating us

Why did God decide to create us and to share with us his life and love? God had two reasons: 1) his glory, and 2) our happiness.

We can speak of God's glory in two different senses. Theologians usually distinguish these two senses by speaking of God's internal glory and God's external glory.

God's glory

God's internal glory is the glory which he has in himself. The Holy Trinity know one another, love one another, and have joy in one another. This trinitarian life of knowledge, love, and joy is God's internal glory.

God's external glory is the glory which he receives from angels and men who, seeing his perfections, love him, praise him, and serve him in this life and in heaven.

50

Man's happiness

Now, it is impossible for angels and men to be with God in heaven without being happy. It follows then that God created angels and men not only for his own external glory but also for their own eternal happiness.

When we know God's purpose in creating us, we also know the end and purpose of our own existences. It is to know, love, and serve God in this world and to be happy with him forever in the next. From this truth emerge three important conclusions to guide us in living our life.

First, one thing alone matters in this life: to know and love God and freely cooperate with him in his plan for us. We give God more glory by winning heaven by our free acts than by receiving it as an unmerited gift.

Second, we can never hope to find perfect happiness in this life. Riches, pleasures, and honors will never fully satisfy our hearts. We ought to use these things insofar as they help us carry out God's plan. We ought to abstain from them insofar as they prove a stumbling block to God's plan.

Third, in the next life complete justice will be done to all. Every good act and every evil deed will receive its reward or punishment.

Study questions

A handsome young soldier lay dying. On his face was a look of pain--and deep confusion. Searching out the eyes of his friend, he said slowly, "Here lies a miserable wretch who is going out of the world without ever knowing why he came into it." Then his eyes closed, and he fell into a coma never to recover.

1 Are there many people in the world like the dying soldier?
2 Did God intend this to be? 3 Who is to blame for ignorance about God's plan for men? 4 Explain in your own words why God created us. 5 List and explain the three conclusions that follow from this.

4

GOD'S KINGDOM INVITATION IS REJECTED

1 Adam rejects God's invitation

After creating Adam and Eve, God invited them to share forever in his love and life. God, also, invited them to rule over the world and to people it with men who would also share his love and life. To the everlasting sorrow of the human race, Adam and Eve rejected God's invitation. Let us read in the Book of Genesis where this is told us.

> He [the serpent] said to the woman,
> "Did God say, 'You shall not eat of any tree of the garden'?"
> The woman answered the serpent,
> ". . . 'Of the fruit of the tree in the middle of the garden,'
> God said, 'you shall not eat,
> neither shall you touch it, lest you die.'"
> But the serpent said to the woman, "No, you shall not die;
> for God knows that when you eat of it,
> your eyes will be opened and you will be like God,
> knowing good and evil."
> Now the woman saw that the tree was good for food,

pleasing to the eyes, and desirable
for the knowledge it would give. She took of its fruit and ate it,
and also gave some to her husband
and he ate.   Genesis 3:1-6

Adam sins

In the third chapter of Genesis God teaches us that Adam rejected his invitation of love. Misled by Satan, man freely and
deliberately turns from God and goes his own way. This first
sin of man is called original sin.

Since the fall of Adam and Eve every human person (except
our Blessed Mother) has, to some extent, freely and deliberately
turned from God or God's plan of love.

Temptation precedes sin

The biblical account of Eve's temptation is a good description
of how Satan still tries to turn us from God and God's plan. Let
us study it closely.

First, there is the temptation. Satan puts a question or idea in
our minds about something that is not a part of God's plan of love
for us. In the case of Eve, Satan asks about the mysterious tree
in the middle of the garden.

Second, there is the failure to reject the temptation immediately. In the case of Eve she begins to talk with Satan.

Third, Satan increases the temptation by proposing that it will
lead to something thrilling and pleasant. In the case of Eve, Satan
says that if she eats of the tree she will become like God--a
thrilling prospect.

Finally, the temptation explodes into sin. Freely and deliberately
Eve rejects God's plan of love for her and casts her lot with Satan.

BIBLE MESSAGE

Christ teaches us today.   Christ said, "If your hand is a
temptation to you, cut if off; it is better for you to go into life
maimed than to keep both your hands and go into the unquenchable
fire." Mark 9:43.

Christ's point here is not to have us cripple ourselves but,
rather, to teach us to be ready to shun occasions of sin even at
the cost of great personal sacrifice.

With the help of your Bible show how Eve's temptation to sin is an accurate description of how Satan tempts us today. Make your explanation concrete. Use the example of a student being tempted to steal while selling tickets at a football game.

Some important biblical background

The "eating of the fruit" from the "tree of knowledge of good and evil" is often discussed. Too often the meaning is missed. The sacred writer's purpose in using this expression is not to reveal what sin Adam and Eve committed. The expression is symbolic; that is, it stands for something else. In this case it stands for the act that our first parents performed which God had forbidden to them.

One biblical scholar explains the symbolic meaning of the "tree of knowledge of good and evil" this way. For the Hebrews knowledge was not so much knowing something as experiencing it. For example, we can know that fire burns by taking another's word for it. But we can also know it by actually going through the experience of getting burned ourselves. It was this experiential knowledge that the sacred writer had in mind. "To eat" from the "tree of knowledge of good and evil" meant to know good and evil by actual experience. It was to sin.

This is just what Adam and Eve did. They learned evil by going through the experience of becoming evil. What they did, we do not know. The Bible merely tells us that after they ate of the fruit (performed the evil act) "the eyes of both were opened, and . . . the man and his wife hid themselves from the Lord God." Genesis 3:7, 8.

LITURGY & LIFE

1 Ignorance of the Bible.   Recently a British botanist caused quite a stir when he said, "There were no apples in the garden of Eden . . . The only edible fruit were apricots and quinces." When a newspaper asked a British clergyman to comment on the botanist's statement, he said, "It doesn't make a hoot of difference . . ."

Would you agree? Does the Bible say anything about an apple? What truth did the sacred writer intend to convey by saying, "She took of its fruit and ate it." Genesis 3:6. Write a short note explaining to the newspaper the Catholic viewpoint on this statement.

2 Loyalty to God.   When George Washington was in his teens
he wrote 110 maxims of good conduct in his copybook. These played a big part in the formation of his character and the respect that
he had for religion during his life. Here are three:

1 When you speak of God let it be seriously and with reverence.
2 Let your recreation be manful, not sinful.
3 Labor to keep alive within you the voice of conscience.

Explain how a high-school student sometimes finds it hard to
keep these three maxims. Using the second maxim as an example,
show how the devil goes about tempting us to be disloyal to God.
Draw up your own list of five maxims of loyalty toward God.

DOCTRINAL POINTS

Temptation

Temptation may be defined as a thought or desire inclining us
to sin. In itself temptation is not a sin; but to yield to it or bring
it on ourselves knowingly and without sufficient reason is sinful.
Temptation ought to be resisted promptly.

To be tempted is not a sign of weakness. Many of the greatest
saints were tempted as much as we. By resisting temptation we
show our loyalty to Christ and our love for God.

Some helps in time of temptation are: 1) turning our thoughts
to other things, 2) quiet prayer, 3) the thought of death and hell,
4) the thought of offending Christ who suffered and died for us.

If temptation persists we are not to be saddened, for as long
as we are fighting, it is a sign that we have not been conquered.
We should remain calm and trust in God.

Two sources of strength against temptation are frequent Communion and confession.

Though temptations to sin can come to us without our wanting
them, most occasions of sin can be avoided. By an occasion of sin
we mean such persons, places, or things that as a rule lead us into
sin unless we keep away from them. These we must try to avoid.

Study questions

"God is faithful and will not let you be tempted beyond your
strength." 1 Corinthians 10:13. Discuss: a) why God sometimes
permits us to be tempted, and b) how we should handle ourselves
in time of temptation.

2 Adam's rejection separates mankind from God

After telling us how Adam and Eve rejected God's invitation,
the inspired writer tells us about the terrible effects of their sin.
It brought shame, suffering, and separation from God. Let us
read the Word of God in the Book of Genesis where these effects
are described.

> Then the eyes of both were opened,
> and they realized that they were naked . . .
> When they heard the sound of the Lord God
> walking in the garden in the cool of the day,
> the man and his wife hid themselves from the Lord God
> among the trees of the garden.
> But the Lord God called the man and said to him . . .
> "You have eaten then of the tree
> of which I commanded you not to eat . . .
> In the sweat of your brow you shall eat bread,
> till you return to the ground,
> since out of it you were taken;
> for dust you are and unto dust you shall return."
> To the woman he said;
> "I will make great your distress in childbearing;
> in pain shall you bring forth children . . ."
> He [God] drove out the man;
> and at the east of the garden of Eden he placed the Cherubim,
> and the flaming sword, which turned every way,
> to guard the way to the tree of life.   Genesis 3:7-24

Effects of original sin

In this Bible passage God teaches us about the five disastrous
effects that flowed from the sin of our first parents.

First, instead of becoming like God, as Satan had promised,
Adam and Eve became more unlike God. After their sin, their
eyes were opened and they saw their nakedness. Before they had
perfect control over their inner drives. Now they no longer have
the harmony that once existed between flesh and spirit. They
control their inner drives only with great effort.

Second, Adam and Eve lose their immunity to suffering and
death. Before they were free from pain and death. Now they feel
pain. They will also return to the dust from which they have come.

Third, Adam and Eve lose their infused knowledge. Before they were able to learn without normal study and effort. Now they must sweat and labor for their knowledge.

Fourth, Adam and Eve lose their special friendship with God. Before they walked in friendship with God. Now they are driven from his sight. Sin robs them of sanctifying grace.

Finally, because Adam and Eve lose these gifts, they can no longer pass them on to their children.

Ever since the time of Adam and Eve, sin has had a similar tragic effect upon every sinner. It brings shame, suffering, and separation from God.

BIBLE MESSAGE

Christ teaches us today. Christ said, "A man cannot be the slave of two masters. He will either hate the one and love the other, or, at least, be attentive to the one and neglectful of the other." Matthew 6:24.

1 How is this illustrated by what happened to our first parents in the Garden of Eden? 2 With the help of your Bible point out how we are taught about the five effects that flowed from Adam's sin. 3 Tell how these effects still make themselves felt in every high-school student's life.

Some important biblical background

The sacred writer describes God as "walking" in the garden, where Adam and Eve lived. The sacred writer has two reasons for doing this. The first reason is to teach the Hebrews that, before sin, Adam and Eve enjoyed the closest friendship and familiarity with God. The second reason is to make God more real for his simple readers. There is no question in the sacred writer's mind that God is far beyond anything human.

Scholars sometimes refer to this "human" way of describing God as "transcendent anthropomorphism"; that is describing God, who is "transcendent" (beyond our imagination), in "anthropomorphic" (human) terms.

Archeologists help biblical scholars

Archeologists, especially, are helping biblical scholars discover the meaning of certain puzzling expressions that occur in the Bible. For example, phrases like "tree of life" and "cherubim"

57

once caused much head scratching. Now, thanks to archeological excavations, the meaning of these expressions is clear.

Tree of life

The expression, "tree of life," was common in early Mesopotamian literature. It referred to a legendary plant that was supposed to confer immortality (freedom from death) on those possessing it. We might compare it to the fountain of youth that the Spanish explorer, Ponce de Leon, hoped to find in Florida. The biblical writer used this Mesopotamian symbol as a device to teach Hebrew people that God originally created man in a state of immortality. The Hebrews understood immediately what he meant.

Thus, too, the Hebrews would know that man lost this state when they read the following: "He [God] drove out the man; and at the east of the garden of Eden he placed the Cherubim, and the flaming sword, which turned every way, to guard the way to the tree of life." Genesis 3:24. Because of his sin, man no longer had access to the tree of life. He had lost his state of immortality and must now die.

The cherubim

The cherubim, mentioned in the above passage, is another mystery that archeologists have helped to solve. The term refers to a fearsome-looking winged bull. Archeologists have discovered this beast on many early Assyrian and Babylonian monuments. The cherubim was a kind of legendary watchdog who protected ancient holy places from unworthy intruders. The sacred writer used the cherubim as a symbol to teach the people that sin had made man unworthy of God's gift of immortality.

During the year ahead you will run across other symbolic expressions like "tree of knowledge" and "cherubim." Make a habit of entering them in your notebook or marking them in your Bible. You'll want to refer to them in the future.

Study questions

1 Discuss the biblical significance and symbolism of the following: a) God's "walking" in the garden, b) the tree of life, and c) the cherubim. 2 Make a list of modern expressions or symbols that readers 2,000 years from now will have great difficulty in understanding.

After Adam's fall

The biblical accounts of what happened after Adam was driven from paradise show a world badly in need of salvation. The first story is that of Cain and Abel. Genesis 4. This story teaches us, in a striking way, the disastrous effect original sin had upon men's lives. Sin not only wrecked man's friendship with God, but it also wrecked his friendship with his neighbor--even his blood brother.

Following the Cain and Abel story is the story of the deluge. Genesis 6:5-9:17. This story, too, has sin as its main theme. Here we see how sin brings down God's punishment. At the same time we see how God rewards those who lead good lives.

Finally, there is the story of the Tower of Babel. Genesis 11:1-9. This story presents still another aspect of sin. Sin is at the root of misunderstandings between nations and groups.

Study questions

How are these three aspects of sin being felt today? Illustrate by current events drawn from the daily paper.

LITURGY & LIFE

1 Effect of sin on the world.   Name four or more buildings and four or more professions that would not exist today if there had never been any sin in the world. Explain each of your selections.

2 Effect of sin on the soul.   The liturgical reading in the Divine Office for the second week in October is from the Book of Machabees. Read 1 Machabees 4:36-58, where the sacred writer describes how the holy temple was cleansed after it had been desecrated.

Using the passage from Machabees as a model, describe how Adam's sin desecrates the soul which was God's temple. By what steps is a desecrated soul restored to its original holiness?

3 Effect of sin on personality.   The English convert, G. K. Chesterton, once wrote that when the Catholic doctrine of original sin was explained to him, it was as though the pieces of a Chinese puzzle began to click into place in his mind. Now he had an answer to the dual personality of man--a personality capable of great nobility, and yet capable of the foulest deeds.

Explain what original sin is.

4 The Church asks God to forgive our sins.

Forgive the sins of Your people, Lord,
that we may be freed by Your goodness
from the power of evil
into which our weakness has betrayed us. Amen.
    Collect: Twenty-third Sunday after Pentecost

DOCTRINAL POINTS

What was Adam like before sin?

After creating the world, God created Adam. He made Adam's
body from the minerals and chemicals of the earth. It shared the
vegetable life of plants in its power to grow. It also shared the life
of animals in its power to sense and to move about. But Adam's
body was not made alive by an animal principle of life that depended
on matter and would cease to exist after a time. It was animated by
a human soul that would live forever. Adam's soul was spiritual
and immortal. It was created directly by God.

Adam was partly spiritual and partly material. He was neither
mere animal nor a pure spirit but a marvelous combination of
soul and body.

Adam had special gifts

But Adam was more. God gave him a special gift so that he
could have greater happiness. God gave Adam a share in his own
life. We call this gift sanctifying grace. Sanctifying grace is
supernatural in every way; that is, it is something to which
created nature has no claim. It is proper to God alone.

God also gave Adam certain other gifts. First, he gave him a
special knowledge that we call infused, because it was not acquired by hard work and study.

Second, God gave Adam the gift of freedom from death. And
since Adam was free from death, he was also free from the
causes of death: disease, accident, and old age.

Because Adam would never grow old, he would never suffer the
weakening effects of old age. He would simply grow stronger and
handsomer. A special providence of God protected him against
anything that would harm him. Adam need never worry about
germs or poisons. Accidents could not touch him.

Third, Adam was given the gift of freedom from concupiscence; that is, he had perfect control over all his animal drives.

Adam was in the state of original justice

We speak so frequently of the state in which Adam was created that it is handy to have a short expression to describe it. The expression used by theologians is "original justice." Original justice included the supernatural gift of sanctifying grace and the preternatural (powers above the natural powers of man, but inferior to God's powers) gifts: infused knowledge and the three freedoms, freedom from death, suffering, and concupiscence.

In God's original plan men would have lived happily in the state that God had created them. Never would one man raise a hand against another or look upon another with anger.

Study questions

Some clever popularizer of chemistry sat down several years back and figured out that after a good going-over with a blowtorch, the human body would amount to enough fat to make several bars of soap, enough iron to make a nail, enough zinc to paint a room, enough sulphur to rid a dog of fleas, and enough phosphorus to make a book of matches. Discuss: a) the makeup of the body, b) the makeup of the soul, c) the meaning of original justice.

What is sin?

Sin is an offense against God. By sin Adam lost the supernatural gift of sanctifying grace and all the preternatural gifts that God had given him. He lost these for himself, and, as head of the human race, he lost them for all his descendants. Had Adam not sinned, his descendants would have been born in the state of sanctifying grace. Because of his sin they are born deprived of sanctifying grace. We say that they are born in original sin.

Original sin

We may define original sin as the state of being born without sanctifying grace because of Adam's sin.

Christ, of course, was born without original sin; and, because of the merits of her Son, the Blessed Virgin was also free from original sin.

Had Adam not sinned, his descendants would have been born with sanctifying grace and with freedom from death, disease, and concupiscence; but every man could have lost these gifts by personal sin. It is probable that man would have, but it was Adam who brought it about that men are born without sanctifying grace and subject to the lifelong battle against concupiscence. He therefore made sin easier; and, in a sense, all moral evil can be said to be due in some measure to original sin.

Actual sin

Opposed to original sin is actual sin. Actual sin is an offense against God that one commits oneself. When this offense is grave, the sin is called mortal (death-dealing) sin.

A mortal sin brings death to the supernatural life of the soul. It makes us enemies of God, robs us of our merits and right to heaven, and brings punishment down on us in this world and eternal damnation in the next.

Mortal sin is the greatest evil in the world. It is an act of ingratitude and rebellion against God and God's love; it is a crime of the worse sort against Christ and his love. "Because as far as lies in their power they again crucify the Son of God and expose him to mockery." Hebrews 6:6.

Requirements for mortal sin

For a sin to be mortal the following three conditions must be fulfilled: 1) grave matter, 2) sufficient knowledge and advertence, 3) full consent of the will. If any one of these is not fulfilled, there is no mortal sin.

If one has had the misfortune of having fallen into mortal sin, he ought immediately make an act of perfect contrition and go to confession as soon as he can. Mortal sin must always be confessed.

Venial sin

Venial sin is a lesser offense against God. Next to mortal sin, it is the greatest evil in the world. Venial sin, if committed frequently, weakens the will and paves the way for mortal sin. Since venial sin is a lesser offense against God, it may be forgiven outside of confession by Holy Communion, prayer, or good works, provided one no longer has an affection for the sin. It is, however, always better to confess venial sins.

Study questions

"It would be better for the sun and moon to drop from heaven, for the earth to fail, and for all the millions who are upon it to die of starvation in extremest agony, as far as temporal affliction goes, than that one soul, I will not say, should be lost, but should commit one single venial sin." 1 Would most people today agree with Cardinal Newman's statement? 2 Define: sin, original sin, actual sin. 3 What three conditions are necessary for mortal sin? 4 What ought one do if he has had the misfortune of sinning mortally?

3 God promises mankind a savior

After Adam's sin God did not abandon man to be forever the slave of sin and Satan. God, who is all good and all loving, promised to free man from Satan and to invite him anew to share in his divine love and life. Let us read about this in the Bible.

Then the Lord God said to the serpent: . . .
"I will put enmity between you and the woman,
between your seed and her seed;
he shall crush your head,
and you shall lie in wait for his heel." Genesis 3:14-15

The Church has traditionally seen in these words the first promise of a redeemer who would free man from Satan. They are merciful assurance that man's initial rejection of God's kingdom-invitation is to be repaired and that man is to be invited anew to share in God's love and life.

BIBLE MESSAGE

Christ teaches us today. When Scribes and Pharisees criticized Christ for eating with sinners, Christ replied, "The sick have need of a physician, not the healthy. It is my mission to call sinners, and not saints, to a change of heart." Luke 5:31-32.

1 Explain Christ's words. 2 Can you recall any other incidents where Christ goes out of his way to get sinners to have a change of heart?

LITURGY & LIFE

1 Salvation achieved by Christ.   Sculptors of the Middle Ages often depicted Christ trampling underfoot symbolic animals. Among these were the asp (a symbol of sin) and the viper (a symbol of death). See page 20.

Why did they show Christ this way? What promise does the adder (snake) remind you of? Through what two sacraments, especially, do we share in Christ's victory over sin and death? Explain your answer.

2 Salvation continued in the Church.   It is a wise plan for every high-school student "to have a regular confessor, some one priest to whom he confesses regularly and quite often. No priest to whom one goes only on occasion will give advice and direction that will fit one's problems exactly without a great many questions and explanations that are as tiring for the confessor as they are unpleasant for the penitent. The penitent, too, will generally feel more secure and more satisfied than he will if he skips at random from one confessor to another.

"If there is a question on your mind, ask it; if you find difficulty putting the question into words, do the best you can." J. R. Kelly, S.J.

What are the advantages of having a regular confessor? How does one choose a regular confessor? How often should one confess? Who really acts through the priest? Why is this sometimes difficult to realize?

3 Salvation history depicted in art.   A stained-glass window in Switzerland has three panels. The first panel shows a foot crushing a snake; the second shows a boat, a net, and a cross-shaped mast; the third shows a net with four fish in it. The fish are white, black, red, and yellow.

What story was the artist trying to tell? How does each panel of the stained-glass window contribute to the story? What is the meaning of: a) the snake, b) the foot, c) the boat, d) the net, e) the cross-shaped mast, f) the sail-like cloth on the mast, and g) the four different colored fish in the net?

Our redemption
is promised
by the Father

Our redemption
is realized
in Christ

Our redemption
is continued
in the Church

DOCTRINAL POINTS

Redemption

Adam's sin was a grave offence against the infinite God. Because of this it was an <u>infinite</u> offence and demanded infinite satisfaction. Now it was impossible for Adam to apologize adequately or to make infinite satisfaction. Human beings--if they unite together--cannot perform infinite acts. Only God can.

But God cannot apologize to himself for an offence of the human race any more than a king can apologize to himself for the offence of one of his servants. The apology must be made by the guilty party.

How then was perfect satisfaction to be made? No mere man could ever make it. It had to be made by a man, but one who was equal in dignity to God. In his wisdom and loving mercy God provided such a redeemer for Adam and the human race. The promised redeemer was his Son, Jesus Christ, true God and true man.

Study questions

1 Why couldn't mere man make adequate satisfaction for this offence? 2 What was the one way that adequate satisfaction could be made?

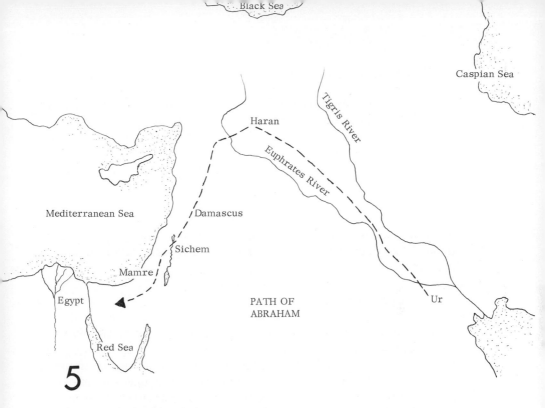

Map labels: Black Sea, Caspian Sea, Haran, Tigris River, Euphrates River, Mediterranean Sea, Damascus, Sichem, Mamre, Egypt, Red Sea, Ur, PATH OF ABRAHAM

5

GOD'S KINGDOM INVITATION IS ACCEPTED

1 God calls Abraham and makes a covenant with him

After a time of preparation, God carried out his promise to redeem man and to invite him anew to his kingdom. God did this in the following way.

Around the year 1850 B.C. there took place in Mesopotamia a migration from the city of Ur to the city of Haran. Among the migrating throng was the clan of a Bedouin sheik named Thare. One of his sons was named Abram. After the family was well established and prospering in Haran, God revealed himself to Abram. God invited Abram to leave his family and country and become the father of a new nation of people, out of which would come the promised redeemer. Let us read how the Bible records this.

The Lord said to Abram: "Leave your country,
your kinsfolk and your father's house,
for the land which I will show you;
I will make a great nation of you. . . .
In you shall all the nations of the earth
be blessed."   Genesis 12:1-3

67

Abram accepts God's invitation

Abram believes in God and accepts his invitation. The Bible records this fact very simply, "Abram went away . . ." Gathering together his servants and herds, Abram, with his wife, Sara, prepares to depart for the land that God will show him. Behind him Abram will leave his many friends and the prosperous life of Haran, his city. Behind him he will also leave the pagan ways of his former life.

When the hour of departure comes, the camel caravan of Abram and his household starts south for the unknown land. As the group disappears over the horizon, a new day begins to dawn in human history.

Abram and Christ

Abram's faith and obedience sets in motion the fulfillment of God's promise that Eve's seed will eventually crush the serpent's head. Genesis 3:15. In God's plan Abram will be the tiny mustard seed from which will grow a new nation. From it will come God's only begotten Son, who will redeem man and invite him anew to God's kingdom.

God makes a covenant with Abram

When Abram accepts God's invitation and departs from Haran, his life changes completely. God makes a covenant with him and invites him to be his special friend. Let us read how the Bible records this.

I am God the Almighty.
Walk in my presence and be perfect.
I will make my covenant between you and me . . .
This is my covenant with you:
You shall be the father of a multitude of nations;
you shall no longer be called Abram,
but your name shall be Abraham . . .
I will make nations of you,
and kings shall descend from you.
I will establish my covenant between you and me
and your descendants after you . . . as a perpetual covenant,
that I may be a God to you
and to your descendants . . .   Genesis 17:1-7

Covenants in Abraham's time

The idea of a covenant is not new to Abraham. It is a ceremony by which desert dwellers enter into a solemn agreement with one another. The ceremony includes a pledge, a meal, and a ritual called "cutting the covenant." In this ritual an animal is cut in two and the contracting parties march between the bleeding halves, showing by this that each would rather die than be disloyal to the other. The covenant between God and Abram is conceived in terms of such a friendship pact. Genesis 15:9-11.

Covenants were usually concluded by some external sign by which the covenant became public. Genesis 31:44-48.

The sign of God's covenant with Abraham

For Abraham the public sign of his friendship pact with God is twofold: 1) a change of name, and 2) circumcision. Genesis 17:11.

Abraham's descendants will also receive a special name; they will be called "Israelites." They will also receive the special mark of circumcision. These will be signs to all that by their faith in God they are true sons of Abraham and sharers in the covenant that God made with him. Circumcision will be for them, as St. Paul put it, "the seal of the holiness which comes from faith." Romans 4:11.

Christ established a new covenant

God's covenant with Abraham lasted until Christ established the New Covenant at the Last Supper. At that time, too, the Old Covenant sign was replaced by a new sign, not made by human hands but by God himself. Ephesians 2:12. This sign is the mark of the Holy Spirit that every Christian receives when he is baptized into Christ's mystical body. This mark seals him forever as a son of Abraham and a special friend of God.

BIBLE MESSAGE

Christ teaches us.   Christ said to the people, "Abraham, your father, exulted in the thought of seeing my day. He did see it, and was glad." John 8:56.

1 What did Christ mean? 2 Discuss and compare: a) Abraham's response to God's invitation to that of Adam's, b) Abraham's

future role in God's plan, c) God's covenant with Abraham, d) how the covenant and its sign were later replaced and fulfilled.

Some important biblical background

Today archeologists are making the time of Abraham come alive. Digging into ruins at Mari, a city destroyed nearly 4,000 years ago, a team of archeologists discovered the hidden archives of an ancient royal palace.

Their find yielded up nearly 20,000 clay tablets. When the ancient Babylonian language on the tablets was translated, the archeologists found themselves in possession of all kinds of data about the Patriarchal Age (named after the three patriarchs: Abraham, Isaac, and Jacob). Archeologists also found valuable clues that may lead to the reconstruction of the very dialect that Abraham spoke.

A similar dig--that's what archeologists call an excavation-- at Nuzu in Iraq has been even more valuable. It has not only yielded up information about the Patriarchal Age but also thrown light on practices mentioned in the Bible but not explained there. For instance, tablets found at Nuzu explain how ancient, pagan marriage contracts obliged a sterile wife to provide her husband with a servant so that the purpose of their marriage--children-- could be fulfilled. This helps explain why Sara readily provided Abraham with a servant for this purpose. (We will see more about this in the next lesson.)

LITURGY & LIFE

1 God's covenant with Abraham.   Speaking of God's covenant with Abraham, a writer said, "From the old decaying trunk of the human race, God broke off a frail shoot and planted it in a new land. The frail shoot would eventually grow into a great tree."

Explain the writer's statement. Why does the writer compare the human race to a "decaying" tree trunk?

2 Abraham's faith turns his life into an adventure.   In the Epistle to the Hebrews we read, "By faith Abraham . . . departed for a country which he was to receive as his property; moreover, he departed without knowing where he was going." Hebrews 11:8.

Abraham's faith in God turned his life into an adventure. It sent him journeying into the unknown. With family and servants,

70

he traveled uncharted lands. Abraham's faith also involved him in risks. He gambled a life and land that were familiar and certain for a life and land that were unknown and only promised. Finally, Abraham's faith demanded courage and trust in God. It forced him to leave the protection of his tribal clan in a period of history when small groups were safe only within the confines of the clan. Once he had to fight an enemy with only a handful of men. Genesis 14:14-16.

How does our faith in God: a) launch us into the unknown, b) involve us in risks, c) demand from us courage and trust in God? Point out how Abraham, our father in the faith, is a model for us in all three of these situations.

3 The true land of promise.   At Catholic burials this prayer is said by the priest: "May the angels lead you to the bosom of Abraham. Lord, grant that he for whom we pray may pass from death to the life which once you promised to Abraham and his descendants."

What is meant by the "bosom of Abraham"? See Luke 16:19-31. Ultimately, what is the life of promise to which God invited Abraham and his descendants?

2 Abraham is loyal to God

Abraham's life as a friend of God is not easy. Years after God promised Abraham that he would become the father of a great people, Abraham's wife Sara is still childless. Moreover, she is quite old. Because of this Sara allows Abraham to take a secondary wife that God's promise may be fulfilled.

Abraham's secondary wife, Agar, gives birth to a boy, Ismael. Abraham is happy. For a number of years Abraham lays plans around Ismael. Then one day God tells Abraham that he must wait for another son by his true wife Sara. Abraham doesn't see how this is possible, but he believes anyway. God rewards his faith as Sara bears a son, Isaac. Abraham's joy knows no bounds. Then comes a trial that tests Abraham's faith in God to the breaking point. Let us read how this is recorded in the Bible.

God said [to Abraham],
"Take your only son Isaac whom you love . . .
and there offer him as a holocaust on the hill
which I shall point out to you." Genesis 22:2

Abraham was stunned. Was God asking him to kill his beloved
son and destroy the one way God had of making him the father of
a great nation? Abraham didn't know what to think, but he resolved
to obey God.

Abraham took the wood for the holocaust
and put it upon his son Isaac
while he himself carried the fire and the knife. . . .
    When they arrived at the place of which God had told him,
Abraham built an altar there and arranged the wood on it.
Then he bound his son Isaac and laid him on the wood upon the altar
    Abraham stretched out his hand,
and took the knife to kill his son.
But an angel of the Lord called to him . . . "Abraham . . .
Do not lay a hand on the boy; do nothing to him.
I know now that you fear God, since you have not withheld
your only son from me."   Genesis 22:6-12

Abraham's faith grows strong

Abraham resolves to trust God no matter the cost--even if it
means the loss of his own beloved son. Through trials and heroic
acts such as this, Abraham's faith grows strong and his friendship
with God grows perfect.

BIBLE MESSAGE

Christ teaches us today.   Speaking to the Pharisees, Christ
said, "If you are children of Abraham . . . you ought to do what
Abraham did." John 8:39.
    1 What do you think Christ was referring to? 2 Compare Abra-
ham's loyalty to that of Adam when he was tested.

Some important biblical background

Isaac is sometimes looked upon as a "type" of Christ. (A "type"
is an Old Testament person, thing, or event intended by God to

foreshadow or resemble a New Testament person, thing, or e-
vent.) Like Christ, Isaac is the beloved son of his father. Like
Christ, he is willingly given by his father to be sacrificed. Like
Christ, he carries the wood of sacrifice. Finally, like Christ,
he is to be sacrificed on a hill.

Jacob

When Isaac grows up, he marries Rebecca. They have two sons:
Esau and Jacob. Before Isaac dies he passes on God's promise to
Jacob. One night Jacob has an extraordinary religious experience.
During it he is told that his name is to be changed. A voice says,
"You shall no longer be called Jacob, but Israel." Genesis 32:29.
Whenever the Bible records a name change it is a sign of something important about the vocation and life of the person. The
name Israel means "may God show him strong." God does exactly
this for Jacob. God passes on his promise to all of Jacob's twelve
sons and their descendants, not merely to one of the sons. From
now on they will be called the children of Israel or Israelites.

Joseph

Of the twelve sons of Jacob, Joseph is especially loved by his
father. This triggers the envy of the other sons, who sell Joseph
into slavery. Genesis 37. Joseph soon finds himself in Egypt. At
the time an Asiatic people known as Hyksos are in control of
Egypt. Among the Hyksos, Joseph soon finds great favor. Genesis
41:37-44. About this time a famine hits Joseph's homeland, and
his father and brothers are driven to Egypt for food. Joseph forgives his brothers and even arranges with Pharao to give them
choice grazing lands in Gesen for their herds. Genesis 47:1-12.

Juda

Before he dies Jacob assembles his twelve sons and blesses
them. On this occasion he prophesies of Juda, "Juda, your brothers
shall praise you . . . The sceptre shall not depart from Juda,
nor the staff from between his feet until he comes to whom it belongs. To him shall be the obedience of nations." Genesis 49:8-10.
In symbolic language Jacob announces that Juda's tribe will be
singularly blessed. From its ranks will come David the king,
who will rule over the chosen people. And from David's line will
come Christ, the king of kings, who will rule over all nations.

73

Study questions

1 Explain how Isaac is a "type" of Christ. 2 How did God show Jacob strong? 3 What precipitated Joseph's being sold? 4 How does Joseph remind you of Christ? 5 Of what are the sceptre and staff symbols? 6 Do you see any connection between these symbols and the crosier which the bishop uses at solemn liturgical functions? Read Luke 1:31-33, and show how it relates to Jacob's oracle.

LITURGY & LIFE

1 The Mass speaks of Abraham's sacrifice. In the Canon of the Mass, just after the Consecration, the priest prays:

Be pleased to look on these offerings . . .
accept them as you were pleased to accept
the offerings of your servant holy Abel,
the sacrifice of our father Abraham,
and that of your high priest Melchisedech --
a holy sacrifice, and unblemished victim.

Explain the prayer. Why do we call Abraham "our father"? Who was Melchisedec? Read Genesis 14:18-20.

2 Christ recalls Abraham's faith. "When he [Christ] returned to Capharnaum, a centurion approached and appealed to him in the following words: 'Sir, my slave lies sick at home; he is paralyzed and suffers frightfully.' Jesus said to him: 'Am I to come and cure him?' By way of answer the centurion said: 'Sir, I am not fit to have you come under my roof. No, only utter a word, and my slave will be cured. . . .'
"On hearing this Jesus was struck with admiration, and said to the accompanying crowd: 'I tell you frankly, I have never found such lively faith anywhere in Israel! I tell you, crowds of people will arrive from east and west and, in the company of Abraham, Isaac, and Jacob, will recline at table in the kingdom of heaven, when, at the same time, the born citizens of the realm will be hurled into the outer darkness.'" Matthew 8:5-12.
Who are born citizens of the realm? Is it enough to receive the "gift of faith" in baptism? Read James 2:20-26. When do we recite the centurion's words at Mass? What is meant by the expression to "recline at table in the kingdom of heaven"?

74

DOCTRINAL POINTS

Faith puts us in orbit

Faith is the power that launches us into the orbit of the supernatural world. It brings us into direct contact with God. Of ourselves we are powerless to make this contact; it must be initiated by God. This is clear from the Bible. It was God who spoke first to Abraham. Because God initiates contact through faith, we speak of faith as a gift. We can do nothing to merit it; it comes as a free invitation from God.

Even after God contacts us, we are powerless to believe in him and in what he tells us. Our human strength is not enough; we need the supernatural help of God's grace. Thus there is a second reason why faith is a gift. God first invites us to faith; he then gives us the power to accept his invitation once it has been made.

Faith and baptism

God freely initiated contact with each one of us. For most of us that took place in baptism. At that time God also pledged us whatever graces we would ever need to continue to believe in him and in all that he tells us.

We may define faith as that supernatural gift by which God invites and empowers us to accept him and to believe on his authority whatever he tells us.

Faith gives us absolute certitude

When we believe something on God's authority, we are absolutely certain that it is true; for God can neither deceive nor be deceived. He cannot deceive because he is all-truthful; he cannot be deceived because he is all-knowing.

Because we know that God always speaks the truth, we always believe him even though we cannot fully understand what he says. A truth of revelation beyond the power of our human reason to understand fully is called a mystery. Though a mystery is beyond reason, it is never contrary to it.

Trials of faith

Trials of faith may arise in our life. If they do, we ought not become unduly alarmed, for we have finite minds, and therefore

75

we do not always see things clearly. It is enough for us to know that God has revealed a certain truth. We do not doubt it, although it is quite possible for us to have a problem in connection with it. We would sin against faith by denying or willfully doubting any truth revealed by God and proposed by the Church for our belief. To deny our faith would be a mortal sin.

How faith is weakened

If we lose our faith, we have lost everything. Only the great mercy of God can set us right again. We ought therefore avoid anything that tends to weaken or destroy faith. We may list these as follows: 1) a sinful and impure life, which makes us try to create arguments against what faith teaches, so that we can have excuses for what we do; 2) pride, which makes us imagine we know better than others and which causes us to attach importance to difficulties against faith that occur to our minds; 3) evil companions; 4) books or papers that tend to break down our faith; and 5) not repelling temptations against the faith. If temptations tend to come back often, we ought to discuss the problem with our counselor or a priest.

How faith is strengthened

Besides avoiding what tends to weaken our faith, we ought to seek out those things that tend to increase our faith. We may list these as follows: 1) leading a good life, 2) frequenting the sacraments, 3) studying our faith, 4) cultivating good friendships, and 5) praying and making acts of faith.

If difficulties of faith arise, we should recall the story of Abraham and imitate his loyalty and trust in God.

Study questions

"And scarce do we guess the things on earth, and what is within our grasp we find with difficulty; but when things are in heaven, who can search them out?" Wisdom 9:16.

1 What is the point of this passage from the Book of Wisdom?
2 Define faith. 3 Give the two reasons why faith is a gift. 4 Why does faith give us absolute certitude? 5 What is a mystery?
6 How is faith weakened? 7 How is faith strengthened and preserved?

6

GOD FORMS A KINGLY PEOPLE

1 God calls Moses

For centuries the children of Israel live at peace in Egypt. During this time they develop from a family into a people. Then, about 1550 B.C., the Egyptians throw off the yoke of the Hyksos. The upshot of this is that the Israelites are no longer welcome in Egypt. Soon they are oppressed and enslaved.

In spite of this, however, the Israelites continue to grow in numbers and strength. This growth worries the Egyptian leaders and they decide on drastic measures to curtail it. Pharao finally orders that from a certain date forward, every newly-born Hebrew boy is to be thrown into the Nile. Exodus 1:22. For the Israelites this begins a time of great trial.

Providentially, a Hebrew boy escapes, when an Egyptian princess rescues him and adopts him as her own, naming him Moses. Exodus 2:10. Though he is brought up as an Egyptian, Moses never forgets his people. One day when he catches an Egyptian maltreating a Hebrew, he turns on the Egyptian and kills him. Exodus 2:11-15. Knowing what will happen if Pharao discovers him, Moses flees to Madian, near Mt. Sinai, where he becomes

a shepherd. Meanwhile God's people continue to suffer, but they
never lose faith. They only increase their prayers for deliverance.

Finally, the hour comes when God answers Israel's prayers.
One day, in the pasture fields of Madian, God appears to Moses
in a burning bush. Let us read how the Bible records this great
event. God says:

"I am . . . the God of Abraham, the God of Isaac,
the God of Jacob. . . . I have witnessed the affliction
of my people in Egypt and have heard their cry . . .
I will send you to Pharao to lead my people,
the Israelites, out of Egypt."
   But Moses said to God,
". . . when I go to the Israelites and say to them,
'The God of your fathers has sent me to you,'
if they ask me, 'What is his name?'
what am I to tell them?"
God replied, "I am who am." Exodus 3:6-14

Moses leads Israel

Moses does as God commands. Leaving his flocks he sets out
for Egypt. There he delivers God's message to Pharao, who treats
it with scorn. But in the days ahead, a series of events makes
Pharao change his mind. Here is an account of the last event in
the series.

The Lord said to Moses . . .
". . . every one of your families must procure for itself a lamb
. . . it shall be slaughtered during the evening twilight.
They shall take some of its blood
and apply it to the two doorposts and the lintel of every house
. . . That same night they shall eat its roasted flesh . . ."
   Moses called all the elders of Israel and said to them,
"Go and procure lambs for your families,
and slaughter them as Passover victims.
Then take a bunch of hyssop, and dipping it
in the blood that is in the basin,
sprinkle the lintel and the two doorposts with this blood.
But none of you shall go outdoors until morning.
For the Lord will go by, striking down the Egyptians.
Seeing the blood on the lintel and the two doorposts,
the Lord will pass over that door and not let

78

the destroyer come into your houses to strike you down.
"You shall observe this as a perpetual ordinance
for yourselves and your descendants.
Thus, you must also observe this rite
when you have entered the land
which the Lord will give you as he promised. . . ."
At midnight the Lord slew every first-born . . .
and there was loud wailing throughout Egypt . . .
Pharao summoned Moses and Aaron and said,
"Leave my people at once,
you and the Israelites with you!"   Exodus 12:1-31

Israel's passover sacrifice foreshadows Christ's sacrifice

The Israelites do as Moses instructs them. By the blood of the passover lamb they are saved from death and freed from the slavery of the Egyptians. By eating the flesh of the passover lamb they are nourished for the long journey about to begin.

Years later by the blood of another passover lamb, the Lamb of God, men will be saved from eternal death and freed from the slavery of Satan. By eating the flesh of the Lamb of God they will receive nourishment for the long journey through life.

Israel's Passover is completed

Filled with joy, the people of Israel set out with their flocks and meager belongings. But more trouble lies ahead.

When it was reported to the king of Egypt
that the people had fled,
Pharao . . . pursued the Israelites . . .
Then the Lord told Moses, "Stretch out your hand over the sea,
that the water may flow back upon the Egyptians . . ."
So Moses stretched out his hand . . .
the sea flowed back . . . it covered the chariots
and the charioteers of Pharao's whole army . . .
Not a single one of them escaped.
Thus the Lord saved Israel on that day from the power of the
Egyptians.
When Israel saw the Egyptians lying dead . . .
and beheld the great power that the Lord
had shown against the Egyptians, they feared the Lord
and believed in him and in his servant Moses.   Exodus 14:5-31

The Passover is Israel's greatest feast

No event etched itself more deeply on the Israelite's mind than did this one. It taught the Israelites God's special love for them. If, in years to come, you asked an Israelite to define God, he would simply say, "He is the Lord, our God, who brought us out of the land of Egypt, the house of bondage."

Future generations of Israelites celebrated the feast of the Passover (the commemoration of God's deliverance of Israel from death and the slavery of Egypt) with great joy. At each yearly celebration, the young Israelite boy listened as his elders retold the thrilling story. The recital of it made him feel a solidarity with his forefathers. For in the gaining of their freedom, he too, in a real sense, gained his.

BIBLE MESSAGE

When our country won its political independence, one of the independence leaders said, "I am apt to believe that [this day] will be celebrated by succeeding generations as a great anniversary festival. It ought to be commemorated as a day of deliverance by solemn acts of devotion to Almighty God. It ought to be solemnized with pomp and parade, with shows, games, sports, guns, bells, bonfires and illuminations from one end of this continent to the other, from this time forward forever more."

1 How is our independence day similar to the Old Testament Passover? 2 On what day do Christians the world over celebrate the anniversary of the New Testament Passover? 3 Describe Moses' role in the Old Testament Passover. 4 Why do you think Christ is often referred to as the new Moses? 5 Describe Christ's role in the New Testament Passover.

Some important biblical background

Exodus means "going out." This is a good title for the second book of the Bible. For the key story of the book tells how God led Israel out of Egypt and made her his chosen people at Mt. Sinai.

Like the Book of Genesis, the Book of Exodus can lead to misunderstandings unless we keep in mind the four rules for reading the Bible, namely: 1) Know the historical background. 2) Know the literary form. 3) Decide the author's purpose in writing. 4) Discover the religious truth God wishes to teach.

80

Historical background and purpose of Exodus

The historical background to the Book of Exodus is this. When
God led the Israelites out of Egypt and made them his chosen people, he commanded them to celebrate this event each year with
a series of holidays, climaxed by a passover banquet. God also
commanded that at each yearly celebration the father must explain to the children the reason for the days of rejoicing. He must
explain to them "the glorious deeds of the Lord . . . and the wonders that he wrought." Psalm 77:4

Literary form of Exodus

The Book of Exodus, as it has come down to us, is a later com-
pilation of many of these stories which for centuries were handed
down by word of mouth from father to son. Because the purpose of
these stories was to teach the Hebrew children how God intervened
in Israel's history to save and bless them, we find that the sacred
author frequently heightened or dramatized the events to make
them easily understood by his young audience. The name given to
this amplified style of writing is epic style. Thus when the
sacred author says in Exodus 12:37 that 600,000 men, not count-
ing children, escaped from Egypt, he doesn't intend this figure to
have mathematical significance. He uses the 600,000 as a symbol to indicate that an enormous number escaped--too many for
a Hebrew boy to count.
So, too, the description of the plagues is made dramatic. Prac-
tically all commentators agree that there is nothing intrinsically
miraculous about the plagues. For example, the first plague could
well be identified with the yearly flooding of the Nile, at which time
it turns a deep red color.
We ought also remember that Hebrews had a different idea of
a miracle from what we have. For us a miracle is had only when
it is certain that the laws of nature have been suspended. For the
Hebrews any dust storm or flash flood that helped them in some
way was considered a special act of God.

The religious truth

The main point behind the plague account is that God delivered
the Hebrew people from Pharao. Their salvation was not due to
any human power; God's hand alone did it. This is the religious
truth God wishes to teach us.

Study questions

Samuel Baker, one of the first explorers of the Nile River, tells how he was once caught in a dust storm so intense that for twenty minutes he could not distinguish his hand before his face. 1 Of what plague does this remind you? Exodus 10:21. 2 What is the main point behind the plague account?

LITURGY & LIFE

1 The miraculous manna and water foreshadow the Eucharist. Shortly after the Israelites escaped over the Red Sea into the desert, they ran out of food and water. God intervened to help them in a special way. Exodus 15:22-16:36. Twelve hundred years later Jesus referred to this intervention. " . . . who comes to me will never hunger, and he who believes in me will never thirst. . . . I am the living bread that has come down from heaven. If one eats of this bread, he will live forever. . . . John 6:35,51.
Describe how God intervened to help the Israelites? How does the food and drink that God gives us through Christ differ from that which he gave through Moses to the Israelites? How are they similar?

2 The saving waters of the Red Sea foreshadow the saving waters of baptism. During the Easter vigil liturgy, the Church prays: "O God, in our time we see the wonders you did of old. As once you showed your power by delivering a single people from Egyptian oppression, so now you save all people by the water of new birth. Grant that the whole of mankind may become sons of Abraham and share the inheritance of Israel's children. Amen."
What sacrament is being referred to? Explain how this sacrament is similar to the passage over the Red Sea. Do you think God intended this similarity? Read 1 Corinthians 10:1-5.

3 God is all-holy. When God spoke to Moses from the burning bush, he said, "Remove the sandals from your feet, for the place where you stand is holy ground." Exodus 3:1-5. The practice of removing the shoes is still observed by Moslems when they enter the mosque.
Why do you think God gave Moses this command? How do Catholics normally show reverence in God's presence? Why show reverence at all?

Then the Lord said to Moses,
"I will now rain down bread
from heaven for you" Exodus 16:4.

But the serpent said to the woman,
". . . when you eat of it,
your eyes will be opened and
you will be like God" Genesis 3:4-5.

Jesus answered . . .
"Your fathers ate the manna
in the desert, and they died.
The bread which I speak of,
which comes down from heaven,
is such that
no one who eats of it will ever die.
I am the living bread that has
come down from heaven" John 6:43-51.

DOCTRINAL POINTS

What is God like?

Earlier we looked at some of God's perfections. For instance, we saw that he was almighty and self-existent. We now look at other perfections.

God's perfections are called attributes. These attributes are not separate perfections which, all added together, make God what he is. We only speak of them as if they were separate because we are trying to describe in human language the infinite perfections of God.

God is all-holy

When Moses approached God in the burning bush, God told him to remove his shoes for the ground on which he stood was holy. The reason the ground was holy is that God is all-holy. When we say that God is all-holy we mean there is no trace of evil in him. He is totally good and perfect. He is the exact opposite of anything that is evil. In his sight the greatest saint appears as a great sinner.

God is eternal

When Moses asked God what his name was, God said, "I am who am." Exodus 3:14. God always was and always will be. He is eternal; that is, he has no beginning and no end. Jesus told the Jews, ". . . I was before Abraham!" John 8:58.

God is infinite

God is also infinite. Finis is the Latin word for "end." A thing is finite if it has an end or limit to it. God is infinite because there is no end or limit to his perfections. He has all perfection possible to the highest degree. Because God is infinitely perfect and thus supreme in every way, he cannot have an equal. Therefore, there can be only one God.

God is unchangeable

God never changes; he remains always the same. If he gained something new, it would mean that he had not been perfect before.

If he lost something, it would mean that he had ceased to be as perfect as he had been. Nor does God change in the sense that he is angry when we sin and happy when we are good. No, that is only our human way of speaking about God.

God is all-knowing

God is all-knowing. He knows all things: past, present, future, and all possible things. He knows our thoughts more perfectly than we know them ourselves. "And no creature is hidden from him: all things are laid bare and are uncovered to the eyes of him to whom we have to render account." Hebrews 4:13.

God is all-present

God is everywhere. He is present, first of all, by his power. He holds all things in existence. He is also present by his knowledge because he knows everything. "Even the hairs on your head are all numbered," said Jesus. Luke 12:7.

God does, however, make the effects of his presence felt more in one place than in another. Therefore, it is right for us to speak of him as particularly present in heaven. Therefore, he can also become present in us in a new way in baptism, in confirmation, and in Holy Communion.

God is a pure spirit

Although God is everywhere, we do not see him. This is because he is pure spirit. Jesus said to the Samaritan woman at the well, "God is Spirit." John 4:24. A spirit is a being without a body, but with an intellect and free will. The angels and devils are spirits, and man is partly spiritual because he has a soul as well as a body.

Since God has no body, when we speak of his eyes and his hands we speak only in a figurative manner to accommodate ourselves to our human way of speaking.

Study questions

"A God we could completely understand would not be God."
1 Why is this statement of St. Augustine true? 2 What do we mean when we speak of an attribute of God? 3 What do we mean when we say that God is: eternal, infinite, unchangeable, all-knowing, all-present, pure spirit?

2 God makes Israel his chosen people

When our forefathers gained their freedom, they were still not a nation. It was not until the framing of our Constitution that they became one people.

The Israelites were in a similar state when they gained their freedom from the Egyptians. They needed a constitution to bind them together into one people: the chosen people of God. They received this constitution from God on Mt. Sinai. Let us read how the Bible records this for us.

In the third month after their departure
from the land of Egypt, on its first day,
the Israelites came to the desert of Sinai. . . .
While Israel was encamped here in front of the mountain,
Moses went up the mountain to God.
Then the Lord called to him and said,
"Thus shall you say to the house of Jacob; tell the Israelites:
You have seen for yourselves how I treated the Egyptians
and how I bore you up on eagle wings
and brought you here to myself.
Therefore, if you hearken to my voice and keep my covenant,
you shall be my special possession,
dearer to me than all other people,
though all the earth is mine.
You shall be to me a kingdom of priests, a holy nation." . . .
    So Moses went and summoned the elders of the people.
When he set before them all that the Lord
had ordered him to tell them, the people all answered together,
"Everything the Lord has said, we will do." . . .
    On the morning of the third day there were peals of thunder . . .
and a heavy cloud over the mountain,
and a very loud trumpet blast,
so that all the people in the camp trembled.
But Moses led the people out of the camp to meet God
 . . . When the Lord came down to the top of Mount Sinai,
he summoned Moses to the top of the mountain . . .
    Then God delivered all these commandments:
"I, the Lord, am your God,
who brought you out of the land of Egypt, that place of slavery.
You shall not have other gods besides me. . . .
You shall not take the name of the Lord, your God, in vain. . . .
Remember to keep holy the Sabbath day. . . .

Honor your father and your mother. . . .
You shall not kill.
You shall not commit adultery.
You shall not steal.
You shall not bear false witness against your neighbor.
You shall not covet your neighbor's house.
You shall not covet your neighbor's wife . . ." Exodus 19-20
    Moses then wrote down all the words of the Lord
and, rising early the next day,
he erected at the foot of the mountain an altar
and twelve pillars for the twelve tribes of Israel.
Then, having sent certain young men of the Israelites
to offer holocausts and sacrifice young bulls
as peace offerings to the Lord, Moses took half of the blood
and put it in large bowls;
the other half he splashed on the altar.
Taking the Book of the Covenant,
he read it aloud to the people, who answered,
"All that the Lord has said, we will heed and do."
Then he took the blood and sprinkled it on the people, saying,
"This is the blood of the covenant
which the Lord has made with you
in accordance with all these words of his." Exodus 24:4-8

The covenant is Israel's most precious heritage

Once at Mt. Sinai, Moses and the people enter into a solemn
covenant with God. By the covenant God becomes Israel's God, and
Israel becomes God's chosen people. Henceforward the covenant
is Israel's most precious heritage. It is the source of her privileges and responsibilities. By the covenant Israel takes on specific
obligations, which she gladly assumes out of love for what God
has done for her. In return she is confident that God will always
protect and guide her as his chosen people.

The covenant sets Israel apart from other nations

Somewhat as the consecration of a priest acts him apart from
other men, so the covenant, which makes Israel "a kingdom of
priests" (Exodus 19:6), sets her apart from other nations. As
with the priest, so Israel's calling results in a blessing for
all men. By her love and obedience to God, Israel becomes a
"light to the Gentiles."

The covenant will last until Christ's time

The covenant which God made with Israel will last for 1300 years. Then Christ will inaugurate a New Covenant which will surpass and fulfill the Old Covenant. The New Covenant will a-chieve men's redemption from sin and make them not just God's chosen people but his adopted sons as well.

BIBLE MESSAGE

Christ teaches us today.   Christ took a cup of wine at the Last Supper, blessed it, and said, "This cup is the new covenant sealed by my blood, which is about to be shed for your sake." Luke 22:20.
1 How did the New Covenant, inaugurated by Christ, surpass and fulfill the Old Covenant? 2 Compare the Old Covenant to: a) our country's Constitution, b) the ordination of a priest. 3 Why was the Old Covenant Israel's most precious heritage?

Some important biblical background

Blood always played an important part in Hebrew covenants. The reason for this is that, for the Hebrews, it symbolized life. "The life of a living body is in its blood." Leviticus 17:11. When two people mingle their blood, it signifies that a life bond now exists between them. This idea is still prevalent. Among certain primitive peoples, when two men enter into a pact of friendship, they jab their wrists and press them together so that their blood mixes. This makes them blood brothers. Thereafter they will fight to death for each other.
This helps us to understand Moses' action at Mt. Sinai. When he took blood and sprinkled half of it on the altar (a symbol of God) and half of it on the people, he was showing by his action the closeness that now began to exist between God and Israel. In a sense, they were blood brothers.

Sharing a meal is also a sign of friendship

Like the mingling of blood, the sharing of a meal is also a mark of special friendship. (This is why the Pharisees criticized Christ when he ate with sinners.)
The meal eventually became the way the Hebrews relived the Passover and renewed the Sinai covenant.

The Mass, our reliving of the new Passover and our renewal of the New Covenant, takes the form of a meal: the Last Supper. In the light of this we can better see the significance of and importance of receiving Holy Communion at each Mass.

LITURGY & LIFE

1 Israel is different from other nations.   A leading Jewish scholar has written, "Israel is not a 'natural' nation . . . like the nations of the world. It is a supernatural community, called into being by God to serve His eternal purposes in history . . . apart from the covenant, Israel is as nothing . . ."
What is a natural nation? Why was Israel different? What purpose did Israel serve in God's plan?

2 Moses is the nation's founder.   A biblical scholar once said, "If Abraham is the father of his people, Moses is the founder of the nation."
How was Abraham the father of his people? Why is Moses the founder of the nation? Why is Christ often referred to as the new Moses? List the similarities between Christ and Moses.

3 The nation's "Constitution": The Ten Commandments. C. B. DeMille, producer of the movie Ten Commandments, says that he thinks the commandment people break the most today is the first. We don't burn incense before the secret idols in our homes. "But," says DeMille, "which of us has not, at some time, worshiped a god of gold or a god of flesh or a god of ambition more than we have worshiped God himself?"
What does DeMille mean by a god of gold, a god of flesh, or a god of ambition? When did the Israelites first break this commandment? Exodus 32:1-29. Are DeMille's examples really sins against the first commandment? Are "gold, flesh, and ambition" wrong in themselves? Discuss.

4 The psalmist sings of the Ten Commandments:

How I love your law, O Lord! . . .
I love your command more than gold . . .
Wonderful are your decrees . . .
May my tongue sing of your promise,
for all your commands are just.   Psalm 118

3 God gives Israel a home

The Sinai covenant made Israel God's chosen people. The next step in God's plan was to give his people a home. To carry out this mission God chose Josue. Let us read of this in the Bible.

After Moses, the servant of the Lord, had died,
the Lord said to Moses' aide Josue, son of Nun:
"My servant Moses is dead. So prepare
to cross the Jordan here, with all the people,
into the land I will give the Israelites." Josue 1:1-2
    Early the next morning, Josue moved
with all the Israelites from Sattim to the Jordan,
where they lodged before crossing over. . . .
    Then the Lord said to Josue, "Today I will begin
to exalt you in the sight of all Israel, that they
may know I am with you, as I was with Moses."
. . . The people struck their tents to cross the Jordan,
with the priests carrying the Ark of the Covenant ahead of them.
No sooner had these priestly bearers of the Ark
waded into the waters . . . than the waters . . . halted . . .
all Israel crossed over on dry ground . . .   Josue 3
    While the Israelites were encamped at Galgal on the plains
of Jericho, they celebrated the Passover . . .   Josue 5:10
    Now Jericho was in a state of siege
because of the presence of the Israelites,
so that no one left or entered.
And to Josue the Lord said, "I have delivered
Jericho and its king into your power."   Josue 6:1-3

Josue leads Israel to victory

With God's guidance, Josue and the Israelites storm the fortified city of Jericho. It falls. The collapse occurs about 1200 B.C., but it will be many years before all Chanaanite resistance ceases. In time, however, Chanaan falls completely into the hands of God's people, and it becomes their home on earth.

Israel renews the covenant

When he was advanced in age, Josue called together the Israelites to renew the covenant with God. Let us read how the Bible records this.

Many years later, . . . when Josue was old and advanced in years,
he summoned all Israel . . . and said to them:
"I am old and advanced in years.
You have seen all that the Lord, your God,
has done for you against all these nations;
for it has been the Lord, your God, himself
who fought for you. . . . Now, therefore, fear the Lord
and serve him completely and sincerely. . . ."
But the people answered Josue,
"We will still serve the Lord." . . .
Then he [Josue] took a large stone and set it up there . . .
And Josue said to all the people,
"This stone shall . . . be a witness against you,
should you wish to deny your God."
Then Josue dismissed the people . . .
After these events Josue, son of Nun,
servant of the Lord, died . . .   Josue 23:1--24:29

Israel divides into tribes

After Josue's death, the Israelites settle in little pockets and
groups in their newly won home. There is no longer a central
leader, so each of the twelve tribes of Israel looks after its own
government. "In those days," says the Bible, "there was no king
in Israel; everyone did what he thought best." Judges 21:25.

One unifying force remains, however. It is the common faith
in God. At a place called Silo, the Israelites build a central sanctuary and place there the Ark of the Covenant, containing the stone
tablets on which are engraved the Ten Commandments received
at Mt. Sinai. By means of this sanctuary, the twelve tribes of
Israel manage to maintain some measure of unity and common
action.

Israel is threatened from within

But in time two forces begin to threaten Israel's religious and
political existence. The first force is an internal one. Even though
Chanaanite power has been crushed, nevertheless, many Chanaanite
citizens survive. Some are rich and influential. It is only natural
that they begin to intermingle and intermarry with the sons of
Israel. Because of this corrupting influence, many Israelites
begin to compromise their covenant promises. In some areas great
numbers of Israelites give way completely to pagan practices.

But God never abandons his people, even though they abandon him. He uses their acts of infidelity and error to teach them of his own mercy and fidelity. Punishment, in the form of some disaster, frequently sweeps down upon the chosen people. They recognize in it the hand of God and repent and return again to him. And always God receives them back.

Israel is threatened from without

The second force threatening Israel's political and religious existence is that of hostile foreign powers, especially the Philistines. What made the Philistines a particular threat was that they had developed iron weapons which gave them an overwhelming military advantage against other armies.

Foreign powers such as the Philistines constantly menace the scattered tribes of Israel. From time to time Judges (inspired leaders), such as Samson and Gedeon, rise up to lead the people. But the Judges are few and far between. Moreover, some of them become involved in infidelity to God.

Israel becomes a kingdom

The situation reaches the breaking point around the year 1050 B.C. Then, during the judgeship of a holy man named Samuel, Philistine armies kidnap the Ark of the Covenant and demolish the holy sanctuary at Silo. This event shakes Israel to her foundations.

Seven months later the Ark is returned, but it is now clear that a more stable form of government is imperative if Israel is to survive as a nation.

After much prayer the holy Samuel decides upon an unprecedented step. He anoints a king, in the hope that this move will help unite the Israelites and preserve them as a nation. The choice falls to Saul.

BIBLE MESSAGE

Christ teaches us.   Christ said: ". . . suppose a family is split into factions: that family cannot possibly last." Mark 3:25.
1 How was this the case with Israel in the promised land? Discuss: a) the similarity between the crossing of the Red Sea and the crossing of the Jordan, b) the renewal of the covenant, c) the political and religious unity after Josue's death, d) the two threats to Israel's unity, e) Samuel's solution.

LITURGY & LIFE

1 Life in the promised land.   If you hold a pure gold nugget
in your hand, it seems perfectly solid. Yet scientists tell us that
within the nugget molecules are racing around at fantastic speeds.
Now press the gold nugget against a block of solid silver. When
you separate the two, they seem unchanged. Yet a physical chemist
can prove that invisible flecks of the gold have crossed over and
embedded themselves in the silver, and invisible flecks of the silver have crossed over and embedded themselves in the gold.

Recently a writer used this fact to point out that something
similar happens with human beings.

Explain what the writer meant. How does the gold and silver
example explain the paganizing effect that the Chanaanites had
on many Israelites? Apply the example of the gold and silver
nuggets to the life of a high-school student.

2 The true promised land.   In his book How to Read the Bible,
Father Poelman says, "The migration of the chosen people [to the
promised land] makes us think of the continual passage of the souls
of the faithful from this vale of tears into the true land of God."

What is he referring to? In what sense is heaven the true promised land? Do you think Father Poelman was thinking about John
14:1-3 when he wrote this? Explain.

7

GOD GIVES HIS PEOPLE A KING

1 <u>God calls David</u>

After Samuel anoints Saul to be king, the Israelites achieve
a certain degree of unity. But it is not long before Saul becomes
unworthy of his kingship. Under God's inspiration Samuel then
anoints David. Let us see how the Bible records this.

And the Lord said to Samuel:
How long wilt thou mourn for Saul
whom I have rejected from reigning over Israel?
Fill thy horn with oil, and come,
that I may send thee to Isai the Bethlehemite:
for I have provided me a king among his sons. . . .
    Then Samuel did as the Lord had said to him. . . .
Isai therefore brought his seven sons before Samuel.
And Samuel said to Isai:
The Lord hath not chosen any one of these. . . .
Are here all thy sons?
He answered: There remaineth yet a young one,
who keepeth the sheep.

And Samuel said to Isai: Send, and fetch him . . .
He sent therefore and brought him.
Now he was ruddy and beautiful to behold,
and of a comely face.
And the Lord said: Arise, and anoint him, for this is he.
Then Samuel took the horn of oil,
and anointed him in the midst of his brethren.
And the spirit of the Lord came upon David
from that day forward. . . .   1 Kings 16:1-13

David foreshadows Christ

David does not immediately take over Saul's post. This comes
later, after Saul's death. Meanwhile God prepares David for his
new calling. David is to be a direct ancestor of Christ; his kingship over Israel will foreshadow Christ's kingship over all men.

We share in Christ's kingship and priesthood

By our baptism we have been called by God in much the same
way as David was called. Like David, we too were anointed with
oil. The most important baptismal anointing (there were two) took
place just after the pouring of the baptismal water. It was performed with holy chrism, the same oil that the Church uses to
ordain priests and to crown kings. The reason why the Church
uses holy chrism at baptisms is to signify that by baptism we
become not only members of Christ's mystical body, but also
sharers in his priesthood and his kingship. Like David, we have
received a high calling from God.

BIBLE MESSAGE

Christ teaches us today.   Christ put this question to the
Pharisees, "'What do you think about the Messias?' he said;
'whose Son is he?' 'David's,' they replied. 'In what sense,
then,' he asked them, 'does David, prompted by the Spirit, call
him "Lord," . . . If, then, David calls him "Lord," In what
sense is he his "Son"?' No one was able to say a word to answer
him." Matthew 22:42-46.
    1 Can you answer Christ's question? 2 Discuss: a) Samuel's
anointing of David, b) how David foreshadowed Christ, c) the
significance of our baptismal anointing with holy chrism.

95

Some important biblical background

After Israel becomes a kingdom it is necessary to have certain young men act as attendants and messengers to the king.
Since these young men will walk daily in the king's court, it is desirable that they be schooled in court ways and court courtesy.

Israel solves this schooling problem by looking to Egypt.
Egypt had a long tradition of courtiers and a detailed program
for the training of these young men. A program of Ptah-hotep,
dating from about 2450 B.C., is still extant today. Among other
things, it counsels the young courtier to be on his guard against
useless talk and pride. It also tells him to be polite and modest
in his dealings with important people.

Israel borrows and adapts Egyptian rules

Since many of the Egyptian rules for courtiers posed noble
ideals, it is not surprising to find that Israel borrowed heavily
from them. Yet, Israel does more than merely borrow. She re-
interprets these rules in the light of her faith and love of God.

Many of the rules for young courtiers are preserved for us
in the Bible in the Book of Proverbs. This book is part of a group
of books called the Wisdom literature of the Bible. Other books
in this group are Job, the Psalms, Ecclesiastes, Wisdom, Sirach,
and the Canticle of Canticles.

Wisdom literature prepares the way for Christ

Some of the maxims found in the Wisdom literature are time-
less. Others seem strange and even humorous to modern readers.
This is not surprising, for they pertain to an age and a culture
completely different from our own. The important thing is that they
represent a major step in the preparation of God's people for the
coming of his kingdom. They served as a foundation and preparation for the new law that Christ would give.

Thus the Israelites understood what Christ meant when he said,
"Take my yoke upon you and master my lessons . . . My yoke is
easy and my burden light." Matthew 11:29-30. They had been prepared by the words of Sirach 6:25, 29: "Put your feet into her
[wisdom's] fetters, and your neck under her yoke. . . . thus will
you afterward find rest in her, and she will become your joy."

Christ did not destroy the old law; he built upon it and fulfilled
it. Moreover, his law was not a code of conduct for men called

to serve in the court of an earthly king, but a way of life for men called to walk in the presence of the King of Kings.

Study questions

Discuss: a) Israel's need for and training of young courtiers, b) Wisdom literature, c) how Wisdom literature helped prepare the way for Christ.

LITURGY & LIFE

1 David prepares for his future role.   Though David was anointed king, still, it would take a long time before Saul died and David could assume the kingship. During this time David performed one of the most inspiring feats of faith and courage recorded in the Old Testament. Read about it in 1 Kings 17.

Why didn't Saul want David to fight? 1 Kings 17:33. Explain how 1 Kings 17:38-40 reveals David's courage. Explain how 1 Kings 17:45 reveals his faith in God.

2 David goes to live with King Saul.   After David's feat of faith and courage, Saul made David a member of his own household. Immediately David and Saul's son Jonathan became the closest of friends. Read the account in 1 Kings 18:1-4.

Explain the statement, "David and Jonathan made a covenant." Why did Saul soon grow jealous of David? 1 Kings 18:6-9. In 1 Kings 20 Jonathan helps David escape from Saul. Do you think Jonathan did wrong in defending David against his own father?

3 David mourns Jonathan.   1 Kings 31 tells how Jonathan died fighting at his father's side. He is loyal to his father in spite of his father's failings. Read David's remarks over the body of his dead friend. 2 Kings 1:26. Explain St. Jerome's statement that "friendship either finds men equal or makes them equal."

4 God calls future "Davids."   Some time ago Time magazine carried an inspiring account of a Protestant minister. The minister recalled how, though he was leading a good life, he always felt he wasn't doing exactly what God wanted him to do. Then one night he decided to settle the matter once and for all. He took a Bible from the shelf, sat down, and wrote in it, "Tonight I give

Melchisedec, Abraham, Moses, Samuel, David
Cathedral of Chartres: Roger-Viollet

in. I'll do whatever you want me to do." That was the turning point in his life. He went on to become one of the most decorated navy chaplains in World War II.

Does God call all men in exactly the same way? Explain. How did God call David? How do you know when God is calling you?

5 Christ foreshadowed.   About an hour's ride from Paris is the famous cathedral of Chartres. On the north side of the cathedral is a doorway flanked by statues of five Old Testament persons. Each person holds an object foreshadowing Christ: Melchisedec holds a chalice, Abraham holds Isaac, Moses holds a staff with a saraph serpent, Samuel holds a lamb, and David holds a scepter and bears a crown of thorns. See the photograph.

Why does Melchisedec hold a chalice? Genesis 14:18. How does it foreshadow Christ? Why is Abraham holding Isaac? Genesis 22:1-12. How does he foreshadow Christ? Why does Moses hold a staff with a serpent? Numbers 21:4-9. How does it foreshadow Christ? John 12:31-34. Why does Samuel hold a lamb? 1 Kings 7:8-10. How does it foreshadow Christ? Why does David hold a scepter and a crown? How do they foreshadow Christ? How does the Old Testament help us understand Christ better?

2 David unites Israel

After Saul dies, David assumes the kingship of Israel. For his capital city, he decides upon the Jebusite-held fortress city of Jerusalem. Because of its central location, it is an ideal spot for bringing about the unification of Israel. A battle ensues, and David's army is victorious.

Immediately David sets to work rebuilding and refortifying the city. When the work is complete, David organizes the new state, probably along the lines of Egyptian models familiar to him.

David brings the Ark to Jerusalem

But Jerusalem becomes more than just a fortress and seat of government. David brings the Ark of the Covenant to the city. In

David's mind it is only right that this symbol of God's presence should reside in a place of honor in the capital. Let us read how David and the Israelites bring the Ark of the Covenant to Jerusalem.

And David gathered together
all the chosen men of Israel . . .
And David and all the house of Israel
brought the ark of the covenant of the Lord
with joyful shouting, and with sound of trumpet.
And when the ark of the Lord was come
into the city of David, Michol the daughter of Saul,
looking out through a window, saw King David
leaping and dancing before the Lord:
and she despised him in her heart.
    And they brought the ark of the Lord,
and set it in its place in the midst of the tabernacle,
which David had pitched for it.
And David offered holocausts,
and peace offerings before the Lord.   2 Kings 6:1-17

Jerusalem becomes a holy city

Because of the presence of the Ark, Jerusalem rapidly becomes a favorite pilgrimage spot for Israelites. In time the city is revered as the holy city. Every Israelite loved the city and visited it as often as possible.

Christ too loved Jerusalem. On the first Palm Sunday, while others cheered, Christ secretly wept over the city. "Jerusalem, Jerusalem! . . . How often have I been willing to gather your children as a mother bird gathers her brood under her wings! But you refused it!" Matthew 23:37. Sadly, Christ prophesied the city's doom. "I tell you plainly, not one stone will here be left upon another. All will crumble to pieces." Matthew 24:2. Forty years later Roman armies under Titus leveled the beloved city.

Jerusalem foreshadows heaven

God never intended the Davidic Jerusalem to fulfill men's dreams. He meant this city of stones to be merely a foreshadowing of the heavenly kingdom. In the Apocalypse St. John says:

I saw a new heaven and a new earth,
for the first heaven and the first earth

had passed away, and the sea was no more.
I also saw the holy city, New Jerusalem . . .
I saw no temple in it, for the Lord God Almighty
and the Lamb are its temple.
The city has no need of the sun or moon to shine on it,
because the glory of God lights it up, and the Lamb is its lamp.
The nations will walk by its light,
and the kings of the earth will offer
their tribute of recognition to it.
Its gates will be wide open all the day long,
which will never be brought to an end by night. Apocalypse 21:1-25

BIBLE MESSAGE

Christ teaches us.   Christ said, "Jerusalem, Jerusalem!
. . . How often have I been willing to gather your children as a
mother bird gathers her brood under her wings? But you refused
it!" Matthew 23:37.
1 To what was Christ referring? 2 Discuss: a) why and how
David seized Jerusalem, b) how Jerusalem became a holy city,
c) the passage from the Apocalypse.

LITURGY & LIFE

1 David and the psalms.   The 150 psalms, making up the
Book of Psalms, are attributed chiefly to the authorship of David.
Some modern authors divide the psalms according to four different
categories: praise, petition, instruction, prophecy. Here are four
selections from four different psalms. Under what category would
you place each?

I am like water poured out; all my bones are racked.
My heart has become like wax . . .
But you, O Lord, be not far from me;
O my help, hasten to aid me.   Psalm 21:15, 20

The heavens declare the glory of God,
and the firmament proclaims his handiwork. . . .
the ordinances of the Lord are true,
all of them just; they are more precious than gold . . .
sweeter also than syrup . . .   Psalm 18:1, 10-11

And he chose David, his servant,
and took him from the sheepfolds . . .
to shepherd Jacob, his people,
and Israel, his inheritance.   Psalm 77:70-71

The Lord said to my Lord:
"Sit at my right hand
till I make your enemies your footstool."
The scepter of your power the Lord will stretch forth
the Lord will stretch forth from Sion . . .   Psalm 109:1-2

Why do the psalms make good prayers? When and how are
psalms used during the liturgy?

2 Liturgical celebrations.   As the people paraded toward
Jerusalem with the Ark, the Bible says they danced, shouted
joyfully, and played trumpets.

Would you say this was irreverent? In other parts of the Bible
we learn that the Israelites frequently chanted and sang during
processions. Among the favorite processional songs was:

Lift up, O gates, your lintels; reach up, you ancient portals,
that the king of glory may come in! Who is this king of glory?
The Lord, strong and mighty, the Lord, mighty in battle. . . .
The Lord of hosts; he is the king of glory.   Psalm 23:7-10

Do you think this psalm was sung when the Ark was brought into Jerusalem? Where do we find the psalms? How many are there?

3 Liturgical processions.   Psychologists tell us that parades
and processions, like the one for bringing the Ark into Jerusalem,
are natural to man.

Make a list of occasions when men make use of parades or processions. How and when does the Church make use of the procession in her liturgy?

4 Liturgical music.   Someone once said, "Music can march
an army to war; it can hush an audience to tears; it can make one
tap one's feet to its rhythm. Music is something spiritual, something which can appeal not merely to the body but to the soul."

What gives music its magic? How does the Church use music
in her liturgy? How can even regular music help us serve God
better? Write an essay on "Why I like the kind of music I do."

3 God makes a promise to David

After David installs the Ark of the Covenant in Jerusalem, he
begins laying plans to build a magnificent temple to house it.
David's plans are hardly underway when God reveals to him that
Solomon, his son, will build the temple. God also reveals to
David that David's family will rule over Israel forever. Let us
read in the Book of Kings where this is recorded for us.

Thus saith the Lord of hosts:
I took thee out of the pastures from following the sheep
to be ruler over my people Israel.
And I have been with thee wheresoever thou hast walked,
and have slain all thy enemies from before thy face.
And I have made thee a great man, like unto the name
of the great ones that are on the earth. . . .
And when thy days shall be fulfilled,
and thou shalt sleep with thy fathers,
I will raise up thy seed after thee . . .
and I will establish his kingdom.
He shall build a house to my name:
and I will establish the throne of his kingdom for ever.
I will be to him a father: and he shall be to me a son.
And if he commit any iniquity, I will correct him . . .
But my mercy I will not take away from him,
as I took it away from Saul,
whom I removed from before my face.
And thy house shall be faithful,
and thy kingdom for ever before thy face:
and thy throne shall be firm for ever.   2 Kings 7:8-16

Christ will come from David's house

Instead of David's building God a house, God promises to
build David a "house," a royal dynasty that will endure forever.
The members of this "house" will be Solomon, his successors,
and eventually the Messia.

This is a milestone in the history of God's plan of love for men.
Through this promise, God makes David the royal ancestor of
Christ; Christ will come from David's "house." From this time
forward a royal Messia is one of the hopes of Israel; and God
begins to prepare his people for the coming of the eternal king,
who will establish the eternal kingdom.

Solomon builds the temple in Jerusalem

After David's death, the kingship passes to his son, Solomon. If David deserves credit for uniting Israel, Solomon deserves credit for leading the people to the high point of national prosperity. This prosperity allows Solomon to fulfill his father's dream of building a magnificent temple to God.

Once completed the temple is a concrete symbol of God's presence among men. For centuries to come it serves as the privileged meeting place of God and men. Each year the Israelites came on pilgrimages to the temple in Jerusalem. It was on such a yearly pilgrimage that our Lord, at the age of twelve, remained behind and conversed with the temple priests.

The temple foreshadows Christ's body

The temple foreshadowed a more perfect temple that was to come. This perfect temple was Christ's own body. "'If you destroy this sanctuary,' Jesus answered them, 'I will build it up again in three days.' The Jews then said to him, 'Six and forty years this sanctuary was in building; and you will build it up again in three days?' He, however, was speaking of the sanctuary of his body." John 2:19-21.

In Christ, says St. Paul, "is embodied and dwells the fullness of the Godhead." Colossians 2:9.

Today Christ lives on in the Church, his mystical body. Through our incorporation into Christ's mystical body by baptism, we, the members of the Church, have "become God's dwelling place." Ephesians 2:22. We are the new temple of the living God. 1 Corinthians 3:16, 17.

BIBLE MESSAGE

Christ teaches us. St. Matthew's Gospel begins by tracing Jesus' ancestory back through David to Abraham. The title Matthew gives to his "family tree" is "A record of the ancestors of Jesus Christ, the Son of David, the Son of Abraham."

1 Why do you think Matthew singled out David and Abraham for special mention in the title? 2 What promise did God make to David? 3 Of what was the temple in Jerusalem a symbol? 4 What "more perfect temple" did it foreshadow? 5 How did Christ reveal this? 6 Where is God's temple today? Explain.

Some important biblical background
_____

The house of David rules politically over God's people until
the Babylonians conquer and exile them in 587 B.C. Though never
exercised after this time, the eternal right of the house of David
to rule God's people remains intact during their exile and sub-
sequent domination by Greek and Roman armies. During all this
time a careful record is kept of the family lists. Thus it comes
about that, when a census is ordered by Caesar Augustus, Joseph
and Mary go to register at Bethlehem, the city of David, because
they are of the house of David. During their stay Christ the King,
the son of David, is born; God's promise to David is fulfilled.

LITURGY & LIFE

1 David and Christ.   Christian artists like to call attention
to the similarities between Christ and David. Both were born in
Bethlehem; both were shepherds; both saved their people and
brought unity to them; both were kings.
Discuss the above similarities. How does David's life and work
help us better understand Christ's life and work? How would you
depict David in art? What symbols might be helpful?

DOCTRINAL POINTS

David's sin and sorrow
_____

God blesses David abundantly. He brings him out of the fields
of Bethlehem. He gives him strength in battle, makes him king of
Israel, and promises him the Messia will come from his house.

David's sin

David recognizes these blessings, too. "Who am I, O Lord
God, and what is my house that thou has brought me thus far?"
2 Kings 7:18. Nevertheless, the day comes when David becomes
involved in a chain of grave sins against God. It happens like
this. One day David allows himself to give in to a desire for a
married woman, Bethsabee. This desire grows, and David next
finds himself plotting to have the woman's soldier-husband,

Urias, sent on a suicide mission in battle. Urias is killed, and David marries Bethsabee.

David's sorrow

Nathan, the prophet, sees through this series of heinous acts and confronts David. Immediately David is struck with sorrow. "I have sinned against the Lord." 2 Kings 12:13. Thereupon, see-David's repentance, Nathan says, "The Lord also hath taken away thy sin." 2 Kings 12:13.

David's sorrow grows out of a double realization: 1) how good God has been to him, and 2) how ungrateful he has been to God by sinning. David is immediately moved to contrition.

Perfect contrition

We may define contrition as a sincere sorrow and hatred of one's sins with the firm resolve to sin no more.

Contrition is called <u>perfect</u> when it proceeds from the love of God; that is, we are sorry for our sins because by them we have offended God, whom we love above all else. We love God "above all else" when we are willing to die rather than offend him in a serious matter. When perfect contrition is accompanied with, at least, the implicit intention of going to confession, it removes mortal sin immediately. The obligation to confess the mortal sin remains, however, because God has commanded that we do so.

Imperfect contrition

Imperfect contrition, called attrition, is had when we repent of having offended God for a supernatural motive less than the motive of love of God; for example, because of the baseness of sin, the loss of heaven, or the pain of hell.

Imperfect contrition is sufficient for forgiveness of sin in the sacrament of penance, even when the sins we confess are mortal.

In going to confession it is good to get into the habit of making our act of contrition before going into the confessional. It is well, however, to renew it while the priest is giving absolution.

Sorrow is not a feeling

It is possible to be truly sorry for our sins and still experience a strong attraction to them. Therefore contrition is not to be

106

judged so much by feelings as by firmness of the will.

But, while we may still fall again because of our weakness, we should not blind ourselves into thinking that we have true contrition unless we are willing to give up the occasion of sin.

By the occasion of sin we mean such persons, places, or things that as a rule lead us into sin unless we keep away from them. If we find that a certain place or a person, as a rule, leads us to commit a serious sin, we must be determined to avoid that place or person in the future.

Study questions

During the last war, a young American pilot was mortally wounded in a crash. Just before he died, he reached into his pocket for a pencil and managed to scrawl these words of assurance to his parents in New York. "Dear Mom and Dad: I had time to say my prayers. Jack."

1 How was this a perfect letter? 2 Supposing that Jack had tragically committed a serious sin just before the crash. How could Jack have put himself right with God? 3 Define: a) contrition, b) perfect contrition, c) imperfect contrition, d) occasion of sin. 4 Discuss the connection between contrition and confession. 5 Read about the contrition of the woman mentioned in Luke 7:36-50. What lesson about contrition does Christ teach us here?

Thus far we have studied:

CHRIST TODAY

    1 Christ attracts men today
    2 Christ remains on earth today
    3 Christ acts in men's lives today

CHRIST TEACHES US ABOUT GOD'S PLAN

    1 Christ teaches us today through the Bible
    2 The Bible reveals God's love for us

GOD'S KINGDOM PLAN UNFOLDS IN HISTORY

    1 God prepares for his kingdom
    2 God creates Adam and extends an invitation to him

GOD'S KINGDOM INVITATION IS REJECTED

    1 Adam rejects God's invitation
    2 Adam's rejection separates mankind from God
    3 God promises mankind a savior after Adam's sin

GOD'S KINGDOM INVITATION IS ACCEPTED

    1 God calls Abraham and makes a covenant with him
    2 Abraham is loyal to God

GOD FORMS A KINGLY PEOPLE

    1 God calls Moses
    2 God makes Israel his chosen people
    3 God gives Israel a home

GOD GIVES HIS PEOPLE A KING

    1 God calls David
    2 David unites Israel
    3 God makes a promise to David

During the season of Advent we will see how:

GOD SENDS PROPHETS TO HIS PEOPLE

    1 God's people split into two kingdoms
    2 God's people are led into exile
    3 From God's people will come a new king and kingdom

GOD PREPARES HIS PEOPLE FOR THE NEW KING

    1 God's people return from exile
    2 God's people are prepared for the new king

Pour out your dew,
you heavens, from above,
and bid the clouds
rain down the Just One.
 Advent Antiphon

O . . . sun of Justice. Come
shed your radiance upon us
who languish in darkness
and the shadow of death.
 O Antiphon: December 21

O Emmanuel,
our king and law-giver.
The nations are waiting
for you, their Savior.
Come to us and save us,
Lord, our God.
 O Antiphon: December 23

ADVENT LITURGY

Christ is our life and our hope

The days of Advent are like the days before a championship football game or a class play. They are days crammed with preparation and anticipation. Advent is a time of extra effort and careful preparation for the celebration of Christmas.

Christmas celebrates Christ's triple coming

Contrary to what many people think, Christmas is more than just a celebration of Christ's birthday. Christ's birth took place once and for all in Bethlehem; but the God-life which Christ brought by his birth continues to flow into our lives each day, especially during the celebration of the liturgy. This daily coming of Christ into our lives by grace will continue until Christ's final coming at the end of time.

Christmas, then, involves a triple celebration: 1) it recalls Christ's historical coming in time; 2) it recalls Christ's liturgical coming each day in Mass and the sacraments; and, 3) it looks forward to Christ's final coming at the end of the world.

Advent involves a triple preparation

Because Christmas celebrates a triple coming, it involves a triple preparation. During Advent we strive 1) to strengthen our faith, so that we may assent more fully to Christ's first coming in history; 2) to increase our charity, so that we may open ourselves more fully to Christ's continual coming in mystery; 3) to build up our hope, so that we may confidently look forward to his final coming in majesty.

The Church helps us

To help us prepare for Christmas, the Church points a liturgical finger at three spiritual giants who played major roles in Christ's first coming. They are Isaia, Our Lady, and John the Baptist.

Isaia buoyed the hopes of Israel during the long centuries before Christ's birth. A "virgin shall be with child, and bear a son . . ." Isaia 7:14.

Our Lady opened the way for Christ's birth. "Regard me as the humble servant of the Lord." Luke 1:38.

Finally, John the Baptist pointed out Christ to the people. "Look, there is the lamb of God." John 1:29.

We announce Christ's triple coming

During the days of Advent, the Church reminds us that, like Isaia, Our Lady, and John the Baptist, we, the members of Christ's mystical body, are called to play a major role in Christ's coming into today's world. By our living faith, we give witness to his first coming in Bethlehem. By our charity, we show that he continues to come daily into our lives. By our hope, we lead others to realize and to prepare hopefully for Christ's glorious coming at the end of time.

Study questions

1 Discuss: a) the threefold coming of Christ that we celebrate on Christmas, b) the threefold preparation that we begin in Advent, c) the symbols shown in the stained glass window on page 110. 2 How are references to Genesis 28:12, Malachia 3:20, and Isaia 45:8 depicted in the window? 3 Bring your missals to class. Show how the Advent Masses prepare us for Christ's triple coming.

8

GOD SENDS PROPHETS TO HIS PEOPLE

1 God's people split into two kingdoms

After Adam's fall God reinvited man to share his love and life by calling Abraham. Abraham accepted God's invitation and became the father of many descendants. At Mt. Sinai, under Moses' leadership, these descendants became God's chosen people. Josue then led God's people to their new home: the promised land. Under David God's people were forged into a powerful kingdom. Under Solomon, David's son, God's people reached the peak of their material power and prosperity.

Israel revolts

When Solomon dies in 922 B.C., a political revolt splits God's people into two separate kingdoms. A group of northern tribes breaks away and forms a northern kingdom, taking the name Israel. Two southern tribes, Juda and Benjamin, remain faithful to the house of David and form the southern kingdom, taking the name Juda. Let us read in the third Book of Kings where this is recorded for our instruction.

And the days that Solomon reigned in Jerusalem
over all Israel, were forty years.
And Solomon slept with his fathers,
and was buried in the city of David his father.
And Roboam his son reigned in his stead.
    And Roboam went to Sichem: for thither
were all Israel come together to make him king. . . .
and they spoke to Roboam, saying:
Thy father laid a grievous yoke upon us.
Now therefore do thou take off a little
of the grievous service of thy father,
and of his most heavy yoke, which he put upon us:
and we will serve thee. . . .
And the king condescended not to the people . . .
And Israel revolted from the house of David . . .   3 Kings 11:42 ff.

A new era begins in salvation history

As so often happens when a nation achieves material success,
the Israelites begin to lose their spiritual balance and direction.
They become enmeshed in political matters. God uses this state
of affairs to usher in a new era in salvation history.

Up until now Israel's formation has, to a large extent, centered
around her external growth and development. She was becoming a
nation, capable of growth and survival among the other nations of
the world. Now begins a period of intense internal formation.

God sends prophets

To serve as his instruments during this period, God raises
up a series of spiritual giants called prophets. The word prophet
means "spokesman" and gives us the key to the prophet's role in
God's plan. Prophets act as God's official spokesmen to Israel.
They do this in two ways: 1) they condemn and threaten Israel for
her infidelity to the covenant, and 2) they announce and promise
certain things concerning the coming of a new king and kingdom
of Israel.

Prophets begin preaching in the northern kingdom

Though the northern tribes separate themselves politically
from the house of David, God does not abandon them. He sends
them prophets to point out their erring ways. Foremost among

114

these is Elias. To understand Elias, we must understand the times that produce him.

After breaking with the southern kingdom, the northern kingdom prospers greatly. This is not surprising because Israel had rich farm land and lay on a main trade route between Damascus and Egypt. With Israel's increased material prosperity comes religious decline. The people of the northern kingdom begin to ignore their covenant promises. This infidelity hits bottom during the reign of Amri (c. 876-869 B.C.). For political reasons Amri marries his son, Achab, to the Tyrian princess, Jezabel. The upshot of this marriage is disastrous. When Jezabel comes from Tyre, she brings hundreds of pagan priests and her pagan gods, Baal and Asherah. In no time Israel becomes infested with idolatrous shrines. Many of God's chosen people begin to kneel in pagan temples before pagan idols.

Elias denounces Israel's infidelity

At this point appears Elias. His denunciation of Israel's infidelity to the covenant is forceful and fearless. Everyone, even the pagan priests, is struck at the wonders that Elias performs in God's name. 3 Kings 18:20-40. Though Elias' efforts seem fruitless at the time, eight centuries later Israelites will still remember his mission. For example, when the angel announces the birth of John the Baptist to Zachary, he says, "Endowed with the spirit and might of Elias; he will . . . prepare for the Lord a people perfect in every way." Luke 1:17. Yet in spite of Elias' impact, many Israelites refuse to mend their ways.

Amos denounces Israel's formalism and social injustice

Years pass, and Israel's infidelity to the covenant continues. Finally, around 785 B.C., God sends a second prophet to the northern kingdom. This is Amos.

Amos inveighs against the formalism (mere show) that begins to taint Israel's temple worship. The sacrifices in the temple lack interior spirit, he charges. Because of this they are empty and meaningless before God. They are merely subtle forms of self-deception or, worse yet, outright hypocrisy.

Amos also attacks the social injustice with which wealthy Israelites begin to treat their poorer brothers. Amos 2:6 ff. This is not according to the spirit of the covenant that made all Israel one family under God.

115

Finally, Amos denounces those Israelites who hold that because God has chosen them, he will make good his promises to them--regardless of their conduct. To this kind of presumptuous thinking, Amos replies that God will honor his promises but only to those who remain faithful. Amos 3:12.

Osee recalls God's love for Israel

A third prophet to the northern kingdom is Osee. In words less biting, but just as firm, Osee condemns Israel's infidelity to the covenant. He recalls how God, out of love, made with Israel a covenant, and how, in return, Israel pledged God love and fidelity. He compares the covenant to a wedding. Israel is like a bride and God a bridegroom. For Israel to turn away from God and to worship pagan gods is like a bride's turning away from her true husband to take to herself other husbands. It is adultery, the worse form of infidelity to a loved one.

The northern kingdom vanishes

The northern kingdom lasts until 722 B.C. Then Assyrians under Salmanasar overthrow Samaria, the capital. Thousands of Israelites are herded off to Ninive to be pressed into slavery. The property of these deportees is parceled out to Assyrians. Eventually these pagan citizens intermarry with Jews still in Samaria. Because these Samaritan Jews intermarry, they are later scorned by Jews of the southern kingdom.

In exile some of the northern kingdom Jews repent their disloyalty to the covenant and turn back to God. The repentent spirit of these exiles is reflected in the inspired Canticle of Tobias.

Give glory to the Lord, ye children of Israel:
and praise him in the sight of the Gentiles.
Because he hath therefore scattered you
among the Gentiles, who know not him,
that you may declare his wonderful works:
and make them know
that there is no other almighty God besides him.
He hath chastised us for our iniquities:
and he will save us for his own mercy.
See then what he hath done with us,
and with fear and trembling give ye glory to him:
and extol the eternal King of worlds in your works. Tobias 13:3-6

116

BIBLE MESSAGE

Christ teaches us. Christ said, "Do not think it is my mission to annul the Law or the Prophets. It is not my mission to annul, but to bring to perfection." Matthew 5:17.

How will Christ bring the work of the prophets to perfection? Discuss: a) the catastrophe that occurred in Israel after Solomon's death, b) the new era in salvation history that now begins, c) the role of the prophets in God's plan, d) the abuse in Israel that set the stage for Elias' appearance, e) the message of Amos, f) the message of Osee, g) the ultimate fate of the northern kingdom.

Some important biblical background

For the most part the prophets lived between 750 B.C. and 450 B.C. God called his prophets from all walks of life without regard for class distinction. For example, Isaia belonged to an aristocratic family, while Amos was a common herder of sheep.

Sometimes the prophets were amazed when God called them to his special service. Read Jeremia 1:6-9 for an almost humorous account of how Jeremia reacted to God's call.

For an awesome and colorful description of what a prophetic experience was like read Isaia 6:1-9.

Study questions

During what Mass prayer does the priest mention Isaia, the prophet, by name? Explain how this prayer is a fitting introduction to the next action that the priest performs.

LITURGY & LIFE

1 Social injustice. "He who spoke with a Samaritan at Jacob's well precisely because the Jews did not speak with Samaritans, and he who gave us the lesson of the good Samaritan, thoroughly cursed racial prejudice. The New Testament is replete with racial justice and condemnations of anything smacking of racial intolerance." Daniel Lyons, S.J.

What prophet to the northern kingdom spoke out against social injustice? How is Christ's action a condemnation of social prejudice, regardless of its origin or nature? Why is it not always easy to follow Christ's example?

2 Religious formalism.   A leading Protestant theologian charges that "religion has been sentimentalized and made easy. The church, itself," he adds "is tending to degenerate into a social institution." His views were echoed by a high-school student who observed, "Religion is getting to be a vending machine. You put in a nickel and you get a reward. It doesn't lead the people; it merely reflects their values."

What have the theologian and the high-school student in common with Amos? Is it easy to be a Catholic? How does the Catholic Church differ from every other social institution?

2 God's people are exiled

When the northern tribes revolt and form their own government, Roboam, heir to the house of David, decides to war against them and force their return. Let us read in the Book of Kings where this is recorded for us.

And Roboam came to Jerusalem,
and gathered together all the house of Juda,
and the tribe of Benjamin . . .
to fight against the house of Israel,
and to bring the kingdom again under Roboam
the son of Solomon.

But the word of the Lord
came to Semeias, the man of God, saying . . .
You shall not go up nor fight against
your brethren the children of Israel.
Let every man return to his house . . . 3 Kings 12:21-24

God sends prophets to the southern kingdom

Roboam obeys God's command and dismisses the soldiers. In the years that follow, life in the southern kingdom is hard. Juda has neither rich farms nor busy trade routes to build her economy. Yet the southern kingdom outlasts the northern kingdom by over a century and a half. It runs until 587 B.C. During this period some twenty kings rule the kingdom. Some are wise and God-fearing; others commit all sorts of crimes, including idolatry.

God raises up prophets for this kingdom, too. Foremost among these is Isaia. Like Elias he leaves an unforgettable mark on Jewish history. Eight hundred years after Isaia's death, Saint Matthew will cite him no fewer than twenty-one times in his Gospel.

Isaia appears

Isaia makes his public appearance in Jerusalem during those hectic days when the whole Near East is in political turmoil. In the north, restless Babylonian armies are itching to march out after new conquests. In the south, Egypt is struggling to maintain her military supremacy. Caught in the middle are the two kingdoms of Israel and Juda.

Isaia is already in the public eye when news comes that the northern kingdom of Israel has fallen to the Assyrians. Achaz, the king of Juda, panics at the news. The Bible says, "The heart of the king and the heart of the people trembled, as the trees of the forest tremble in the wind." Isaia 7:2. To save himself and his kingdom, Achaz contemplates making a deal with the Assyrians, even offering to adopt their pagan worship.

Isaia demands fidelity to the covenant

At this Isaia explodes. He condemns the king roundly. To sell out to Assyria is not only political suicide, but also a grave offense against God. Isaia insists that the only way to survive is to remain faithful to the covenant with God.

But Achaz ignores Isaia and sells out to Assyria. The result is that Juda becomes a puppet state of the powerful Assyrian empire.

In 716 B.C. Achaz dies, and his throne passes to his son, Ezechia. Unlike his father, Ezechia turns out to be a noble king. Around 700 B.C. the Assyrians become infuriated with Ezechia's policies, especially his growing political friendship with Egypt. They decide to teach him a lesson. Sennacherib sets out for Jerusalem with a vast army. Once again panic seizes Juda, and once again Isaia counsels fidelity to the covenant. Ezechia listens to Isaia, and God rewards him. Sennacherib's army meets with a surprising disaster that forces it to turn back to Assyria.

Babylonian armies attack Juda

After Ezechia's death, God's people begin to drift (except for a brief period under King Josaia) from her covenant promises. Finally, around 597 B.C. things come to a head. The king of Juda, growing tired of the repeated warnings of another prophet, Jeremia, jails the holy man. Shortly after this rejection of God's holy spokesman, the city is pounced upon by the Babylonians and many of its leading citizens are taken prisoner and deported to Babylon. It is the beginning of a dark hour for God's chosen people.

Jeremia preaches a message of hope

But God does not abandon his people. Jeremia is released from prison and begins to exhort those who fight on. He reveals that God is preparing his people for the day when he will replace the Old Covenant with a New Covenant. Unlike the Sinai covenant, where God wrote his law on stone tablets, God will write the New Covenant on the hearts of men. Jeremia 31:31-33.

More than ever, in this time of trial, Juda prays that God will hasten the day of her deliverance.

BIBLE MESSAGE

Christ teaches us. Christ used the words of the prophet Isaia to rebuke the Scribes and Pharisees. "This race honors me with its lips, but its heart is far away from me." Matthew 15:7-8.

1 What did Christ mean? 2 Discuss: a) the political crisis in Juda that caused Isaia to rebuke the king and people of Israel, b) the effect Isaia's rebuke had upon King Achaz, and later, upon King Ezechia, c) the catastrophe that struck Juda in 597 B.C., d) the important message of Jeremia to the people.

1 Trust in God.   All Europe was growing panicky. Even Pope Innocent IV was disturbed. Rumor had it that ferocious hordes of Mongols, with horses three times as fast as European horses, were massing for an all-out attack on Christendom. Filled with horror at these reports, the Queen of France rushed hysterically to the bedside of the ailing King Louis IX, the famous soldier-saint. "What will become of us?" she cried. The king turned to her and said quietly, "Be brave and calm . . . God will send us comfort . . . If he but will it, these barbarians will be driven back to their native haunts. Or if it is his good pleasure to allow them to wreak out fury on us, why then let them do their utmost!"

Compare King Louis' trust in God's providence to that of King Achaz. What do you mean by God's providence?

2 Cooperate with God.   Another great soldier-saint, Ignatius of Loyola, used to say, "Work as though everything depends on you; pray as though everything depends on God."

Is it enough to sit back and trust in God's providence? Does God ever let us down? How do you explain the fact that God sometimes does not seem to answer our prayers?

3 Know God.   "One of the chief reasons why so many men lack effective trust in God," says an author, "is that they have only the vaguest and most inadequate idea of him."

Explain what the author means? How does one go about getting an adequate idea of God? Write a short essay on "Why I trust God."

4 Fear is natural.   Upon hearing that a certain group of people were supposed to be without fear, Aristotle remarked, "Someone who does not fear is either a beast or a god."

What did he mean? Do you think that King Achaz was any more afraid of the Assyrians than Isaia was? Is there a difference between fear and cowardice?

5 Prayer helps.   A group of 400 marines--veterans of World War II and all wearers of the Purple Heart--were asked this question: How do marines overcome their fear in battle? Ninety-seven percent of them gave the same answer: "Prayer!"

How does prayer help us control fear? Pyschologists tell us that fear prepares the body for fight or flight. What do they mean? How does this show that some fear is not only good but necessary?

3 From God's people will come a new king and kingdom

The deportation to Babylon took place in three stages. The
first group comprised mostly skilled artisans and court officials.
In this group of exiles was Ezechiel, the son of a Jerusalem priest.
During the fifth year of exile God called Ezechiel to be his spokesman. Let us read in the Bible where Ezechiel himself tells what
happened.

> While I was among the exiles by the river Chobar,
> the heavens opened, and I saw divine visions. . . .
> I fell upon my face
> and heard a voice that said to me:
> Son of man, stand up!
> I wish to speak with you.
> As he spoke to me, spirit entered into me
> and set me on my feet, and I heard the one who was
> speaking say to me: Son of man,
> I am sending you to the Israelites . . .   Ezechiel 1:1; 2:1-3

Ezechiel announces Jerusalem's destruction

Ezechiel's work as God's spokesman to Israel divides itself
into two periods: before and after 587 B.C. (the fall of Jerusalem).
In each period Ezechiel deals with different problems.

Before the fall of Jerusalem, the major problem is the presumption of the people. The first wave of prisoners, shipped off
to Babylon in 597 B.C., feel that no real harm can befall Jerusalem. Although the city is under siege, they feel that Jerusalem
will never fall. They wait daily for good news from home--news
of dramatic intervention on God's part to save the city. Ezechiel's
answer to these false hopes is crushing. He announces that not only
Jerusalem but also the temple will soon be totally destroyed. But
the people refuse to believe him.

Jerusalem and the temple are demolished

Then one day in 587 B.C. refugees bring news that Jerusalem
and the temple have been leveled. At first the people can hardly
believe what they hear. But as the last survivors from the siege
limp in, it becomes clear that Israel is finished as a political power.
From a human point of view there is nothing more to hope for.
Black despair engulfs God's people.

Ezechiel announces a new king and kingdom

Once more Ezechiel steps forward. Now the tone of his preaching changes. Instead of portending woe, it reflects hope. Ezechiel describes a vision given him. He sees a valley full of dried bones which God restored to life, signifying that from defeated Juda, God will raise up a new kingdom. Ezechiel 37:1-14.

Ezechiel also describes the coming of a "new David," a great king from David's line, who will rule the new kingdom. "I will appoint one shepherd over them to pasture them . . . and be their shepherd. I, the Lord, will be their God, and my servant David shall be prince among them. I, the Lord, have spoken." Ezechiel 34:23-24.

BIBLE MESSAGE

Christ teaches us.   Christ said to the people, "I am the good shepherd; and I know mine and mine know me, as the Father knows me and I know the Father; and I lay down my life to save the sheep. Still other sheep I claim as my own, which are not of this fold. I must lead them also to pasture, and they will listen to my voice, and there will be one flock, one shepherd." John 10:14-16.

1 Of what words of Ezechiel does Christ's statement remind you? 2 What does Christ wish to teach us by his statement? 3 Discuss: a) Ezechiel's calling, b) Ezechiel's work as God's spokesman, c) the significance of Ezechiel's vision of the "dry bones."

LITURGY & LIFE

1 God draws good from evil.   One day the chaplain of a state prison received a letter from a former convict. As the chaplain opened it, his eyes fell on this line: "I now look back upon that time (my imprisonment) as an act of God. He used it to teach me about himself. I owe the gift of my faith to that time of my life."

How does this true story illustrate how God brings good from evil, if we cooperate with him? How did God draw good from evil during Israel's exile in Babylon? Write a short paragraph or story on "How God can draw good from evil."

2 God's power is infinite.   How does Ezechiel's vision of the dry bones remind you of John the Baptist's words to the Jews, "I

tell you, God is able to raise children to Abraham out of these stones." Luke 3:8? How were the Israelites "dead" after the collapse of the temple and Jerusalem? How is the parable of the dry bones realized each time a soul returns to God in confession?

3 Our hope is in God.   The virtue of hope may be defined as a supernatural gift from God empowering us to trust that God can and will make good all he has promised concerning his kingdom and the means we need to reach it.

In what two ways did many of the Israelites sin against this virtue? How do men still sin against it?

4 Hope and art.   Artists frequently try to express the virtue of hope by a concrete image. One way is by using an anchor. Near the door of the cathedral of Amiens, however, is a slightly different image of hope. It shows a seated figure holding a shield with a cross-shaped emblem on it. With the one hand, the figure reaches out confidently toward a crown (a medieval symbol for our future glory).

Is the anchor a Christian symbol for hope? What does St. Paul say about it in Hebrews 6:19? What do you think is the idea behind the hope image at Amiens? How else might hope be symbolized? For some inspired examples read Psalm 30. How is Advent a time of hope?

For a sun and a shield is the Lord God;
grace and glory he bestows . . .   Psalm 83:12

124

DOCTRINAL POINTS

Hope keeps us in orbit

Faith is the power that launches us into the orbit of the supernatural world. It makes us believers: people who accept God and
believe what he tells us. But it is not just enough to believe; we
must also hope. Hope keeps us in orbit once we have been launched
there by our Catholic faith. This means we pursue with complete
confidence what God promises--namely, the kingdom of heaven and
the grace needed to reach it.

Hope is a supernatural power

When we were baptized, we received sanctifying grace and along
with it the three infused theological virtues of faith, hope, and
charity. These virtues are called infused because God simply gives
them to us. They are called theological, because theos in Greek
means "God"; and these virtues propel us toward God. We believe in
God; we hope in God; we love God. Finally, they are called virtues
because virtus in Latin means "power." Faith, hope, and charity
are supernatural powers to help us reach God and his kingdom.
We may define hope as a supernatural gift from God, empowering us to trust that God can and will make good all he has promised
concerning his kingdom and the means we need to reach it.

Sins against hope

We sin against hope by despair and presumption. Presumption
is hoping to reach God's kingdom without taking the necessary
means to do so. It is like a young man who wants to be a doctor,
but who will not go to medical school. Despair is giving up all
hope of salvation and the means to attain it.

Study questions

"Notwithstanding the sight of our miseries, which press upon
us and take us by the throat, we have an instinct which we cannot
repress, and which lifts us up." (Pascal)
1 What is the difference between natural hope (the one Pascal
speaks of) and supernatural hope? 2 Define supernatural hope.
3 Why do we call faith, hope, and charity infused theological
virtues? 4 How are faith and hope related?

9

GOD PREPARES HIS PEOPLE FOR THE NEW KING

1 God's people return from exile

Prophets foretold it. The people prayed for it. And now it happened. Freedom! The Persians under Cyrus marched into Babylon in 538 B.C., and the proud city fell without a fight.

Cyrus' victory sent Juda's hopes soaring. The great Israelite prophet, called Second Isaia, detected God's hand in the victory.

> Thus says the Lord to his anointed, Cyrus . . .
> For the sake of . . . Israel my chosen one,
> I have called you by your name, giving you a title,
> though you knew me not.   Isaia 45:1-4

Cyrus immediately issued an edict, urging the people to return to Jerusalem to rebuild the temple.

> Thus saith Cyrus king of the Persians:
> The Lord the God of heaven . . .
> hath charged me to build him a house
> in Jerusalem, which is in Judea.
> Who is there among you of all his people?

His God be with him.
Let him go up to Jerusalem . . . and build the house
of the Lord the God of Israel.   1 Esdras 1:2-3

Only a remnant returns

Not all the people accept Cyrus' invitation. Some have aban-
doned their faith. Others have made ties in Babylon that are hard
to break. The faithful few that do respond, however, leave Babylon
with a deeper understanding of God's plan for them.

Jerusalem and the temple are in ruins

The sight of Jerusalem turns the joy of the returning exiles into sorrow. The city has been in ruins for half a century and is
largely deserted. The temple is an empty shell, and weeds grow
in the courtyard. Some of the survivors around Jerusalem have
intermarried with pagans; others have neglected their faith. This
is hardly the joyful hour of return that the exiles had dreamed of
during their long days of captivity in Babylon.

The exiles rebuild Jerusalem and the temple

The exiles immediately set to work rebuilding the temple and
the city. The progress is slow and discouraging. While the people
rebuild with one hand, they defend themselves with the other. For
as soon as neighboring peoples see that reconstruction is proceed-
ing in earnest, they grow alarmed. They fear lest a new power
emerge in their midst. Sabotage is a constant danger.
Finally, after endless trials and difficulties, the monumental
task is completed. The temple does not have the same splendor as
it did in the days of Solomon; but it is, nonetheless, the symbol
of God's presence among his people.

Juda renews the covenant

In the days that follow, a Jewish leader, Nehemias, and a holy
priest, Esdras, prepare the people for a solemn renewal of the
covenant. When all is ready, Esdras brings "the law before the
multitude" and reads it. "And all the people answered: Amen, Amen
. . . And they bowed down, and adored God . . ." 2 Esdras 8:2-6.
After an absence of half a century, the Israelites are established
anew as God's people in God's holy city: Jerusalem.

BIBLE MESSAGE

Christ teaches us.   Christ said to the people, "If anyone wants
to be my follower, he must renounce himself and shoulder his cross;
then he may be a follower of mine." Mark 8:34.

1 What is Christ's point? 2 How was this especially true for
the returning exiles? 3 Discuss: a) the reason why not all of the
people returned, b) the difficulties faced by those who returned,
c) the renewal of the covenant.

LITURGY & LIFE

1 Carrying Christ's cross.   "To be able to suffer is to be a
man; to accept it when it comes is to be noble; voluntarily to choose
it for a worthy cause is to be a hero." Archbishop Goodier, S.J.

List some of the sufferings that the returning remnant of Israelites either accepted or voluntarily chose. List some sufferings a
high-school student can accept, or can voluntarily choose for a
worthy cause. How can Christ help us?

2 God's people are prepared for the new king

Israel's new peace lasts for about 200 years. Then a new series
of trials begin. In 331 B.C. powerful Greek armies under Alexander
the Great sweep down across the Near East. Among the kingdoms
they capture is Juda.

But just as suddenly as Alexander's star streaks across the
sky, it vanishes. The young general contracts a deadly fever and
dies. After Alexander's death, his empire is split four ways. At
first Palestine falls under Egyptian control, but eventually it is
taken over by the Seleucids. The upshot of this proves disastrous.
In 175 B.C. a fanatic, Antiochus Epiphanes IV, ascends the throne
and tries to impose Greek customs and Greek worship on Juda. A
statue of Zeus is even erected in the Holy of Holies. Let us read
about this in the Bible.

And king Antiochus wrote to all his kingdom
that all the people should be one
and every one should leave his own law. . . .
And the king sent letters by the hands of messengers
to Jerusalem and to all the cities of Juda:
that they should . . . forbid
holocausts and sacrifices and atonements
to be made in the temple of God,
And should prohibit the sabbath
and the festival days, to be celebrated.
And he commanded the holy places to be profaned
and the holy people of Israel.
And he commanded altars to be built, and temples and idols . . .
And many of the people of Israel determined with themselves
that . . . they would not break the holy law of God:
and they were put to death.   1 Machabees 1:43-66

The vision of Daniel encourages Juda

In these difficult days there appears in Juda a scribe writing
under the name of Daniel. He encourages God's people to keep
faith, reminding them that all history is under the control of God,
who directs it according to his own mysterious purposes. Then the
writer describes a vision. "I saw one like a son of man coming,
on the clouds of heaven; when he reached the Ancient One and
was presented before him, he received dominion, glory, and
kingship; nations and peoples of every language serve him. His
dominion is an everlasting dominion that shall not be taken
away, his kingship shall not be destroyed." Daniel 7:13-14.

Machabeus leads a revolt

Inspired by Daniel's words, young Israelites take heart. In
167 B.C. in the Judean hills, a band of freedom fighters rises
up around the gallant leadership of Judas Machabeus.
"Remember," says Machabeus, "in what manner our fathers
were saved in the Red Sea, when Pharao pursued them with a
great army. And now let us cry to heaven: and the Lord will have
mercy on us and will remember the covenant of our fathers . . .
And all nations shall know that there is one that redeemeth and
delivereth Israel." 1 Machabees 4:9-11.
A revolt follows. For thirty long years it rages. Finally, after
much bloodshed, it ends in victory for the freedom fighters.

129

Roman armies move into Palestine

For years all goes well. But this peace, too, is not to be permanent. Soon civil war breaks out and divides God's people into rival camps. One camp asks military help from the Romans. The invitation is accepted, and in 63 B.C. Pompey's armies clank into Jerusalem. After the civil uprising is stamped out, the Romans stay on. Palestine is now a Roman colony.

In 40 B.C. the Roman Senate appoints a foreigner, Herod the Great, to rule the Jews. To please his subjects, Herod rebuilds and enlarges the temple that was destroyed during the fighting. Herod the Great rules until his death in 4 B.C. Then the Romans divide the rule of Palestine among his three sons. Herod Antipas rules Galilee and Perea; Philip rules the districts east and north of Galilee; and Archelaus rules Judea, Samaria, and Idumea.

An angel appears to the Virgin Mary

Meanwhile in Rome, Octavian, better known as Caesar Augustus, succeeds Mark Anthony to the throne in 27 B.C. Unlike his predecessor, Augustus doesn't engage in new military expeditions; rather, he consolidates his empire. As part of his consolidation program, Caesar Augustus decrees that a census be taken of the whole Roman world. And so the world is at peace. It is time for the angel to visit the Virgin Mary.

In the course of the sixth month, the angel Gabriel came
. . . to speak to a virgin espoused to a man named Joseph,
a descendant of David. The name of the virgin was Mary.
    On coming into her presence, he said:
"Greetings! child of grace! The Lord is your helper!
You are blessed beyond all women!"
But she was profoundly disturbed by the address,
and debated within herself what this greeting might mean.
    So then the angel said to her: "Do not tremble, Mary!
You have found favor in the eyes of God.
Behold: you are to be a mother,
and to bear a son, and to call him Jesus!
He will be great: 'Son of the Most High' will be his title,
And the Lord God will give to him the throne
of his father David.
He will be king over the house of Jacob forever,
and to his kingship there will be no end!" Luke 1:26-33

BIBLE MESSAGE

Christ teaches us.   Christ said to the people: ". . . if one is ashamed of me and my message before this adulterous and sinful race, of him the Son of Man will, in turn, be ashamed when he returns wrapt in his Father's glory and escorted by his holy angels." Mark 8:38.

1 What is the point of Christ's teaching here? 2 How was this especially true under the Greek tyrant Antiochus? 3 How did the vision of Daniel encourage Juda? 4 Discuss: a) the Machabean revolt, b) the coming of the Romans, c) the coming of the angel Gabriel.

LITURGY & LIFE

1 Dignity and freedom.   Addressing a meeting of the American Jewish Congress, Robert Kennedy said that American armed forces were in the Caribbean, West Berlin, South Vietnam, and South Korea "for the same reason that the Machabees stood their ground against Antiochus--for human dignity and freedom."

How did Antiochus violate the principle of human dignity and freedom? How did Judas Machabeus' men stand their ground against Antiochus? Why should we be concerned with the human dignity and freedom, not only of citizens of our own nation, but also of those of other nations?

CHRISTMAS LITURGY

The new king comes

Now it happened that an important letter was sent from Rome to the officials of the Jewish government. It informed them that Caesar Augustus wanted a census to be taken in all the Roman provinces.

Accordingly, the people went,
each to the city of his ancestor, to be registered;
and so Joseph, too, being a member of the house
and family of David, went up from the town of
Nazareth in Galilee to David's town in Judea,
called Bethlehem, in order to be registered.
He was accompanied by his espoused wife, Mary,
who was with child.
　　In the course of their stay there,
the time came for her delivery;
and she gave birth to her first-born son.
She wrapped him in swaddling clothes,
and laid him in a manger,
because there was no accommodation for them in the lodging.
　　In the same region shepherds were camping
in the open and keeping watch over their flocks by night.
Suddenly, an angel of the Lord stood facing them,
and the glory of the Lord shone round about them,
so that they were struck with terror.
"Do not fear," the angel said to them.
"Listen: I am bringing you good news of great joy
which is in store for the whole nation.
A Savior, who is the Lord Messias,
was born to you today in David's town!" Luke 2:3-11

Christmas is the feast of light

The custom of celebrating Christ's birthday on December 25 began in Rome more than 300 years after Christ's birth. The date was picked purposely to coincide with the pagan feast of light, celebrating the winter solstice.

Perfect symbol

The Church's decision to pick this date was wise for two reasons. First of all, it would have been foolish to pass a law trying to ban the celebration of a feast so deeply rooted in the culture of the people. It was far wiser to retain the feast and Christianize it. Secondly, the winter solstice (the day on which the hours of light increase and the hours of darkness decrease) naturally symbolized the spiritual truth contained in Christ's birth. By his coming Christ, the Son of Justice and Light of the World, broke the reign of sin, death, and darkness that had engulfed the world since Adam's fall.

Christ is our light

This theme of Christ's victory over sin and darkness weaves through all the Christmas Masses. At midnight we pray to God, "You have made this sacred night shine with the brightness of the true light." In the dawn Mass we say, "Almighty God, we are drenched in the new light of the Word become Man." Finally, in the day Mass, we pray, "Come, you nations, adore the Lord, for today a great light has come down upon the earth."

Christ is our life

Parallel to the theme of light is that of life. Christ came not only to rescue us from darkness, but also to communicate to us his life. This idea of new life in Christ is beautifully expressed by Pope St. Leo in a famous Christmas sermon.

Let us rejoice. It would be unlawful to be sad today, for today is Life's birthday, the birthday of that Life which, for us mortal creatures, takes away the sting of death and brings the bright promise of an eternal hereafter . . . Rejoice if you are a saint, for you are drawing nearer to your crown! Rejoice if you are a sinner, for your Savior offers you pardon! And if you are a pagan, rejoice, for God calls you to life . . .

Let us then put off the old man with his deeds, and, having obtained a share in the sonship of Christ, let us renounce the deeds of the flesh . . . Remember whose body it is of which you are a member, and who is its head. Remember that it is he who has delivered you from the power of darkness and has transferred you into God's light and God's kingdom.

From the liturgy

In him was life, and his life
was the light of men.   Gospel: Christmas Day Mass

Study questions

The poet Crashaw referred to Christmas as "love's noon in nature's light." 1 Show how this is not only good poetry but good theology. 2 Did Christ ever say that he is our light and our life? Read John 8:12. 3 Mark in your missal the references to light and life in the Christmas Masses.

During the season of Advent we saw how:

GOD SENT PROPHETS TO HIS PEOPLE

1 God's people split into two kingdoms
2 God's people are exiled
3 From God's people will come a new king and kingdom

GOD PREPARED HIS PEOPLE FOR THE NEW KING

1 God's people return from exile
2 God's people are prepared for the new king

During the season of Epiphany we will see how:

CHRIST IS THE PROMISED KING

1 Christ is proclaimed Messia-King of all men
2 Simeon proclaims Christ the promised one
3 Christ proclaims his divine mission

. . . as I love you, so I want you, too
to love one another.
By this token all the world must know
that you are my disciples . . .   John 13:34, 35

LITURGY AFTER EPIPHANY

We manifest Christ to the world

The word Epiphany means "to manifest." During this season
the Church's liturgy proclaims that Christ is the Son of God. He
is the Messia-King, come to establish God's kingdom on earth.

On the feast of the Epiphany the priest, as spokesman of
Christ's mystical body, prays in the Divine Office:

We celebrate a day
made glorious by three miracles.
Today the star led the Wise Men to the crib.
Today water was made wine for the marriage.
Today, in the Jordan,
Christ consented to be baptized by John,
for our salvation. Alleluia!

Triple manifestation

This prayer telescopes into one, joyful song the three main
manifestations that we recall and relive during the Epiphany season: the adoration of the Magi, the baptism of Jesus, and the marriage feast at Cana.

Through the episode of the Magi, Christ manifests himself, in
a special way, to the non-Jewish world. He teaches us that he is
the Messia-King whose reign and salvation will extend to all nations.

Through his baptism at the Jordan, Christ manifests himself, in
a special way to the people of Israel. He is the one promised by
the prophets.

Through the Cana miracle, Christ manifests himself, in a special way to his disciples. On that occasion, St. John says, "He
revealed his glory and his disciples believed in him." John 2:11.

We proclaim Christ's kingship to the world

During the season of Epiphany, the Epistles of the Sunday Masses invite us, the members of Christ's mystical body, to continue to
manifest Christ to the world. The best way we do this is by the
example of our Christ-like charity toward one another. ". . . as I
love you, so I want you, too, to love one another. By this token all
the world must know that you are my disciples . . ." John 13:34-35.

By our Christ-like charity, we, the members of Christ's mystical body, continue to proclaim and manifest Christ's kingship and
messiaship to all men.

From the liturgy

Allelulia, allelulia! The Lord is king:
let the earth exult; let the islands of the world rejoice.
Allelulia!   Gradual: Sundays after Epiphany

Study questions

1 Explain to whom and how Christ manifests himself in a special
way at Bethlehem, the Jordan River, and Cana. 2 Bring your missals to class, and be prepared to show how the Epistles of Epiphany
and the Sundays after Epiphany give us the basic principles by which
we are to continue to manifest Christ to the world. 3 Be prepared
to give five concrete examples showing how these principles can be
applied to a high-school student's daily life.

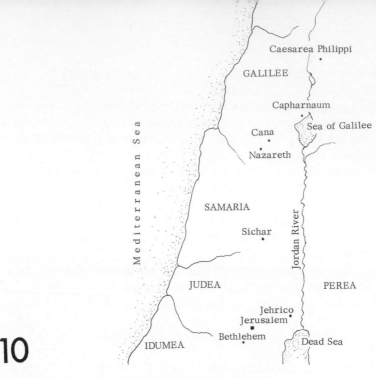

10

CHRIST IS THE PROMISED KING

1 Christ is proclaimed Messia-King of all men

It surprises many people to discover that St. Matthew devotes only one line to Christmas and a whole page to the Epiphany. The reason for this is most important. Let us read St. Matthew's account and discover his purpose.

> After Jesus was born at Bethlehem in Judea,
> in the days of King Herod, a commotion arose
> in Jerusalem when Magi from the East arrived
> and inquired:
> "Where is the newborn King of the Jews?
> It was his star we saw in the East,
> and we came to offer homage to him."
>   The news threw King Herod into consternation,
> shared by all Jerusalem.
> Assembling the whole body of the chief priests
> and Scribes--the nation's Council--
> he inquired of them where the Messias was to be born.
> "At Bethlehem in Judea," they said to him . . .

Then Herod secretly summoned the Magi and . . .
sent them to Bethlehem with this injunction:
"Go and make careful inquiries about the child,
and, when you have found him, report to me.
I, too, wish to go and do homage to him."
So they obeyed the king and went their way;
and, unexpectedly, the star they had seen
in the East preceeded them till it came
and stopped over the place where the child was! . . .
And so, entering the house and seeing the child
with his mother Mary, they threw themselves down
to do homage to him. Opening also their treasure chests,
they presented him with gifts: gold, frankincense, and myrrh.
But advised in a dream not to return to Herod,
they departed for their country
by a different route.   Matthew 2:1-12

Christ comes to save all men

If you read St. Matthew's Gospel closely, you will be struck at
the number of times he refers to the salvation of Gentiles: non-
Jewish peoples. Matthew 4:15, 10:18, 24:14, 28:19. St. Matthew
devotes several parables specifically to this theme (the laborers
in the vineyard, 20:1-16; the two sons, 21:28-32; the vine dressers,
21:33-46; and the marriage feast, 22:1-14). The reason St. Matthew
does this is to teach that Christ came to save all men. Though this
teaching seems perfectly obvious to us today, it was not always so.

Proclamation of Christ's universal kingship and messiaship

In the light of this, we can now see why St. Matthew gave so
much more time and space to the Epiphany than to Christmas.
He wanted to make this story stand out and be the official New
Testament proclamation of the fact that Christ has come to save
not just the Jews but all men. God's kingdom and Christ's kingship is to extend to all nations, even the Gentile nations.
And so after 2,000 years, the promise God made to Abraham
is fulfilled. "In you," God told Abraham, "shall all the nations
of the earth be blessed." Genesis 12:3. Christ is that blessing.
This is why Matthew makes so much of the Epiphany.
Because of its great importance, especially to the non-Jewish
world, the Epiphany is celebrated in many countries with a
solemnity greater than that of Christmas.

BIBLE MESSAGE

Christ teaches us today. When Pilate asked Jesus if he were a king, Jesus replied, "I am a king." But Jesus also said to Pilate, "My kingdom is not a worldly one." John 18:36.

Explain Christ's teaching here. Discuss: a) the reason for the many references to the salvation of the Gentiles in Matthew's Gospel, b) the reason for Matthew's great emphasis on the Epiphany.

LITURGY & LIFE

1 Religious message of the Magi story. A famous biblical scholar says, "Matthew contrasts Israel's infidelity with the faith of pagan astrologers or wise men . . . The religious message Matthew sees in the story concerns God's plan for the pagan's salvation: Magi through their natural science discover by faith what Herod and the religious leaders of Judaism miss, despite their possession of 'the Scriptures.'" David Stanley, S.J.

Put in your own words the religious message God is trying to teach us through the Magi story. How is the Magi story a kind of preview of what many future Jews will do? Point out in the biblical account where the Magi specifically call Christ a king. How is the Magi story a preview of Christ's kingship over all men?

2 Artists and the Magi. A panel of TV experts was asked to identify famous men from symbols flashed on a studio screen. One team won ten points for identifying three crowns as standing for the three men who paid homage to Christ. The other team objected, saying that crowns didn't symbolize these men because a Magi (wise man) is not necessarily a king.

If you were the quiz master, how would you answer this objection? Why do you think so many people think of the Magi as kings? What is the important point to keep in mind about the three men who came to pay homage to Jesus?

3 Gifts of the Magi. From earliest times Christian artists and writers have regarded the three gifts of the Magi as symbolic representations of Christ's kingship, divinity, and humanity.

How is this idea in keeping with the purpose of the account in St. Matthew? Can you figure what gift was symbolic of: 1) Christ's kingship, 2) his divinity, 3) his humanity?

140

4 Modern day Magi. From January 18 until January 25, the Church celebrates the Chair of Unity Octave. During these eight days the Church prays in a special way that lapsed Catholics, separated brethren, and unbaptized persons find their way into the one fold of Christ.

How is the Epiphany season an excellent time for such an Octave of prayer? How can a high-school student best help his non-Catholic friends find Christ? Prepare a classroom display and report for each day of the Unity Octave.

2 Simeon proclaims Christ the promised one of Israel

Following his birth Jesus receives the rites and blessings that Jewish children normally receive. During one of these rites a great announcement is made. Let us read about it in the Bible.

When seven days had elapsed,
it was time for him to be circumcised;
and he was named Jesus.
It was the name pronounced by the angel before his conception.
    When the prescribed days had elapsed, it was time for them
to be purified according to the Law of Moses.
So they took him up to Jerusalem
in order to present him to the Lord . . . Just at that time
there was a man in Jerusalem by the name of Simeon. . . .
Now it had been revealed to him by the Holy Spirit
that he was not to see death
before seeing the Lord's Anointed;
and so, impelled by the Spirit, he betook himself to the temple.
And there, just when the parents
had brought in the child Jesus,
intending to perform in his behalf
the customary rites of the Law,
he took him into his arms and spoke this hymn to God:
    "Now you may release
    your bondsman, O Master . . .

141

For my eyes have looked upon the salvation
which you have prepared
for all nations to behold,
a Light to illumine the Gentiles,
a Glory to grace your people Israel."
His father and his mother were wrapt in wonder
at what was being said about him.
Simeon blessed them, and then said to Mary his mother:
"Alas! This babe is destined
to be the downfall no less than the restoration
of many in Israel!
His very name will provoke contradiction,
and your own soul, also,
shall be pierced by a sword! . . ."
When they had complied with every detail
of the Law of the Lord,
they returned to their own town Nazareth in Galilee.
The child grew strong in body and soul
as his intelligence developed;
and the grace of God rested upon him.   Luke 2:21-40

Jesus is circumcised and receives his name

God commanded Abraham and his male descendants to be
circumcised as a sign of his covenant with them. Genesis 17:10.
In fulfillment of this law, eight days after his birth, Jesus submits to circumcision. By this act he officially becomes a member
of the chosen people. On this occasion our Lord also receives the
name which the angel prescribed for him before his conception.
He is called Jesus. The name Jesus means "God saves" and foreshadows Jesus' vocation.

Jesus is presented at the temple

According to Jewish law, the firstborn of men and animals
and the firstfruits of the harvest were to be offered to God.
Exodus 22:28-29. Offering the firstborn and the firstfruits was
a symbolic act by which the Jews humbly acknowledged that both
life and the means to sustain life were gifts from God and right-
fully belonged to him. In accordance with this ancient law, Jesus,
who is the firstborn of Mary and Joseph, is offered to the Father
in the temple.
But since God forbade human sacrifice, Jewish law provided a

ransom for buying back the firstborn child. In the case of Jesus, the son of a poor family, the ransom was two turtle doves. Luke 2:24.

It is on the occasion of Jesus' presentation at the temple that the Holy Spirit reveals to the holy man, Simeon, that Jesus is the promised savior who will, indeed, some day sacrifice his life for the ransom of mankind. Moreover, Christ's death will not be for the Jews alone but for all men. He will be a "Light to illumine the Gentiles" and a "Glory to grace your people Israel."

Mary is purified

Jewish law further required that all Jewish mothers present themselves to the temple to be purified forty days after having given birth to a son.

In fulfillment of this law, Mary presents herself, along with her son, at the temple. Mary's humble act of submission becomes the occasion for Simeon to announce to her that she will be most closely associated with the sacrifice of her son. Simeon says to her, "And your own soul, also, shall be pierced by a sword." Luke 2:35.

BIBLE MESSAGE

Christ teaches us.   Christ was above the Jewish law, and the Virgin Mary had no need of "purification." But Christ chose to obey the law and use it as an occasion to teach us some important truths about himself and his future mission.

1 What important announcements concerning Jesus and Mary are made at this time? 2 Discuss the Jewish laws concerning a) circumcision, b) presentation of the firstborn, c) purification of mothers.

Some important biblical background: Mary's role

Mary's role in God's plan has a double aspect. First of all, she is the mother of Jesus.

Mary is mother

God announced to Mary her vocation of motherhood when the Angel Gabriel appeared to her and said, "You are blessed beyond all women! . . . you are to be a mother, and to bear a son, and to call him Jesus." Luke 1:29-31. Following her call, Mary went to the home of Elizabeth, her cousin. Elizabeth realized God's presence within Mary and addressed her as "the mother of my Lord." In ancient eastern courts this title was reserved for the mother of a king. For in those days, because of polygamy, the mother of the king acted as queen. This brings up the second aspect of Mary's role in God's plan.

Mary is queen

In addition to being the mother of Christ, Mary is also his close associate in the work of salvation. She is queen of God's kingdom, interceding for kingdom members before the throne of her son, Christ the King.

The third Book of Kings 2:19 gives us an insight into the favor which certain (but not all) queens enjoyed in biblical times. In this passage Solomon's mother, Bethsabee, enters the royal presence of her son to ask of him a favor for one of the subjects of the realm. The Bible records the incident saying, "the king arose to meet her and bowed to her, and sat down upon his throne. And a throne was set for the king's mother: and she sat on his right hand." 3 Kings 2:19.

Mary's role as our queenly intercessor manifested itself for the first time at Cana. John 2:3-5. Later it was revealed in even more striking ways beneath the cross (John 19:25-27) and in the upper room on Pentecost (Acts 1:14). Finally, Mary's role reached perfection when she was gloriously assumed, body and soul, into heaven. There she now reigns and intercedes for men.

Study questions

1 What is Mary's dual role in God's plan? 2 Briefly discuss how Mary carried out, and continues to carry out, each role.

Joseph's role in God's plan

Joseph's role in God's plan was to be Jesus' foster-father and Mary's husband. Joseph was of David's line. He was young when he married Mary. In keeping with a marriage custom, Mary and Joseph lived apart for a specified time after their betrothal. It was during this time that Joseph found Mary was with child.

Joseph, "being right-minded and unwilling to expose her, resolved to put her away without public formalities. He had just
made up his mind to this course when an angel of the Lord appeared to him in a dream and said: 'Joseph, son of David, do not scruple
to take Mary, your wife, into your home. Her conception was wrought
by the Holy Spirit. She will bear a Son and you are to name him Jesus; for he will save his people from their sins.'" Matthew 1:19-21.

Husband and father

With tenderness and honor, Joseph took Mary into his home.
He was at her side when Jesus was born. Luke 2:16. He led the
Holy Family to safety during Herod's massacre. Matthew 2:13.
When all was safe again, Joseph brought the Holy Family back
to Nazareth. There he supported them with his carpenter trade.
Matthew 2:23, 13:55.

Except for the mention of his yearly trip to Jerusalem at the
time of the Passover, the Gospel makes no further mention of
Joseph. It is assumed that he died in Nazareth when his vocation
as earthly foster-father to Jesus and protector of the Holy Family
were gloriously fulfilled.

Today St. Joseph is honored throughout the world as protector
and patron of Christ's mystical body, the Church.

Study questions

1 What was Joseph's role in God's plan? 2 How did Joseph first
learn of his role? 3 How did Joseph carry out this role? 4 What
is Joseph's role today? 5 Using your missal, list the liturgical
feasts in honor of St. Joseph and show how they relate to Joseph's
role in God's plan of love for men.

LITURGY & LIFE

1 Baptism replaces circumcision.   When Jesus inaugurated
the New Covenant, circumcision lost its significance as a mark
of God's covenant with the Jews. It was replaced by baptism and
the mark of the Holy Spirit. Colossians 2:11 ff.

Explain how baptism achieves for the New Testament Christians
what circumcision achieved for the Old Testament Jews. When do
we celebrate the liturgical feasts of: a) Jesus' circumcision,
b) Jesus' name?

2 Jesus' presentation and Mary's purification.   The Church
recalls and relives the event of Jesus' presentation and Mary's
purification in the Mass liturgy on February 2. Drawing inspiration from Simeon's words that Jesus is the "Light" who will
"illumine the Gentiles," the Church makes her liturgy on February
2 a festival of lights. The ceremony consists of: 1) the blessing
of candles, 2) the distribution of candles, 3) the procession with
lighted candles, and 4) the Mass.

The Purification "liturgy of light" reminds us that Christ is
the Light of the World. It also reminds us of the entrance of Christ
into our lives at the time of baptism (our circumcision). Then the
priest handed a lighted candle to our sponsors and said, "Receive
this lighted candle, and keep your baptism beyond reproach. Keep
the commandments of God, so that when the Lord comes to his
marriage feast you may meet him in the halls of heaven with all
the saints, and may live with him forever." A candle will again be
lit at our deathbed.

With the help of your missals outline the Purification liturgy
service. Briefly, put in your own words the general idea and
meaning of the prayers accompanying the service.

3 Presenting the firstborn in the temple.   Besides serving as
a dramatic reminder of God's dominion over human life, the custom of offering the firstborn to God also recalled for the Jews a
great event in Israel's history.

What was the event? To refresh your memory see Exodus 11:4-7.

4 Blessing mothers.   Christian tradition has kept the memory
of the rite of purification in a ceremony called "The Blessing of
Mothers after Childbirth."

In this ceremony, which frequently takes place after the baby's
baptism, the priest, vested in a surplice and white stole, proceeds
with a server to the entrance of the Church. There the mother and
baby await him with a lighted candle. The priest then sprinkles
them and all present with holy water. Next the priest says a series
of short prayers. The last prayer of the series reads:

The woman shall receive the Lord's blessing,
and mercy from God, who has saved her,
for she is one of the family of those who seek the Lord.

Then the priest puts one end of the white stole into the mother's
hand and leads her and the child toward the altar, saying:

Come into God's temple
and worship the Son
of the blessed Mary the Virgin,
worship him who has granted
that you should bear a child.

The mother then kneels with her baby at the foot of the altar,
thanking God for his blessings. The priest then says another
short series of prayers. He concludes the ceremony by sprinkling
the mother and baby with holy water and saying:

May the peace and blessing of almighty God,
The Father, the Son, and the Holy Spirit,
come down on you, and be with you forever. Amen.

3 Christ proclaims his divine mission

When Jesus was twelve he visited his Father's house in Jerusalem.
Let us read in the Bible where this is recorded.

Year after year his parents went to Jerusalem
for the feast of the Passover.
And so, too, when he was twelve years old,
they went up according to their custom at the time of the feast.
    After spending there the required number of days,
they prepared to return,
but the child Jesus remained behind at Jerusalem,
without his parents knowing about it.
Supposing him to be in the caravan,
they finished a day's journey, and began to search for him
among their relations and acquaintances.
When they did not find him,
they retraced their steps to Jerusalem,
there to renew their search for him.
    It was only on the third day that they
discovered him in the temple, seated among the rabbis,

now listening to them, now asking them questions,
while all those that heard him
were charmed by his intelligence and his answers.
They were overjoyed to see him.

His mother said to him: "Child, why did you behave
toward us in this way? Oh, our hearts were heavy--
your father's and mine--as we searched for you!"

He said to them: "Why did you search for me?
I had to answer my Father's call, and did you not know it?"
But they did not grasp the meaning
of the reply he made to them.

He then went down in their company and came to Nazareth,
where he was subject to them.
His mother treasured all these incidents in her memory,
and Jesus made steady progress,
proportionately to his age, in understanding
and in favor with God and men.   Luke 2:41-52

Christ comes to do his Father's will

It is significant that the first recorded words of Jesus in the
Bible refer to the mission his Father has given to him. Jesus has
come to carry out the will of his Father. Jesus' mission is to
establish his Father's kingdom, and through it, to invite all men
to share in his Father's love and life.

Christ replaces the Jerusalem temple

It is also significant that the only recorded event in the Bible
concerning Christ's life between infancy and adulthood is a Passover visit to the temple in Jerusalem. The event becomes even
more significant when we recall that on the very first Passover
of his public life, Jesus returns to Jerusalem to announce that
the temple of Jerusalem (the symbol of God's presence on earth)
is being replaced by the temple of his body (the reality of God's
presence on earth). John 2:13-22.

Christ's mystical body is God's new temple on earth

Today that presence is still realized in Christ's mystical body,
the Church. Moreover, by our membership in Christ's mystical
body, we have become a part of God's new living temple among
men. 1 Corinthians 3:16-17; Ephesians 2:22.

BIBLE MESSAGE

Christ teaches us.   In telling about our Lord's public life,
St. John records that on Jesus' first Passover visit to Jerusalem,
he engages in a discussion with temple authorities. He tells them:
"'If you destroy this sanctuary . . . I will build it up again in
three days.' The Jews then said to him: 'Six and forty years this
sanctuary was in building; and you will build it up again in three
days?' He, however, was speaking of the sanctuary of his body.
After he had risen from the dead, therefore, his disciples remembered that he had said this; and they believed both the Scripture and the statement Jesus had made." John 2:19-22.

1 Why do you think the Jews misunderstood Jesus? 2 How was
Jesus the reality of God's presence, whereas the temple was only
its symbol? 3 Where is God's temple today?

LITURGY & LIFE

1 Christ's mission.   St. Luke lists as Christ's first recorded words, "Why did you search for me? I had to answer my Father's call, and did you not know it?" Luke 2:49. St. Luke lists as
Christ's last recorded words, "Father into your hands I commit
my spirit." Luke 23:46.

Do you see any connection between these two statements? Review Christ's role in his Father's plan of love for men. Do you
think Mary and Joseph understood Christ's role from the start?

2 The observance of Jewish feasts.   In Jesus' time, Jewish
law required that every adult male be present in Jerusalem for
the feast of the Passover at least. This great insistence on the
observance of Jewish feasts kept Israel's faith living and vital.
An old Jewish proverb seems to have this in mind when it says,
"More than Israel kept the Sabbath, the Sabbath kept Israel."

Explain the proverb. Explain how the proverb could also be
applied to our Sunday and holydays.

What was Jesus' boyhood like?

The first years of a Jewish boy's life were spent in his mother's
care. Once the boy grew older, however, his father took over the
responsibility of teaching him.

149

Father's role

Among the father's first duties was to teach his son about the wonderful works that God had performed for Israel. The Bible directed him to do this, in particular, by explaining the meaning of all the great feasts. "On this day [the Feast of the Unleavened Bread] you shall explain to your son, 'This is because of what the Lord did for me when I came out of Egypt. . . .'" Exodus 13:8.

After teaching his son about what God had done for Israel, the father next taught his son how to respond gratefully to God for being so good to Israel. The father taught his son to be loyal to God's commandments. "He [God] . . . established it as a law in Israel, that what he commanded our fathers they should make known to their sons." Psalm 77:5.

In addition to the father's instructions, there were also schools for Israelite children. These were connected with the synagogues. In Christ's time these schools were somewhat informal. They usually consisted in having the Israelite boys sit on the ground around a teacher and repeat after him, from memory, sentences that the teacher had read aloud. For the most part these sentences were from the Torah (the first five books of the Bible).

The boy becomes a man

The Israelite boy began his school around five; he finished at about thirteen. At that age he was supposed to know the whole law of Israel and practice it faithfully. From then on he was considered as having left childhood behind him. He became a "son of the Law"; and, like his elder, he would recite daily the "Shema Israel," a prayer of faith in God. He would also fast regularly, make the traditional pilgrimages to Jerusalem, and take his place in the "court of the men" in the temple.

For this reason the "Bar Mitzvah," the day on which the Israelite boy officially became a "son of the Law," was celebrated with great festivity. A highpoint in the celebration came when the boy stood and read aloud a passage from the Law.

What did Jesus do on the Sabbath?

Each Sabbath morning the Israelite boy attended the synagogue in his village. The seating arrangement of having all the men sit in one area and all the women in another is still preserved in synagogues today.

The synagogue service

The service opened with a prayer and hymn. It was followed
by a series of readings from Sacred Scripture. These readings
usually recounted the wonders God had done for his people and
were followed by a short sermon-like commentary. Services
closed with a blessing and a prayer. The Israelite boy then returned home to spend the rest of the day in prayer and rest.

The closest thing to a prayerbook or hymn book that the Jewish
boy knew was the Psalter: a collection of 150 psalms.

The Psalms: the Bible set to prayer and music

Someone once remarked that if the whole Old Testament had
been lost, except for the Book of Psalms, we could probably re-
construct its basic outline from just this one book. For in this
book we have the great events of the Old Testament set to prayer
and music (psalms were usually sung).

The psalms are the prayers that Christ prayed during his life.
Today every priest prays all 150 psalms each week in the Divine
Office. They are the official prayer of Christ's mystical body.

Study questions

1 Identify: Torah, Shema Israel, Bar Mitzvah, Psalter. 2 Compare the synagogue service to the Mass of the Catechumens.
3 Read Psalms 8, 135, 136, 126, and explain how they set the Old
Testament to prayer and music.

During the season after Epiphany we saw that:

CHRIST IS THE PROMISED KING

1 Christ is proclaimed the Messia-King of all men
2 Simeon proclaims Christ the promised one of Israel
3 Christ proclaims his divine mission

During the season of Septuagesima we will see how:

CHRIST BEGINS HIS MISSION

    1 Christ is announced by John the Baptist
    2 Christ is anointed for his divine mission
    3 Christ previews his mission

With my eyes fixed on the goal,
I press on to the prize in store for those
who have received from above
God's call in Jesus Christ.   Philippians 3:14

SEPTUAGESIMA LITURGY

Christ invites us to follow him

Septuagesima means seventieth. It reminds us that we are now
seventy days away from Easter. It also reminds us that we are
entering the second half of the liturgical year.

During the first half of the year, we saw how Christ became
like us. During this second half of the year, we will see how we
are to become like Christ. Christ took on our humanity (Christmas) that we might take on his divinity (Easter).

The Church's liturgy helps us

To help us reach this lofty goal, the Church launches us on a
period of preparation. Septuagesima Sunday marks the start of
that period.

The message of the Gospels

The Gospel of Septuagesima Sunday begins by recalling how
Christ invited us to work in his vineyard (to help him bring about
God's kingdom). The Gospel for the second Sunday recalls that
Christ planted in us his powerful words of life. It urges us to hold
fast to these words. The Gospel of the third Sunday assures us
that if we hold fast to Christ's words, we will some day reach God,
our goal, and rejoice forever in his glory.

The message of the Epistles

If the Gospels of Septuagesima recall for us our goal, the Epistles recall for us how we can best reach that goal. The Epistle of
the first Sunday tells us to train and to condition ourselves for the
spiritual struggle that lies ahead of us. The second Sunday teaches
us to trust in Christ, no matter what happens in the struggle. The
third Sunday reminds us that the key to our victory is charity:
love of God and love of neighbor.

Follow Christ

The Gospels of Septuagesima are invitations to spend ourselves
for Christ; the Epistles are training plans for victory. The purpose
of this season of Septuagesima is to rally us behind Christ, our
head and leader, for the spiritual contest that lies ahead.

From the liturgy

. . . whenever men run a race in a stadium,
all run but only one wins the prize?
So run that you will surely win.
Every contestant submits to all sorts of privations
and that to win a perishable crown,
but we an imperishable one.
Epistle: Septuagesima Sunday

Study questions

Bring your missals to class, and discuss in detail the message
of the Gospels and the message of the Epistles. Be ready to give
several concrete examples, showing how a high-school student
can carry out the message of each in daily life.

11

CHRIST BEGINS HIS MISSION

1 <u>Christ is announced by John the Baptist</u>

Not far from where the Jordan River flows into the Dead Sea is a natural ford over the Jordan. Since earliest times this ford has been used by caravans from all over the Near East. On an afternoon one may see Arabs from Transjordan, Babylonians with rings in their noses, and bronze-colored Abyssinians. It has therefore become a favorite place for people to gather and exchange the news.

One day, however, a new attraction sends people flocking to the ford. For weeks word has been circulating about a strange figure, dressed in the garb of a prophet, who is preaching there. Not for 500 years has a prophet been heard in Israel. So it is not surprising that people come all the way from Jerusalem to look over the matter. Let us read about this in the Bible.

In those days John the Baptist arrived
to preach in the desert of Judea, and his theme was:
"You need a change of heart;

156

the kingdom of heaven is close at hand."
This is the man spoken of by Isaia the prophet,
who says: "A herald's voice rings out:
'Make ready the way of the Lord in the desert;
make straight his paths.'"

John wore a distinctive garment of camel's hair
and a leather belt was round his loins;
his food was locusts and honey of wild bees.
Soon Jerusalem and the rest of Judea,
as well as the entire region on either side of the Jordan,
went out to meet him. They confessed their sins
and were baptized by him in the Jordan River.

On seeing many of the Pharisees and Sadducees
coming to the scene of his baptism he said to them:
"Brood of vipers! Who advised you to flee
before the gathering storm of anger?
Well, then, let your conduct show your change of heart!
And do not presume to say to yourselves:
'We have Abraham for our father!'
I tell you, God is able to raise up children to Abraham
out of these very stones.
Besides, from now on the axe lies ready to strike
at the root of the trees;
any tree, therefore, that does not produce sound fruit
is cut down and thrown into the fire.
I baptize you with water to help you make a change of heart;
but One shall come after me who is mightier than I
and whose sandals I am not worthy to take off his feet.
He for his part will baptize you
in the Holy Spirit--and in fire.
His winnow in hand,
he will thoroughly cleanse his threshing floor:
the wheat he will store in his barn,
and the chaff he will burn in unquenchable fire." Matthew 3:1-12

Repent, the kingdom is at hand

When the tall, bronzed figure of John appears on the banks of
the Jordan, it is clear to all that he is a prophet. His dress and
spirit show this. But the big question in everybody's mind is,
"Just who is he?" Some think he is Elias come back to life.
John 1:21. Others don't know what to think. This is certain,
John's appearance creates a great stir in Israel.

157

Men from everywhere come to hear John. It is a long time since the voice of a prophet rang out in Israel. The people listen to him eagerly. John's preaching centers around two points. The first point is this. Prepare and repent, for the kingdom of God is close at hand. It is not enough that you are children of Abraham. You must return to the spirit of Abraham and do what he did. You must have a change of heart. Leave the ways of the world, as Abraham did, and go to a new life. As a sign of your desire to do this, do penance and be baptized.

A mighty person will soon appear

John's second point stirs even greater excitement. He says that there will soon appear a great person in Judea. What your penance and my baptism are only a sign of, says John, his baptism will achieve. For this man is much holier and mightier than I am. His very sandals, I am not worthy to loosen.

BIBLE MESSAGE

Christ teaches us.   Speaking about John the Baptist, Christ said to the people, "What did you go into the desert to look at? A reed waving in the wind? Well, then, what did you go out to see? A man dressed in fine, soft clothes? But notice: the people that wear fine clothes and live in luxury are in the royal palaces! Well, then, what did you go out to see? A prophet? Yes, I tell you, and more than a prophet!" Luke 7:24-26.

1 How was John more than a prophet? 2 Discuss the two main points of John's message to the people.

LITURGY & LIFE

1 John's appearance begins a new era.   St. Luke precedes his account of the appearance of John the Baptist by pinpointing the exact year of the event six different ways. "In the fifteenth year of the reign of Emperor Tiberius--when Pontius Pilate was governor of Judea; Herod, tetrarch of Galilee; Philip, his brother, tetrarch of Iturea and Trachonitis; Lysanias, tetrarch of Abilene; under the high priest Annas and Caiaphas--a summons from God came in the desert to John, the son of Zachary." Luke 3:1-2.

Why do you think St. Luke took so much trouble to pinpoint the date of John's appearance? What was Zachary's position in Israel? Read Luke 1:5 ff. Describe the events preceding and following John's birth.

2 John is strong.   In the Divine Office for June 24, the feast of John the Baptist, the following hymn occurs: "You left the busy cities, when still a child, and chose to live in desert caves to avoid the discredit of even the slightest sin of speech. The camel provided your holy body with coarse clothing, and oxen your belt. A spring gave you your drink, honey and locusts your food. All other prophets had spoken in their messages of the future coming of the Light, but you pointed out with your finger the One that takes away the sin of the world. In the whole wide world there is no child of man more holy than John, found worthy as he was to baptize him who washes men clean of sin." Hymns of the Roman Liturgy: Connelly.

In the early days of the Church when few could read or write people often used to learn the truths of their faith by singing hymns like this. From your reading of the Gospel would you say this hymn contains the important truths about John the Baptist? What eventually happened to John? Read Mark 6:17-29. How did Jesus regard John? Read Luke 7:24-28. Why do you think the Church made use of songs to teach the people who couldn't read or write? What Mass prayer takes over the words of John the Baptist found in John 1:36? Explain why this prayer is well placed in the Mass. How might you symbolize John the Baptist in art? In what sense was John a bridge between the Old Testament and the New Testament?

3 John is not soft.   A famous football coach once said, "If I have learned one fact in my twenty years of work with boys, it is this--the most dangerous thing in American life today is that we're getting soft inside and out! We're losing a forceful heritage of mind and body that was once our most precious heritage."

What does it mean to be soft inside and out? How can a person guard against becoming soft? How would John the Baptist be a good model for us today?

4 Learn to sacrifice.   A mother once asked General Robert E. Lee, the great Civil War leader, what she should teach her son. Lee's answer shocked her. "Teach him," said Lee, "to deny himself."

Why do you think General Lee told her this? How is self denial both naturally and supernaturally enriching? Did Christ ever say anything about self denial? Read Matthew 10:38-39. What does the Church have to say about external penance? Give examples.

5 The spirit is what counts.   Writing about "Lenten Practices" a writer says, "Supernaturally speaking, the important thing is not the external penance but the internal spirit. Without an internal spirit, the external act is meaningless. It could even be harmful because success in performing external penance could end in inflating the ego rather than eliminating it."

Explain the writer's statement. How did John the Baptist express this same idea? What did Christ say about showy penances? Read Matthew 6:16-18.

2 Christ is anointed for his divine mission

One day, not long after John's announcement, Jesus arrives at the banks of the Jordan River. There he presents himself to be baptized by John. Let us read how this is recorded in the Bible.

At that time Jesus arrived from Galilee
to meet John at the Jordan and be baptized by him.
John tried to stop him.
"It is I who should be baptized by you," he said,
"and you come to me?"
Jesus remonstrated.
"Let me have my way for the present," he said to him;
"after all, it is only so that we fulfill,
as is proper for us, all just demands."
Then he let him have his way.
No sooner was Jesus baptized, than he came up out of the water,
and there and then the heavens opened to his view:
he saw the Spirit of God descend in the shape of a dove,
and alight on him. And a voice rang out upon the air:
"This is my Son, the beloved,
with whom I am well pleased."   Matthew 3:13-17

Christ identifies himself with us

When John sees Jesus, he immediately realizes his own un-
worthiness and asks Jesus to baptize him. But Jesus insists that
justice must be accomplished. In other words, it is his Father's
will that it be done this way.

John baptizes Jesus. Christian tradition has always regarded
Jesus' submission to John's baptism as a sign showing how closely
Jesus, by becoming man, identified himself with our sinful race.
This identity is so perfect that Christ's victory over sin will be-
come our victory. 1 Corinthians 15:21.

Christ is anointed king

No sooner does John baptize Jesus, than the Holy Spirit descends
upon Jesus, not to sanctify him but to anoint him for his future
mission: the eternal king of God's kingdom.

To the ancients' way of thinking every king had to be officially
anointed. Just as Saul and David were anointed kings by Samuel,
so Jesus is now anointed by the Holy Spirit.

From now on Jesus will be known as the "anointed one." The
Hebrew word for "anointed one" is <u>Messia</u>; the Greek word
is <u>Christos</u>.

At the moment of Christ's anointing, a voice rings out from
heaven saying, "This is my Son, the beloved, with whom I am
well pleased." The heavenly Father affirms that Jesus is not
only the promised Messia but also his own Son.

From the liturgy

"You are my son; this day I have begotten you. . . .
I will give you the nations for an inheritance
and the ends of the earth for your possession. . . ."
And now, O kings, give heed;
take warning, you rulers of the earth.
Serve the Lord with fear, and rejoice before him . . .
Happy are all who take refuge in him! Psalm 2:7-12

BIBLE MESSAGE

Christ teaches us.   Discuss: a) Christ's similarity to us,
and b) Christ's anointing and its significance.

Some important biblical background

Christians have always wondered how Christ looked. Though the Gospel is silent on the subject, it does leave some interesting clues. For example, Jesus held crowds spellbound for hours (Mark 6:34-36); children liked him (Luke 18:15-16); and many people developed a deep affection for him (John 11:1-6). These clues suggest that Jesus had an attractive appearance and personality.

Moreover, Christ and his apostles lived a strenuous life. For example, Christ walked miles in all kinds of weather (John 4:1-6), fasted for long periods of time (Matthew 4:2), spent nights in prayer (Luke 6:12), and frequently slept out in the open (Luke 9:58). These facts suggest that Christ was physically fit and strong.

Finally, Christ was the perfect kind of man God had in mind when he created him. Thus Christ's soul was the noblest and most perfect ever created. Since Christ's body formed a natural unity with his soul, there must have been some reflection in his body of the dignity and nobility of his soul.

For these reasons a famous theologian thinks we can safely assume that Christ was attractive and noble in appearance; but the simple fact is that we are not sure how he looked.

What about the Holy Shroud?

Recently much has been said about the Holy Shroud of Turin. It has been referred to as a "photograph" of Christ as he lay in the tomb. Actually we don't have the complete history of the Holy Shroud from the earliest ages. We only know that it has been reverenced for some centuries. The Church, always cautious, does not tell us that we must look upon the shroud as genuine. But the Church allows it to be honored by the faithful.

Study questions

Do you know of any other passages or incidents in the Gospel that suggest something about Christ's physical appearance?

LITURGY & LIFE

1 The day of Jesus' baptism is important. After Jesus' death the apostles decided to select a twelfth apostle to replace Judas.

One of the qualifications that St. Peter laid down for the successor was that he had to be a man who had been one of their company since the time of Jesus' baptism by John. Acts 1:22.

What does this stipulation teach us about the importance of this event? Is there anything significant in the fact that St. Peter should be the one who made this stipulation?

2 The Holy Trinity. "No sooner was Jesus baptized, then he came up out of the water, and there and then the heavens opened to his view: he saw the Spirit of God descend in the shape of a dove, and alight on him. And a voice rang out upon the air: 'This is my Son, the beloved, with whom I am well pleased.'" Matthew 3:16-17.

How does this passage point to an important truth about God? Why do you think Jesus waited so long to teach this truth to his followers? Will we ever be able to understand this truth completely in this life?

DOCTRINAL POINTS

The Holy Trinity

When Jesus came up from the water, he became aware of a remarkable happening. John the Baptist also perceived it. John 1:32. The Holy Spirit descended on Jesus in the form of a dove, and the voice of the Father "rang out upon the air: 'This is my Son, the beloved, with whom I am well pleased.'" Matthew 3:17.

Up until now neither John the Baptist nor any other person of Old Testament times suspected the depths of the mystery presented at this moment on the banks of the Jordan.

The mystery of the Trinity

The Holy Trinity is the mystery of three Divine Persons in one God. The Holy Trinity is a strict mystery. We know of the existence of the Holy Trinity because God revealed the fact. But even after its revelation we cannot fully understand how the details of the truths fit together.

Basic truths about the Trinity

The things that we know and believe concerning the Holy Trinity are the following: 1) There are three Persons in God. 2) God the

Father is the First Person of the Blessed Trinity; God the Son is the Second Person; and God the Holy Spirit is the Third Person. 3) The Father is God; the Son is God; and the Holy Spirit is God. 4) The three Divine Persons are really distinct from one another. 5) The three Divine Persons are all eternal and equal in glory and in power. 6) The divine attributes and the external works of God are common to all three Divine Persons. When God, for example, created the world, all three Persons created it. But in human speech we attribute or "appropriate" certain works to each Person. The work of creation is attributed to the Father, redemption to the Son, and sanctification of men to the Holy Spirit.

Happiness of the Trinity

It is something of a help for us in trying to understand how God could be eternally happy without creatures to remember that in God there are three Divine Persons. Without company men feel lonely, but the three Divine Persons have no need of companionship, for they are infinitely happy with and in themselves.

Imitation of the Trinity

As the three Divine Persons dwell together in infinite love and extend this love to men and angels, we cannot imitate them better or please them more than by cultivating a deep love of God and of our fellow men who are made to God's image and likeness.

The Trinity within us

We are temples of the Holy Trinity. 1 Corinthians 3:16. This means that the three Divine Persons live and abide with us as long as we are in the state of grace. Jesus said, "Anyone who loves me will treasure my message, and my Father will love him, and we shall visit him and make our home with him." John 14:23.

It is our incredible privilege to have God closer to us than any friend could be. We ought to respond to this great act of love on God's part by loving God in return and by doing nothing that would ever break the friendship that now exists between us.

Study questions

The story is told that St. Augustine was one day walking by the seashore meditating upon the Trinity. Coming upon a child who

was pouring water from the sea into a hole in the sand, he asked
him what he was doing. "Trying to empty the ocean into this hole,"
was the reply.

"You can never succeed," said the saint smiling. "I will
succeed in this before you will be able to understand the mystery
of the Trinity," replied the child, who then disappeared.

1) State the mystery of the Holy Trinity. 2) Discuss: a) the
basic truths about the Trinity, b) happiness of the Trinity,
c) imitation of the Trinity, d) the Trinity within us.

3 Christ previews his mission

After describing Jesus' baptism, St. Matthew records a striking
experience that happens to Christ immediately afterwards. The
experience reveals important truths about Christ and his mission.

Then Jesus was led on by the Spirit into the desert
to be put to the test by the devil.
Forty days and forty nights he fasted
and after that time he was hungry.
Now, then, the tempter approached and said to him:
"If you are the Son of God,
command these stones to turn into loaves of bread."
But he met the proposal by replying:
"It is written, 'Man does not live by bread alone:
but by every word coming from the lips of God.'"
    Then the devil took him up into the holy city
and set him down upon the battlement of the temple.
"If you are the Son of God," he said to him,
"fling yourself down; for the Scripture says:
'to his angels he will give charge of you'
and 'Upon their hands they will bear you up
that you may not stub your foot against a stone.'"
Jesus answered him:
"On the other hand, the Scripture says:
'You shall not tempt the Lord your God!'"

Again, the devil took him up
to a very high mountain and let him see
all the kingdoms of the world and their splendor.
"All these things will I give to you,"
he said to him,
"if you go down on your knees and do homage to me."
Then Jesus said to him:
"Go out Satan! The Scripture says:
'You shall do homage to the Lord your God,
and him alone shall you adore!'"
So then the devil left him undisturbed and, presently,
angels approached and waited on him.   Matthew 4:1-11

A dramatic preview

By his temptation in the desert, Christ previews in dramatic
fashion: 1) who he is, and 2) how he will go about carrying out the
mission his Father has given him.

Christ is the new Adam

God blessed Adam and put him in a garden of plenty. He invited
him to be the father of a great kingdom of men who would share
his happy lot. But in spite of God's goodness, Adam rejected God's
invitation.

Christ's mission is to repair the damage of Adam's sin. He is to
redeem mankind and be the means by which God will reinvite men
to his kingdom. Christ is the new Adam of the human race. Where
the first Adam failed, Christ, the new Adam, will succeed.

In the light of this it is not surprising that Christ, like Adam,
is tempted by Satan at the very outset of his vocation. But where
Adam fell, Christ triumphs. In doing so he assures victory to all
those who will follow him. Through the old Adam all men were
condemned to death; through Christ, the new Adam, all men are
raised to life. Romans 5:18.

Christ is the new Israel

Christ is also the new Israel. The old Israel became God's
"firstborn son" when he saved them from Egypt and made them
his own at Mt. Sinai. After this, Israel wandered for forty years
in the desert before reaching the promised land. There Israel,
tempted by Satan, fell into sensuality, presumption, and pride.

166

Now history repeats itself in a marvelous way. Christ is to be the "firstborn" of a new Israel. Where the old Israel had failed, it will be Christ's job to succeed. He will, as it were, relive its life and undo its mistakes. He will do this in the name of all future members of God's kingdom, the new Israel.

Thus it happens that after Jesus is anointed and announced to be the beloved Son of God, he is led into the desert to face the same trials as his ancestors. Like old Israel he is without food and remains there for forty days (symbolic of the forty years Israel spent in the desert). Like old Israel, he is tempted with the same three temptations as they were. But where they failed, Jesus triumphs. After each temptation Jesus quotes to Satan from Deuteronomy, the book that records the three falls of old Israel.

Christ, thus, reveals who he is. He is the new Adam and the new Israel. Through him all men will be reconciled with God and be invited anew to membership in God's kingdom.

How Christ will carry out his mission

At the time of Christ's coming, the people had expected a Messia-King as dashing as David had been. They also expected that the new king would establish an earthly kingdom of God renowned for its power and wealth, like the one in Solomon's time.

In scorning Satan's request to perform spectacular feats, Christ says, "No, God's kingdom will not be one of earthly power and show. Nor will Israel's king be one who will overwhelm Israel's enemies by brute physical force."

Christ, thus, gives us a preview of how he will carry out the mission his Father has given him.

BIBLE MESSAGE

Christ teaches us.   Christ said to the people, "It is not my mission to condemn the world; but, on the contrary, to save the world." John 12:47.

Discuss Christ's mission as: a) the new Adam, b) the new Israel, c) the long awaited Messia-King.

LITURGY & LIFE

1 Christ is the new Adam.   The entrance to a modern church in Germany has a pair of unusual doors. The one door shows two

people under a tree; the other door shows two people on a tree.

Identify the people and the trees. What idea do you think the artist was trying to get across by this design? Why do you think Christ is sometimes called the second Adam? Read Romans 5:18 and 1 Corinthians 15:22. Why do you think Mary is sometimes called the second Eve? Do you think this is a good design theme for church doors? Discuss.

By a tree we were enslaved,
and by the cross we are set free.
The fruit of a tree was our undoing;
the Son of God has redeemed us.
                    Good Friday Liturgy

2 Enemy of Christ's mission.   The Bible is filled with references to Satan. It leaves no doubt that "the devil, like a roaring
lion, prowls about looking for someone to devour." 1 Peter 5:8.
Yet, today Satan seems to have disappeared. Many people seem
to have forgotten that he exists. Why is this?

"Some of Christianity's greatest minds," says Life magazine,
"have a simple explanation for the Devil's disappearance from
common consciousness: he planned it that way. 'The Devil's
cleverest wile,' says Baudelaire, 'is to convince us that he
does not exist.'"

Discuss Baudelaire's observation. Christ once called the Devil the "father of lies." John 8:45. How does Christ's remark fit
in perfectly with the Devil's modern underground strategy?

3 The enemy's strategy.   St. Ambrose, a great writer and
theologian of the fourth century, wrote, "The devil's snare does
not catch you, unless you are first caught by the devil's bait."

What did St. Ambrose mean? Illustrate by an example.

DOCTRINAL POINTS

Devils are fallen angels

Angels are pure spirits. That is they have no body. Angels
were created before man. Like man, they were free to accept
God's invitation of love or to reject it. Those who accepted were
made sharers in God's love and life for all eternity. Those who
rejected were, by their own choice, separated forever from God.
They were plunged into hell, which was created to punish them.

When we say that the angels were in heaven during their proba-
tion, we mean that, like Adam and Eve in the garden, they were happy where God had placed them. We do not mean that they enjoyed the
Beatific Vision, for they could not lose this once they obtained it.

Angels have a special role in God's plan

In the Bible angels frequently appear as God's messengers to
man. Thus we find them coming to Mary at the time of the Annun-
ciation (Luke 1:26); to the shepherds at the Nativity (Luke 2:9);
to St. Joseph after the departure of the Magi (Matthew 2:13); to
Joseph after the death of Herod (Matthew 2:19); to Mary Magdalene
at the tomb (John 20:12); to the apostles just after our Lord's

Ascension (Acts 1:10); and to St. Peter in prison (Acts 12:7).

Angels also appear as guardians. The Psalmist says, "No evil shall befall you, nor shall affliction come near your tent, for to his angels he has given command about you, that they guard you in all your ways. Upon their hands they shall bear you up, lest you dash your foot against a stone." Psalm 90:10-13. Satan quoted this passage to Christ. Matthew 4:6. In a later passage in St. Matthew, Christ infers that each person has a guardian angel who watches over him from birth to death. Our Lord says of a group of little children before him, "Take care you do not despise any one of these little ones. I tell you, their angels in heaven look continually upon the face of my Father . . ." Matthew 18:10.

Finally, Sacred Scripture presents the angels as offering our prayers to God. St. John speaks of an angel offering "the prayers of the saints" to God. Apocalypse 8:4.

On October 2 the Church celebrates in her liturgy the feast of the Guardian Angels, and that entire month is dedicated to them.

Study questions

Artists frequently depict angels with wings to show that they are messengers of God. They also depict them as small children to show their innocence and eternal youth.

Discuss: a) the advantages and disadvantages of showing angels this way, b) the creation and fall of the angels, c) the role of the angels in salvation history.

The combat between Christ and Satan

Satan has been described as commander-in-chief of the fallen angels. Christ once referred directly to Satan's fall from heaven when he said, "I was watching Satan fall like lightning that flashes from heaven." Luke 10:18.

The earthly combat between Christ and Satan began in the garden when God said to Satan, "I will put enmity between you and the woman, between your seed and her seed . . ." Genesis 3:15

This combat manifested itself openly for the first time when Christ entered the desert after his baptism. Luke 4:1-13.

The combat continued to wage during the days of Christ's teaching in Galilee. One of Christ's daily activities was to free people who were under the power of the devil. Mark 5:1-20.

The combat reached a peak in the Garden of Gethsemani just

170

before Christ's passion. Luke 22:40-46.

Christ's victory over Satan manifested itself completely and gloriously on Easter morning. Luke 24:2-8.

Today the combat between the forces of good and the forces of evil continue. We, the members of Christ's mystical body, are in the thick of this combat. We are assured of victory but only by remaining close to our head, Christ.

From the liturgy

Do not let your people
touch the things of Satan, Lord,
but enable them in simplicity of heart
to follow you, the only God. Amen
    Collect: Seventeenth Sunday after Pentecost

Study questions

Why do you think Satan is as successful as he is in the combat against Christ today? What appeal does Satan make to modern man? Contrast Satan's appeal with Christ's.

During the season of Septuagesima we saw how:

CHRIST BEGAN HIS MISSION

1 Christ was announced by John the Baptist
2 Christ was anointed for his divine mission
3 Christ previewed his mission

During the season of Lent we will see how:

CHRIST TEACHES THE PEOPLE

    1 Christ teaches the people through signs
    2 Christ teaches about God's kingdom through parables
    3 Men respond differently to Christ's teaching
    4 Christ teaches how to enter God's kingdom
    5 Christ teaches how to live in God's kingdom
    6 Christ chooses leaders for God's kingdom

CHRIST REDEEMS MANKIND

    1 Christ foretells his death and resurrection
    2 The leaders of the people plot Christ's death
    3 Christ inaugurates the New Covenant
    4 Christ suffers and dies for us

Grant, Lord, that we, Christ's soldiers,
may enter on this campaign with holy fasting,
so that self-denial may strengthen us
in our warfare with the spirits of evil.
Through Christ our Lord. Amen
Ash Wednesday Liturgy

LENTEN LITURGY

We prepare to pass with Christ to the Father

To look upon Lent only as a time of extra penance and prayer
would be a mistake. It would be like confusing the means to a goal
with the goal itself. The goal of Lent is not penance and prayer;
it is preparation for the paschal celebration of Easter. To see
Lent in its rightful relationship to Easter is to recover, at the same
time, an understanding of what our Christian faith is all about.

Easter is the key feast of the liturgical year

Once Easter was the only feast that the Church celebrated, and the Church celebrated it each Sunday. Only later were other feasts of the liturgical year added. They were added primarily to help the Christian better understand and more fully participate in the central mystery of our faith: the paschal mystery of Easter.

Easter celebrates Christ's passage to the Father

The word paschal comes from the word pasch which means "passover" or "passage." The paschal mystery of Easter commemorates Christ's passage from death to life. What took place once in history, in the history of Christ's humanity, is now renewed in the unfolding of the liturgy. Easter is the celebration of Christ's victory over sin, death, and Satan by his passage from death to risen life and glory with the Father.

In dying and rising, Christ was the first of the human race to pass to the Father. In a sense he took the human race with him. For he represents mankind just as Adam did. St. Paul says, "He [Christ] is the first fruits of those that have fallen asleep in death, because since man is the cause of death, so man is the cause of resurrection from the dead. Just as in Adam all men die, so too in Christ all men are brought to life." 1 Corinthians 15:21-22.

We pass with Christ to the Father

But something more is needed. Each member of the human race must personally return to God, by dying in union with Christ and rising to new life in union with Christ. St. Paul explains how this is achieved: ". . . all of us who have been baptized into union with Christ Jesus have been baptized into union with his death . . . Now since we have grown to be one with him through a death like his, we shall also be one with him by a resurrection like his . . . The death that he died was a death to sin . . . you too must consider yourselves dead to sin, but alive to God in Christ Jesus. Romans 6:3-11.

Lent ends with the renewal of our baptismal vows

In the early days of the Church, Lent was a time when adult converts were sent through the final stages of preparation for baptism. This explains the many references to baptism in the

Lenten liturgy. It also explains why Lent culminates in the renewal of our own baptismal vows at the Easter vigil service.

The purpose of Lent, then, is to help us renew our determination to die to sin in order to rise in Christ--and, in union with Christ, to pass to the Father. All our Lenten prayers are directed toward this end.

Study questions

Discuss: a) the goal of Lent, b) the meaning of <u>pasch</u>, c) in what sense Christ took us with him when he passed to the Father, d) how we share in Christ's passage, e) the centrality of Easter in the liturgical year.

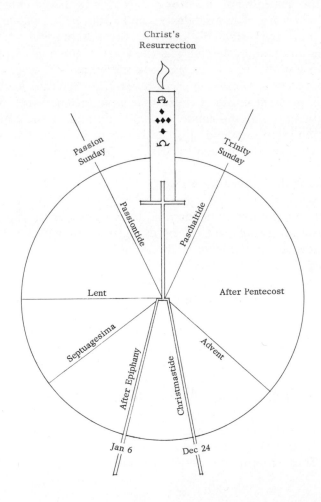

12

CHRIST TEACHES THE PEOPLE

1 Christ teaches the people through signs

After his victory over Satan in the desert, Jesus begins his teaching mission in Galilee. He announces to the people that the time has come when he will establish God's kingdom on earth. Let us see how the Gospel describes this.

Jesus returned to Galilee to preach God's Good Message.
This was his theme:
    "The time of waiting is over;
    the kingdom of God is close at hand.
    Change your evil ways;
    believe in the Good Message. . . ."
The people were lost in admiration of his teaching.
He had a way, certainly, of teaching them
as one possessed of authority, and not as their Scribes.
    Presently there came into the synagogue a man
under control of an unclean spirit, who shouted the words:
"Ha! Why do you meddle with us, Jesus of Nazareth?
Have you come to destroy us?

I know who you are--God's Holy One!"
Jesus sternly rebuked him:
"Hold your peace, and come out of him!"
The unclean spirit then threw the man into convulsions,
uttered a shriek, and went out of him.
A sense of awe came over all, so much so that,
in discussing the incident with one another, they said:
"What does this mean?"
"A novel way of teaching with authority!"
"He even commands the unclean spirits, and they obey him!"
As a result, the report about him spread
within and beyond the boundaries of Galilee.   Mark 1:14-28

Jesus teaches through miracles

In Old Testament times God taught Israel by signs and wonders.
He led them safely over the Red Sea; he fed them miraculously in
the desert; and he revealed himself dramatically on Mt. Sinai.

In a similar way Jesus uses signs and wonders to instruct the
people of Galilee. Outstanding among these is the miracle. We
may define a miracle as a remarkable event beyond scientific
explanation, produced by God for special religious purposes.

Miracles announce the coming of the kingdom

First of all, Christ uses miracles to teach the people that God's
kingdom is at hand. Old Testament prophets have described the
coming of God's kingdom in these terms: "Then will the eyes of
the blind be opened, the ears of the deaf be cleared; then will the
lame leap like a stag, then the tongue of the dumb will sing."
Isaia 35:5, 6. Christ presents his miracles as fulfillments of
this Old Testament prophecy. When John the Baptist sends his disciples to ask Jesus if he is the promised one, Jesus answers:
"Go and bring word to John about all you see and hear: the
blind recover sight, the lame walk, lepers are made clean, the
deaf hear, dead men rise again, the humble have the Good News
preached to them." Luke 7:22. By his answer Jesus teaches that
he is the one whom the prophets foretold.

Miracles announce Satan's downfall

Secondly, Christ uses miracles to teach the people that Satan's
dominion over the world is now ended. Christ teaches this, first

of all, by driving out demons. Speaking to the Pharisees, he says, "If . . . I drive out demons by the Spirit of God, then evidently the kingdom of God has by now made its way to you." Matthew 12:28. Christ also teaches this truth by showing his power over sin, sickness, and death. These three disorders entered the world with Adam's fall and held sway over men since that time. Now Christ teaches that their mastery is ended and God's kingdom is being established. Jesus forgives sin, heals the sick, and raises the dead to life.

Miracles reveal truths about the kingdom

Thirdly, Christ uses miracles to teach invisible truths about his Father's kingdom. By showing his power over nature, Christ prepares the people to realize that he has the power to change bread and wine into his own body and blood. At the marriage feast of Cana, Christ changes water into wine. John 2:1-11. Near the Lake of Galilee, Christ feeds a crowd of 5,000 by multiplying five loaves and two fishes. John 6:1-13. Both of these miracles foreshadow and prepare men for the institution of the Eucharist.

Miracles show Jesus' divine authority

Fourthly, Christ uses miracles to teach that his authority came from God. Even Christ's enemies, the Pharisees, get this idea. "A member of the Pharisaical party, Nicodemus by name, a leader in the Jewish community, came to him one night, and said to him: 'Rabbi, we know that you have a mission from God to teach. Surely, no one can give such striking proofs of his claims as you are giving, unless God is with him.'" John 3:1-2.

Miracles reveal truths about the Father

Lastly, Christ uses miracles to teach people about their Father in heaven. Miracles show God's power and wisdom. They also show his mercy and love for men. Miracles are proof that God is intervening to save men from the sin, suffering, and death to which Adam's sin had doomed them.

BIBLE MESSAGE

Christ teaches us.   The Gospels record more than thirty

miracles worked by Christ during his lifetime. 1 Define miracle. 2 List and explain the five main teaching purposes of Christ's miracles.

LITURGY & LIFE

1 Miracle project. Divide the blackboard (or a clean sheet of paper) into five columns. At the top of each column write one of the five main teaching purposes of Christ's miracles. Now, classify, under the proper column heading, the various miracles you are able to recall from the Gospel. Briefly, explain why you put a particular miracle in the column that you do. Don't be surprised if some miracles fit under several column headings. Why?

2 More miracles. Miracles did not cease after Christ's ascension into heaven. God used St. Peter as an instrument for working miracles. Read about one of these miracles in Acts 3:1-11.

In whose name did Peter work the miracle? Why do you think God continued to work miracles through Peter? According to Peter, what did miracles prove concerning Christ? See Acts 2:22.

3 Miracles today. God still works miracles in our time. The saints we honor during the liturgical year are living examples of this. Before a saint is beatified, proof of at least two miracles is required. Two more miracles must be approved before canonization.

Why do you think the Church accepts miracles as proof of sanctity? Why do you think that more than one is required? Describe miracles from saints' lives that you have read.

2 Christ teaches about God's kingdom through parables

Besides using miracles to teach people about God's kingdom, Christ also used parables. A parable may be defined as a comparison of one thing with another, usually expressed in story form. Let us read the Gospel to see how Christ used these literary forms to teach the people about God's kingdom.

That same day Jesus left the house to linger by the sea,
and so great was the concourse of people that
he went into a boat and sat down.
While the throng stood crowding the shore,
he taught them many lessons in parable style. . . .
"The kingdom of heaven reminds me of a man
who has sown good seed in his field.
But, while everybody is asleep, his enemy comes
and sows weeds among the wheat, and goes away.
Eventually the blades spring up and put forth heads,
but by that time the weeds also crop out.
So the help of the landowner approach him and say:
'Sir, was it not good seed that you sowed in your field?
How, then, is it overrun with weeds?'
'That is the work of an enemy!' he replies.
'Well,' say the help to him, 'do you want us to go
and gather them up?'
'Not at all,' he answers;
otherwise, in gathering the weeds,
you might pull up the wheat along with them.
Let both grow until the harvest,
and, when harvest time has come,
I will say to the reapers:
'Gather up, first of all, the weeds
and bind them in bundles to be burnt;
after that, store the wheat in my barn.'"
   Still another parable proposed by him was this:
"The kingdom of heaven reminds me of a mustard seed
which a man carefully plants in his field.
This is the tiniest of all seeds;
but the full-grown plant is larger than any garden herb
and, in fact, becomes a tree,
so that the birds of the air come
and settle in it's branches."
. . . All these lessons
Jesus taught the crowds in parable style;
indeed, without the use of parables
he would not teach them anything.
Thus his practice fulfilled the prediction
made through the prophet, who says:
"I will open my mouth to speak in parables;
I will utter things that have lain hidden
since the world's foundation."   Matthew 13:1-35

The idea of a kingdom was familiar to the Jews

A kingdom may be thought of as a land ruled by a king, such as the 12,000 square miles of land ruled by the king of Belgium. A kingdom may also be thought of as the spiritual union of millions of people united under the rule of one king, such as the people of Great Britain.

In biblical times, the word kingdom was much more familiar to people than it is today. Then, most countries had a king; and everyone knew what a kingdom was.

Therefore, when Jesus speaks of the coming of God's kingdom, the Jews automatically think of the day when God will rule as king over the people and land of Israel. The Jews even have a name for the day when this will happen: the Day of Yahweh. On this day, the Israelites think that God will give them power and dominion over all their old enemies: Egypt, Babylon, Greece, and even the powerful Romans. Thus the Jews are whipped into an excited frenzy when John the Baptist and Jesus preach that the kingdom of God is close at hand.

Christ preaches a different kind of kingdom

This excitement cools, however, when it becomes clear that the kingdom that the Jews expected and the one that Christ preaches are different. The kingdom that Christ speaks of is not a material one, consisting of land, wealth, and power. It is a spiritual one. Moreover, the kingdom will not come about in one great burst of glory in which God will set himself up over all nations. It will come about slowly and gradually, like a seed planted in the ground. Only later will it grow into something great for all to see. Matthew 13:31-33.

Indeed God will set himself over all nations, but in a completely different way than the Jews expect. God will do this in a spiritual way. Rather than force them into submission with armies, he will freely invite them to follow him.

God's kingdom is a union of men with God

But the greatest difference between God's kingdom and all other kingdoms is that God's kingdom will not be a mere legal union of people under one king. It will be much more. It will be a personal union in which all people will be intimately united to their King. Ephesians 2:6. The people will actually form one body with

Christ their king. Ephesians 1:23. We may define God's kingdom as a happy union of mankind with God.

BIBLE MESSAGE

Christ teaches us.   One day when Jesus is teaching, the high priests and the Pharisees dispatch policemen to arrest him. When the policemen return empty-handed, the Pharisees are enraged. "'Why did you not bring him?' 'Never,' the policemen explained, 'has man spoken as this man speaks!' The Pharisees replied: 'Have you, too, perhaps, been led astray?'' John 7:46-47.

1 Give two reasons why Christ is an excellent teacher. 2 Define: a) parable, b) God's kingdom. 3 How does the kingdom Christ teaches differ from the one the Jews expect? 4 What is the greatest difference between God's kingdom and other kingdoms?

LITURGY & LIFE

1 Parable project.   On the blackboard (or on a piece of paper) list in one long column the names of as many kingdom parables as you can think of. Next, by yourself or with the help of the class, determine the main point Jesus was trying to get across by each kingdom parable. Record your conclusions opposite each title. For some kingdom parables read Matthew 13:1-52.

2 Parable screen. Artist David Hayes designed a "Screen of Parables" for the newspaper office of the Hartford "Catholic Transcript." See the photograph on page 184. The design features several parable images used by Christ: 1) the narrow gate to heaven (Luke 13:24-30), 2) the lamp upon the stand (Luke 11:33), 3) the vine with grape bunches, representing the parable of the workers (Matthew 20:1-16), as well as Christ (John 15:1-8), 4) wheat stalks, symbolizing the "bread of life" (John 6:32-40), as well as the seed springing from good ground (Matthew 13:4-9), 5) a lamb, symbolizing Christ the victim (John 1:29), as well as Christ the Good Shepherd (John 10:11-18), 6) ten gold coins, representing the ten talents given by the master (Matthew 25:14-30), and 7) the sign of Jonas, symbol of the key mystery of Christianity: the Resurrection (Matthew 16:1-4).

Identify and discuss the biblical significance of each image shown in the parable screen.

"Screen of Parables" designed by artist David Hayes

3 Men respond differently to Christ's teaching

Not all the people of Israel respond to the teaching of
Christ in the same way. Some, like the "poor" of Israel, respond with faith. Others, like the Pharisees, refuse to believe. Let us read St. John's Gospel, where this is taught us.

One day he [Jesus] saw, in passing, a man blind from birth.
So his disciples asked him:
"Rabbi, who has sinned, this man or his parents,
to account for his being born blind?"
"Neither this man has sinned," replied Jesus,
"nor his parents. No. God simply wants
to make use of him to reveal his ways. . . .
As long as I am in the world,
I am the light of the world."
   With these words spoken, he spat on the ground,
and by means of the spittle made a lump of mud,
and then spread the mud over his eyes, and said to him:
"Go, and wash in the pool of Siloam"--
a word which in our language means "Ambassador."
So he went, and washed, and came back able to see. . . .
   The man who had been blind
was then taken before the Pharisees.
Now it happened that the day on which
Jesus had formed the lump of mud
and opened his eyes was a Sabbath.
So the Pharisees, for their part, asked him
how he had obtained sight.
He replied: "He put a lump of mud on my eyes,
and I washed, and now I see."
   Then some of the Pharisees said:
"That man has no authority from God;
he does not observe the Sabbath."
Others argued:
"How can a sinner give such proofs of power!" . . .
   So they summoned a second time
the man who had been blind, and said to him . . .
"What did he do to you? How did he open your eyes?"
"I told you already," he replied,
"and you did not take my word for it.
Why do you want to hear it again?
Do you, too, perhaps, want to become his disciples?"
Then they heaped abuse on him.
"You are a disciple of that man," they said;
"we are disciples of Moses.
We know that Moses is God's spokesman,
but whose mouthpiece this man is we do not know."
"Why," the man retorted, "the strange thing is
that you do not know whose mouthpiece he is when,

as a matter of fact, he has opened my eyes!
We know that God does not listen to sinners;
but when one is God-fearing and does his will,
he does listen to him.
Since the world began, it is unheard of
that anyone opened the eyes of one born blind!
If this man had no mission from God,
he could do nothing!"
By way of answer they said to him:
"You were wholly born in sin, and you mean to teach us?"
And they expelled him.

　　Jesus was informed that they had expelled him.
When he met the man, he said:
"Do you believe in the Son of God?" . . .
"I do believe, sir," he said;
and he fell on his knees before him.
Jesus continued: "To be the parting of the way--
that is my mission to the world:
henceforth the sightless are to have sight,
and those who see are to become blind."
Some of the Pharisees, who happened to be near,
heard this and said to him:
"Maybe we, too, are blind, are we?"
"If you were blind," replied Jesus,
"you would have no sin; as it is,
you claim to have sight. Your sin remains."   John 9:1-41

Christ is the Light of the World

　　Unless we keep in mind the Old Testament prophecy of Isaia,
we will miss much of the significance of this Gospel incident.
Isaia, the prophet, had predicted that the Messia would be a light
to the nations and give sight to the blind. Isaia 42:6-7. On this
occasion Christ proclaims, "I am the light of the world"; and
he heals a blind man. He teaches by words and signs that he is
the Messia spoken of by Isaia. He is the one sent by God to establish God's kingdom.
　　The two responses to Christ's teaching are typical of the
responses men still make to it. The blind man's response is
one of faith. By his belief in Christ, his eyes are opened not
only to the light of the day but also to the light of faith. His
physical healing is thus a sign of a deeper spiritual healing.

The response of the Pharisees to Christ's teaching is one of rejection. Though they know the prophecy of Isaia backwards and forwards, they willfully blind themselves to its fulfillment in Christ. Thus the Gospel episode is a second fulfillment of Isaia's words. St. Matthew says: "Thus the prophecy of Isaias is more and more fulfilled in them. It says: 'Your ears will hear, yet you will not understand; your eyes will look, yet you will not see. For blunted is the sense of this people . . . they are not converted and healed by me.'" Matthew 13:14-15.

BIBLE MESSAGE

Christ teaches us.   In a prayer just before the Gospel at Mass, the priest, Christ's spokesman, refers to an incident in the life of the prophet Isaia.

1 How and why does he do this? 2 How does Christ fulfill the prophecy of Isaia: a) by what he says, and b) by what he does? 3 What is meant by saying that the physical healing of the blind man is a sign of a deeper spiritual healing? 4 How does Christ teach us that the reaction of the Pharisees further fulfills the prophecy of Isaia?

LITURGY & LIFE

1 Enraged leaders.   The parable of the vinedressers, which Jesus tells in Matthew 21:33-41, enraged the high priests and the Pharisees. They realized it was aimed at them. Matthew 21:45. This parable is an excellent example of an allegorizing parable. Unlike the pure parable, which makes only one comparison and one point, the allegorizing parable makes many comparisons and many points. Each detail in the story stands for someone or something.

With this in mind identify the following in the parable: 1) the man who planted the vineyard, 2) the vineyard, 3) the vinedressers, 4) the servants or agents of the owner, 5) the son of the owner, 6) the new vinedressers hired by the owner.

2 Light of faith.   In her liturgy the Church uses the story of the man born blind for the Gospel reading of the Wednesday of the fourth Sunday in Lent.

In view of the fact that Lent was once a period of last-minute instruction for converts who were to be baptized at the Easter Vigil service, why did this Gospel story make appropriate reading? How is our own baptism recalled in the liturgy of the Easter Vigil service? Why do you think catacomb artists used the cure of the man born blind as a symbol for the sacrament of baptism?

3 Response to Christ.   In the light of the lesson, discuss the parable of the sower which Jesus tells in Matthew 13:1-23.

What makes some people respond generously to Christ's teaching and others not?

4 Christ teaches how to enter God's kingdom

After revealing that God's kingdom is completely different from earthly kingdoms, Christ teaches the people what they must do to enter God's kingdom. Let us read about this in the Gospel.

A member of the Pharisaical party, Nicodemus by name,
a leader in the Jewish community,
came to him [Jesus] one night,
and said to him:
"Rabbi, we know that you have a mission from God to teach.
Surely, no one can give such striking proofs of his claims
as you are giving, unless God is with him."
Jesus seized the opportunity and said to him:
"I must be frank with you: if one is not born anew,
he cannot see the kingdom of God."
"But how," replied Nicodemus,
"can a man be born in his old age?
Can he really enter his mother's womb a second time
and have another birth?"
Jesus answered: "I am telling you the plain truth:
unless a man is born of water and the Spirit,
he cannot enter the kingdom of God!
What is born of the flesh is flesh,
and what is born of the Spirit is spirit."   John 3:1-7

We enter God's kingdom by being baptized into Christ

Because God's kingdom is different from other kingdoms, we can't join it merely by raising our right hand and swearing allegiance to Christ the king. Membership in God's kingdom means personal union with Christ the king. This union is achieved by baptism. Baptism grafts us into Christ's mystical body. It makes us live with Christ's life, just as truly as a branch grafted into a vine lives by the sap that passes to it through the vine.

The life which Christ gives us in baptism is really a share in the divine life of the Holy Trinity. 2 Peter 1:4. This does not mean that we become God or a part of God. This is absurd. We never lose our individuality. What it does mean is that we now possess the power that will make it possible for us some day to see and love God face to face, "just as he is." 1 John 3:2.

Baptism gives us a new relationship to the Trinity

Because of the divine life which Christ gives us in baptism, we enter into a special, new relationship with each member of the Holy Trinity. We are now related to God the Father not merely as creature to creator but as son to Father. Similarly, we now become brothers of Christ. Finally, we become living temples of the Holy Spirit.

Baptism gives us a new relationship to others

Because of the life which Christ gives us in baptism, we also enter into a special, new relationship with our fellow Christians. Since we are all incorporated into Christ, we all become one in Christ. "Just as the body is a unit, although it has many members, and all the members of the body, many though they are, form but one body, so too is the Christ. In fact, by a single Spirit all of us, whether Jews or Greeks, slaves or free men, were introduced into the one body through baptism, and were all given to drink of a single Spirit. . . . You are Christ's body and individually its members." 1 Corinthians 12:12, 13, 27.

The life we receive in baptism is frequently called sanctifying grace. It is called sanctifying (holy-making) because it gives us a share in the life of God and makes us temples of God. It is called grace because it is a gift, something to which we have no right. We have a right to our human life, because we were created human beings. Human life is natural to us. To share in God's life, however, is something far above what is natural to us. For this reason sanctifying grace is also called supernatural life.

BIBLE MESSAGE

Christ teaches us.   Christ called baptism a "rebirth." For this reason early Christians used to regard the baptismal font as the womb of the holy Mother Church. At the font Christians are reborn with the life of God himself.

1 What does it mean to say that we share God's life? 2 What does Christ teach us regarding the new relationship that begins to exist after baptism: a) between the baptized person and the Holy Trinity, and b) between the baptized person and other members of the mystical body? 3 Why is our divine life frequently called sanctifying grace? 4 Why is sanctifying grace frequently referred to as supernatural life?

LITURGY & LIFE

1 Membership in God's kingdom.   King Louis XII said that the greatest honor of his life was not when he received his kingship over the kingdom of France but when he received his membership in the kingdom of God.

Why is membership in God's kingdom a greater honor than kingship over an earthly kingdom? How does the way one becomes a member of God's kingdom differ from the way one becomes a member in any other kingdom?

2 New life in Christ.   Some of the most delicious fruit that we eat today is produced by grafting a shoot from one tree on another tree. The shoot lives with the life of the tree on which it is grafted. It truly becomes a part of that tree. The fruit which it produces is different and better because of the new life and strength which it receives from the tree on which it is grafted. In his Epistle to the Romans, St. Paul says that we have been cut off from the wild olive tree which is natural to us and grafted on the cultivated olive tree; that is, on Jesus Christ. Romans 11:24.

Discuss: a) when and how we were grafted on Christ, and b) why our actions are richer and better because of our new relationship with Christ.

190

DOCTRINAL POINTS

Membership in Christ's mystical body

"Only those are really to be included as members of the Church," says Pius XII, "who have been baptized and profess the true faith and who have not unhappily withdrawn from Body-unity or for some fault been excluded by legitimate authority." Therefore baptism and profession of the Catholic faith are necessary for full membership in the mystical body of Christ. All baptized Catholics are such members unless they have lost their membership by heresy, schism, or excommunication.

We must distinguish, however, between living and dead members. Those Catholics who are in the state of sanctifying grace are living members; those in the state of mortal sin are dead members. The latter are supernaturally dead, but, as long as they do not deny their faith, they retain this visible connection with the mystical body and can still be called members.

What about non-Catholics in the state of grace?

Pope Pius XII says that non-Catholics in the state of grace are "unsuspectingly related to the mystical body of the Redeemer in desire and resolution." Certainly they are not complete and perfect members of the mystical body, since they do not fulfill the conditions of baptism and the profession of the true faith. Nor do they have the rights and privileges that go with membership; for example, the right to receive the sacraments of penance, Holy Eucharist, and confirmation. They may perhaps be called invisible or imperfect members; "invisible" because their connection with the mystical body is not known to men, but to God alone; "imperfect" because they do not have the rights of full-fledged members.

Are there substitutes for baptism?

What about people without baptism? Are they doomed to die separated forever from God's kingdom? The answer is no. The effects of baptism of water may also be achieved by baptism by blood or baptism by desire.

Baptism by blood is the term applied to the death of martyrs killed out of hatred of Christ before having been baptized. Martyrdom borne willingly and patiently for Christ can supply for the lack of baptism by water. Such martyrs are said to be "baptized" in their own blood. St. Augustine says of them: "The newly baptized confesses his faith in the presence of the priest; the martyr in the presence of the persecutor. The former is sprinkled with water, after he has confessed; the latter with his blood."

Baptism of desire is an act of perfect contrition or perfect charity made by one who has not received baptism but who would receive it were it not for the fact that he knows nothing about it or has no one to administer it. A person's desire may be either explicit or implicit. It is explicit if he knows what baptism is and desires it. It is implicit if he doesn't know about the necessity of baptism, but wishes to do all that is required for salvation. If he is truly ready to do everything required for salvation, he would certainly be ready to receive baptism if he knew of its necessity. Therefore he has an implicit desire for baptism.

This desire of baptism is an act of love of God, and no one can love God without being loved by God in return. Such a person, the Church teaches, is justified (made holy) by his act of love, and is not required by God to receive the sacrament which because of circumstances he cannot receive. But he is of course obliged to do so if circumstances change, so that he no longer lacks knowledge of the sacrament or a minister to give it to him.

Salvation outside the Church

The Catholic teaching that "outside the Church there is no salvation" does not mean that everyone who is not a Catholic will be damned. It means that salvation comes to men in and through the Catholic Church. Therefore non-Catholics who are in the state of grace are in the Catholic Church, though invisibly; and if they persevere in grace, they will be saved through the merits of the mystical body of Christ--the Catholic Church with Christ as its head.

Study questions

A courageous nonbaptized friend of yours dies while trying to rescue a drowning boy. Discuss: a) the possibility that your friend will some day be in heaven with you, b) the requirements for membership in the mystical body, c) the distinction between live and dead members of the mystical body, d) membership of non-Catholics in the mystical body, e) substitutes for baptism, f) salvation outside the Church.

192

5 Christ teaches how to live in God's kingdom

Because God's kingdom differs from earthly kingdoms, life in
it also differs from life in earthly kingdoms. Let us see how Jesus
taught this to the people assembled on the mountainside.

One day when his eyes fell on the crowd,
he went up a mountainside, where he sat down,
with his disciples close to him.
Opening his lips he gave to his hearers
a lengthy instruction, saying:
"Blessed are the humble souls,
for theirs is the kingdom of heaven.
Blessed are the meek and gentle,
for they will inherit the land.
Blessed are the sorrowing, for they will be consoled.
Blessed are those who hunger and thirst after holiness,
for they will be fully satisfied.
Blessed are the merciful,
for they will have mercy shown to them.
Blessed are the singlehearted,
for they will see God.
Blessed are the promoters of peace,
for they will rank as children of God.
Blessed are the victims of persecution for conscience' sake,
for theirs is the kingdom of heaven.
. . . Do not think it is my mission
to annul the Law or the Prophets.
It is not my mission to annul, but to bring to perfection. . . .
You have heard it said:
'An eye for an eye, and a tooth for a tooth.'
I, on the contrary, declare to you:
do not meet evil with evil.
No, if someone strikes you on your right cheek,
turn to him the other as well. . . .
You have heard it said:
'Love your neighbor, and hate your enemy.'
I, on the contrary, declare to you:
love your enemies and pray for your persecutors,
and thus prove yourselves children of your Father in heaven.
. . . Take care not to practice your religion before your
fellow men just to catch their eyes;
otherwise, you have no reward with your Father in heaven.

. . . When you give alms, your left hand
should not know what your right is doing.
Thus your alms is given in secrecy,
and your Father, who sees what is secret, will reward you.
. . . The following, then, must be the pattern of your prayer:
"Our Father in heaven!
May you be known and glorified,
your kingdom come,
your will be done, on earth as well as in heaven;
give us this day
our daily bread;
forgive us our debts
as we also forgive our debtors;
and do not expose us to temptation,
but deliver us from evil.
. . . In short, in all respects do to your fellow men
exactly as you wish them to do to you.
This, surely, is the gist of the Law and the Prophets."
. . . When Jesus had finished these discourses,
the crowds were lost in admiration of his teaching;
he certainly had a way of teaching them
as one that has authority,
and not as their Scribes and Pharisees.
He then came down the mountainside
and great crowds followed him.   Matthew 5:1--8:1

Love is the way of life in God's kingdom

Because we form one body in Christ, we are infinitely closer
to our head and to one another than are the citizens of earthly
kingdoms. For this reason our response to Christ and to one
another ought to differ from that of the response of citizens of
an earthly kingdom toward one another.

The Christian way of life is one of love. "'Love the Lord your
God with your whole heart, and with your whole soul, and with
your whole mind.'" said Christ, "This is the great and first
commandment. But a second commandment is like it: 'Love your
neighbor as yourself.' On these two commandments hinge the
whole Law and the Prophets." Matthew 22:37-40.

"A new commandment I give you," said Jesus, "Love one
another; as I love you, so I want you, too, to love one another.
By this token all the world must know that you are my disciples
--by cherishing love for one another." John 13:34-35.

Commenting on Christ's command, St. Paul wrote to the Ephesians, "Thus, let everyone of you lay aside falsehood and speak the truth to the neighbor, because we are members of one another. . . . Therefore, follow God's example, as his very dear children, and let your conduct be guided by love, as Christ also loved us and delivered himself for us." Ephesians 4:25--5:2

Special powers help us to love

We would not be able to love God or neighbor according to our Christian vocation were it not for special help from God. We received this help in baptism, when in keeping with our new life, we received new permanent powers: the supernatural virtues of faith, hope, and charity. These three powers, together with the gifts of the Holy Spirit, make it possible for us to live as members of Christ's mystical body and as sons of God.

Moreover, after baptism, God continues to put at our disposal special helps called actual graces. We need only ask for them through prayer, and our Father in heaven will give them to us. These actual graces give light to our minds and strength to our wills; they help us keep alive and increase divine life within us.

Life in the kingdom is happy

Christ promises the members of his kingdom happiness both in this life and in the life hereafter. This is what he meant when he said to the people on the mountainside, "Blessed are you." The word "blessed" means happy.

But the kind of happiness Christ promises in this life is not the kind of happiness that the world normally thinks of. Christ does not promise pleasure and wealth. On the contrary, he tells us that we will be happy doing, for his sake, the very things that we think will make us unhappy. Christ tells us to fight temptation, to forgive our enemies, and to suffer for him, if necessary. By the world's standards, these things are distasteful and should make us unhappy. But Christ, who is Divine Wisdom incarnate, promises just the opposite.

BIBLE MESSAGE

Christ teaches us.   During the last war, a hardened army surgeon said he was moved to tears when he saw a dying soldier

strip off his own blanket and place it across the shivering body
of the soldier next to him.

1 What does this act teach us about the dying soldier? 2 What
does Christ teach us regarding the attitude that we should try to
develop: a) toward the members of the mystical body, and b) toward the head of the mystical body? 3 How did Christ express
this attitude in the form of a new commandment? 4 What helps
does Christ give us through baptism to live out our Christian
calling? What reward does Christ promise us?

LITURGY & LIFE

1 New law.   St. Matthew is at pains to note that Jesus teaches
the new law of love while the people are gathered at the foot of a
mountain. Jesus, thus, resembles Moses who taught the old law
at the foot of Mt. Sinai. Matthew's aim is to connect the teaching
of the new law as closely as possible with the teaching of the old
law, and to show that the old law is now being brought to perfection by the new law.

How are the old law and the new law connected? How does
Christ show this connection? How does even the phrasing of the
first part of Christ's Sermon on the Mount recall the phrasing
of the ten commandments given at Mt. Sinai?

2 Brotherly love.   An unknown poet once wrote: "I sought my
soul, but my soul I could not see. I sought my God, but my God
eluded me. I sought my brother--and I found all three."

In your own words, explain what the poet meant. How does the
poet's experience tie in with the new law of love taught by Christ?
Who is your brother? Read Christ's answer in Luke 10:29-37,
and apply it to modern life.

3 Our Father.   It is significant that the only prayer Christ
prescribed for the members of God's kingdom, speaks of God as
Father and as our Father.

Why is it fitting that members of the kingdom address God as
Father? What is significant about the fact that we address God as
our Father rather than my Father? Discuss the need and necessity
of prayer in a high-school student's life. To see where, when,
and how Christ prayed read Mark 1:35, Luke 6:12, and Luke 22:
42-44. To see what Christ said about prayer read Luke 11:1-13
and Matthew 6:5-7.

DOCTRINAL POINTS

What is love?

One day Jesus said, "'Love the Lord your God with your whole heart, and with your whole soul, and with your whole mind.' This is the great and first commandment. But a second commandment is like it: 'Love your neighbor as yourself.'" Matthew 22:37-39.

We may define the virtue of charity as that supernatural gift from God that empowers us to love him above all things for his own sake and our neighbor as ourself.

We love God above all things when we are willing to lose all rather than be disloyal to him by mortal sin. We love God for his own sake when we love him because he is infinitely good and perfect in himself and is thus worthy of our best love. Such love of God is called perfect love. It is quite easy to make an act of perfect love if we try. God will always give us the grace to do so.

Love of God is imperfect when we love God for his gifts rather than for himself.

Love is the greatest virtue

Charity (love) is a greater virtue than either faith or hope. It is the only one of the three virtues that we shall keep in heaven. Faith will cease to exist, because we will no longer have need of it. We will see God face to face. Hope will also cease to exist, because we will then have what we now hope for.

Charity is increased by prayers and good works. We show our love of God by acts of love, receiving the sacraments, being loyal to God's law, and serving man for God's sake.

Charity is lost only through mortal sin. Venial sin diminishes the fervor of charity but does not destroy it.

Love of God is not a feeling

When we speak of love or charity, we must remember not to confuse true love of God with feelings. It may happen that we feel love for God, but it is not necessary that we should.

In time of war, air terminals are packed with people saying good-bye. Everybody is sad; many cannot hold back tears. But the young men and women are going to war, and all are letting them go without trying to prevent them. Why? Because these young men and women put their country and duty ahead of their feelings.

When a person does this, we say that he loves his country.

We love God above all things when we can say sincerely, "God comes first in my life; I will be loyal to him no matter what the cost."

Charity along with faith and hope are the three virtues, above all others, that make Christians what they are. It is therefore evident that we will want to make acts of these virtues often, especially in time of temptation, when receiving the sacraments, in time of danger, and on our deathbed.

Study questions

In one of his famous letters, St. Paul wrote: "And if I should distribute all I have bit by bit, and should yield my body to the flames, but have no love, it profits me nothing.

"Love is long-suffering; love is kind, and is not envious; love does not brag; it is not conceited; it is not ill-mannered; it is not self-seeking; it is not irritable, it takes no note of injury; it is not glad when injustice triumphs; it is glad when the truth prevails. Always it is ready to make allowances; always to trust; always to hope; always to be patient." 1 Corinthians 13:3-7.

Discuss: a) the reason why love is so important, b) the meaning of love, c) the meaning of perfect love, d) why love is the greatest of all virtues, e) how love is increased, f) how love is lost, g) why love is not necessarily a feeling.

6 Christ chooses leaders for God's kingdom

Because Christ intends that his Father's kingdom should continue to build up after his ascension, he entrusts its work and government to certain chosen men. Let us read in the Gospel where Christ teaches us how he did this.

He then called to him his twelve apostles
and gave them power to drive out unclean spirits,
as well as power to heal any disease and any infirmity.
The names of the twelve apostles are as follows:

First, Simon, surnamed Peter;
then Andrew, his brother;
James, the son of Zebedee,
and his brother John;
Philip and Bartholomew;
Thomas and the tax collector Matthew;
James, the son of Alpheus, and Thaddeus;
Simon the Cananaean;
and Judas Iscariot, the same that eventually betrayed him.
    These Twelve Jesus sent on a missionary tour,
after giving them the following instructions. . . .
    "As you go along, preach on this text:
'The kingdom of heaven is close at hand.'
Attend to the sick; raise the dead;
make lepers clean; drive out demons.
Gratis you have received; gratis you must give.
Do not procure pocket money,
whether gold or silver or copper. . . .
    Once you enter a town or village,
search out a worthy citizen, and in his home
make your headquarters till you leave that locality. . . .
He who befriends you befriends me . . ." Matthew 10:1-40

Upon Simon Peter, Christ conferred special power and authority.

You are Peter,
and upon this rock
I will build my Church,
and the gates of hell
shall not prevail against it.
I will give you the keys of the kingdom of heaven,
and whatever you bind on earth
shall be bound in heaven,
and whatever you loose on earth
shall be loosed in heaven.   Matthew 16:18-19

Finally, just before ascending to his Father Christ said to
his apostles.

Absolute authority in heaven and on earth
has been conferred upon me.
Go, therefore,
and make all nations your disciples:

baptize them in the name
of the Father
and of the Son
and of the Holy Spirit,
and teach them to observe
all the commandments I have given you.
And mark:
I am with you at all times
as long as the world will last.   Matthew 28:18-20

Christ appoints his successors

Christ entrusts the work and government of God's kingdom to
his apostles. He shares with them his own threefold office of
prophet (teacher), priest (sanctifier), and king (ruler).

At the Last Supper, Christ shares with his apostles his priestly office, ordaining them to offer sacrifice. Luke 22:19. After his
Resurrection, Christ shares with them his kingly office, conferring
on them the power to forgive sins. John 20:22-23. Finally, just
before he ascends into heaven, Christ shares with his apostles
his prophetic office, commissioning them to teach. Matthew 28:
19-20.

To Peter, Christ promises special power and responsibility.
"You are Peter, and upon this rock I will build my Church, and
the gates of hell shall not prevail against it. I will give you the
keys of the kingdom of heaven, and whatever you bind on earth
shall be bound in heaven, and whatever you loose on earth shall
be loosed in heaven." Matthew 16:18-19.

Christ's successors continue his work

Christ's newly-formed representatives do not immediately
begin their work after Christ's ascension. Jesus instructs them
to remain in Jerusalem in prayer until the promised Holy Spirit
comes upon them to strengthen and to enlighten them. Acts 1:
7-8. Finally, on the day that we now call Pentecost, the Holy
Spirit comes upon the apostles and forms them into Christ's
mystical body, the Church: God's kingdom on earth. After the
coming of the Holy Spirit, the apostles understand Christ's
teachings in a new light, and they go forth fearlessly, preaching,
praying, and administering the sacraments.

Through his apostles Christ continues the work of redemption
which he began on earth. Through them he still: 1) offers himself

in Mass, 2) acts in the sacraments, 3) prays to the Father, and
4) teaches men. Through his successors, Christ is preparing
mankind for the day when God's kingdom will be complete, and
he will come again to lead it triumphantly to his Father. 1 Corinthians 15:24.

BIBLE MESSAGE

Christ teaches us.   St. Francis of Assisi, who was not a
priest, once said, "The Lord gave me and He gives me so much
faith in priests . . . that if they persecuted me I would have re-
course to them . . . in them I see the son of God."
1 How is the Son of God present in a special way in his priests?
2 With the help of the Bible, or from memory, show exactly how
and when Christ commissioned successors to continue the work of
God's kingdom, especially with regard to: 1) teaching, 2) ruling,
and 3) sanctifying. 3 By what words did Christ confer on Peter
a special commission? 4 When did the apostles begin to carry out
their commission in its fullness? 5 By what four ways, especially,
does Christ continue the work of God's kingdom through his successors?

LITURGY & LIFE

1 Christ today.   "For the first Christians, Christ was a
personal reality who not only had redeemed us in the past, who
was not only the One whose return was awaited at the end of time,
so that they were merely looking to the future. He was much
rather 'someone who was living today,' keeping in touch with
them now. Christ is truly a person present to us, who although
invisible because of his glorification, remains alive among us."
E. Schillebeeckx, O.P., Worship.
How does Christ still live among us today? How does Christ
still act in our lives today?

2 Finding Christ.   St. Ambrose said: "You have shown yourself to me face to face, O Lord; for it is you that I find in your
sacraments."
In what sense do we "find Christ" in the sacraments? Where
else do we "find Christ"? Explain how Christ is still present on
earth and acting in men's lives.

13

CHRIST REDEEMS MANKIND

1 Christ foretells his death and resurrection

After having taught the people about his Father's kingdom,
Jesus next makes it clear to them that he will soon suffer and
die at the hands of their leaders. He also reveals that he will
rise from the dead on the third day. Let us read how St.
Matthew records this for our instruction.

When Jesus had reached the environs of Caesarea Philippi,
he put this question to his disciples:
"Who do the people say the Son of Man is?"
"Some say, John the Baptist," they replied;
"others say, Elias;
still others, Jeremias, or some other prophet."
"But you," he went on to say, "who do you say I am?"
Then Simon Peter spoke up:
"You are the Messias, the Son of the Living God."
Jesus acquiesced and said to him:
"Blessed are you, Simon, son of Jona.

It was my Father in heaven that revealed this to you,
and not flesh and blood.
And I, in turn, say to you: You are Peter,
and upon this rock I will build my Church,
and the gates of hell shall not prevail against it."
. . . From that time on Jesus began to make plain
to his disciples that it was necessary for him
to go to Jerusalem,
suffer much at the hands of the elders,
high priests, and Scribes,
be put to death, and on the third day rise again.
At this Peter drew him aside
and proceeded to lecture him.
"May God spare you, Master," he said:
"this must never happen to you!"
But he turned on Peter with the words:
"Get out of my sight; follow me, Satan!
You are a stumbling block to me,
for you do not take God's view of things, but men's."
    Then Jesus said to his disciples:
"If anyone wants to become my follower,
he must renounce himself and shoulder his cross;
then he may be a follower of mine.
Indeed, he who is bent on saving his life,
must part with it anyway;
but he who freely parts with his life for my sake
will secure it in the end.
Clearly, what will it profit a man to gain the whole world
when his life is forfeited in any case?
Or, what price can a man pay down to purchase life forever?
Furthermore: the Son of Man is to come hereafter
wrapt in his Father's glory and escorted by his angels;
and then he will repay everyone
according to his conduct." Matthew 16:13-28

Christ's words alarm the apostles

At the time of Christ's coming, the Jews were expecting a
powerful Messia-King who would overwhelm Israel's enemies.
From the first days of his ministry Christ undertook to correct
this wrong notion and to teach the people gradually that this was
not to be. Now Christ takes a major step forward. He foretells
that their king will not overwhelm the world. Rather, he, himself,

will apparently be overwhelmed by it. Israel's king will wear a crown of thorns, not a crown of gold.

This disturbing news catches the apostles, especially Peter, off guard. It shows that, though Peter understands that Christ is the Son of God, there are other things that he does not understand. One is that the promised Messia is to suffer and die for the people and thereby repair the damage of Adam's sin. Years before, Second Isaia prophesied of the promised one, "The will of the Lord shall be accomplished through him. . . . through his suffering, my servant shall justify many, and their guilt he shall bear. Therefore I will give him his portion among the great . . . because he surrendered himself to death and was counted among the wicked; and he shall take away the sins of many, and win pardon for their offenses." Isaia 53:10-12.

Jesus suffers out of love

Why did God's plan permit the cruel death of his only begotten Son? Was it necessary to free men from sin and admit them to God's kingdom? The answer is no. Any action of Christ would have been more than ample to redeem man. But God permitted his Son's death to reveal to men two truths: 1) the depth of his love for men, and 2) the malice of sin.

Throughout his life Christ taught men by his words that they ought to love one another. By his death Christ teaches men of his own infinite love for them. "No one can give a greater proof of his love than by laying down his life for his friends." John 15:13

Throughout his life Christ also taught men the serious evil of sin. He said that it was better to go through life without a hand or foot than to give in to serious sin. Mark 9:43. By his death Christ teaches men even more graphically the malice of sin. It led him to be scourged and crucified.

BIBLE MESSAGE

Christ teaches us.   Christ teaches us in the Gospel that "No one can give a greater proof of his love than by laying down his life for his friends." John 15:13.

1 Why is this the greatest proof of love? 2 Discuss: a) why Christ chose to redeem us as he did, b) why Christ foretold his passion, death, and resurrection, c) why Christ's passion prophecy took the apostles by surprise.

2 The leaders of the people plot Christ's death

The last week of Christ's earthly life in Palestine draws near.
Among the people of Palestine, the Master's teachings and miracles have provoked different reactions. Some, like the apostles
and the "poor" of Israel, open their minds and hearts to the
Light of the World. Others, like the Scribes and Pharisees, shut
out the light and prefer the darkness to their own selfishness
and ignorance. Still others don't know what to think.
It is thus that Christ's entrance into Jerusalem on Palm Sunday
causes a mixture of joy and sadness. Those who believe in Jesus
wave palms and shout Hosannas. Those who reject Jesus stand
in the background and lay plans to kill him. Finally, those who do
not know what to think, merely follow the crowd. Christ, himself, weeps. He weeps especially for those who reject him, for
in rejecting him, they are rejecting his Father and his Father's
plan of love for them. Let us read how all of this is recorded in
the Gospel.

> When he [Jesus] arrived at the outskirts of Bethphage and Bethany,
> on the slope of the so-called Mount of Olives,
> he sent two of his disciples on an errand, with this instruction:
> "Go into the village directly in front of you and,
> as you enter, you will find hitched a foal
> on which no man has ever sat.
> Unhitch it and bring it here . . ."
> They brought the foal to Jesus, and,
> after throwing their cloaks on it, seated Jesus upon it. . . .
> the people carpeted the road with their cloaks. . . .
> and now the whole throng of the disciples
> became enthusiastic and burst into praising God . . .
>> "A blessing on the King
>> who comes in the name of the Lord!
>> Peace in heaven
>> and glory in the heights above!"
> Then some of the Pharisees in the crowd said to him:
> "Rabbi, reprove your disciples!" But his answer was:
> "I tell you, if these are dumb, the stones will cry out."
>> When at last he came near enough to have a view of the city,
> he sobbed out his grief over it, saying:
>> "O if you, too, did know, at least on this your day,
>> what makes for peace!
>> But alas, it is hidden from your eyes!

Days are coming upon you when your enemies
will throw a rampart round you, and encircle you
and press hard upon you on every side;
and they will dash to the ground
both you and your children within,
nor will they leave stone upon stone within your walls;
because you did not recognize the time of your visitation." . . .
Meanwhile, the chief priests and the Scribes,
as well as the leaders of the people,
were scheming to destroy him;
but they could not discover just what to do,
for the mass of the people hung upon his words. Luke 19:29-48

The Scribes and Pharisees plot Christ's death

The stage is now set. The sides are drawn. The people accept
Christ. They shout his praise, "A blessing on the King who comes
in the name of the Lord." The leaders of the people reject Christ.
They plot his death. "Thereupon the chief priests and the Pharisees
convened a meeting of the Supreme Council. 'This man,' they
urged, 'is giving many proofs of power! What, then, are we to do?
If we let him go without interference, all the world will believe
in him; and then the Romans will come and put an end to our rank
and race alike.'

"One of them, however, Caiaphas, who was chief priest in
that year, said to them: 'You are not men of vision! Can even you
not understand that it is to our advantage that one man should die
for the people so that the whole nation may be saved from ruin?'
In saying this, he was wiser than he knew; the truth is, being chief
priest in that year, he revealed God's design that Jesus was to die
for the whole nation; and not only was he to save the whole nation,
but to unite in one body all the scattered children of God. . . .
accordingly, they passed a resolution to put him to death." John
11:47-53.

BIBLE MESSAGE

Christ teaches us.   The Palm Sunday crowd greets Jesus in
a way reminiscent of the way the people greeted the political
victories of the Machabees. 2 Machabees 10:7. They greet Jesus
with a political enthusiasm.   To correct their political notions
Jesus acts out the prophecy given in Zacharia 9:9.   He comes

206

riding on a donkey to show that, like the king promised in Zacharia, he has come to bring salvation and peace to Israel. The Jews still expected a political kingdom. Jesus is saying by his action that this is not the kind of kingdom he brings.

1 What effect do you think this truth had upon the people in the days that followed? 2 List and discuss the motives that prompted the chief priests and Pharisees to pass a resolution to put Jesus to death.

LITURGY & LIFE

1 Liturgical themes. Passion Sunday occurs two weeks before Easter and marks the beginning of what the Church calls Passiontide. Strictly speaking, Passiontide does not form a new liturgical season, but is the continuation of Lent. The liturgical texts of the Masses of Passion Week (the week following Passion Sunday) highlight Christ's rejection by the people, especially by the Scribes and Pharisees.

Palm Sunday follows Passion Week and marks the beginning of Holy Week, the second and final week of Passiontide. Whereas Passion Week highlighted Christ's rejection by the people, Holy Week highlights Christ's passion and death.

Take your missals and show how the Mass texts, especially the Gospels, stress these two main themes.

2 More than a king. In The Robe, a book about Christ, Lloyd C. Douglas describes a slave, named Demetrius, elbowing his way through the crowd on the first Palm Sunday. Demetrius is trying to see the man on the donkey. Finally he gets close enough to see the face of Jesus. Later another slave asks Demetrius, "See Him--close up?"

Dazed, Demetrius merely nodded.

"Is he crazy?"

Demetrius shook his head.

"A king?" asked Demetrius' friend.

"No," answered Demetrius, "not a king."

"What then?" demanded the second slave.

"I don't know," said Demetrius slowly, "but He is something more than a king."

What do you think Demetrius saw in Christ's face that made him say what he did? How would you go about explaining to Demetrius who Christ really is?

And after receiving a cup and saying grace, he said . . .
"This cup is the new covenant sealed by my blood, which
is about to be shed for your sake." Luke 22:18-20

3 Christ inaugurates the New Covenant

The last week of Jesus' earthly life advances. Finally, the day arrives for the celebration of the Jewish Passover. In spite of the death plots afoot, Jesus and his apostles prepare to go to Jerusalem to celebrate the feast. Let us read how the Gospel describes this.

At last the day of the Unleavened Bread arrived,
and the paschal lamb had to be sacrificed.
So Jesus sent Peter and John on an errand,
with this instruction:
"Go to prepare the paschal supper for us to eat."
"Where," they asked him, "do you want us to make preparations?"
"Listen," he replied; "on entering the city,
you will meet a man carrying a pitcher of water;
follow him into the house he enters,
and say to the proprietor of the house:
'The Rabbi asks, Where is the dining room
in which I can eat the paschal supper with my disciples?'
He will show you a room upstairs
which is spacious and well furnished.
There get things ready."
They went and found everything as he had told them,
and prepared the paschal supper.
   When the hour had come, he took his place on a couch,
and so did the apostles.
"It has been my heart's desire," he said to them,
"to eat this paschal supper with you before I suffer.
I tell you, I shall not eat it again
till it is fulfilled in the kingdom of God."
And after receiving a cup and saying grace, he said:
"Take this, and divide it among you.
I tell you, I shall not again drink of the produce
of the vine till the kingdom of God is set up."
He also took bread into his hands and, after saying grace,
broke it into portions, which he gave to them with these words:

"This is my body, which is about to be given for your sake.
Do this as my memorial."
He did the same with the cup when supper was over, and said:
"This cup is the new covenant sealed by my blood,
which is about to be shed for your sake."   Luke 22:7-20

Christ eats the Last Supper with his apostles

The night before he dies, Christ meets with his followers to eat
the paschal supper.

For 1200 years the Jews had celebrated Passover, as a memorial of their deliverance from Egypt and of their covenant with
God at Mt. Sinai. But the Passover did not look just to the past;
it also looked to the future: the day when the promised Messia
would deliver Israel not just from Egypt but from all its
enemies.

The paschal supper was always celebrated in Jerusalem. This
was prescribed by law. Jerusalem's normal population was about
25,000 people. During the Passover it swelled to over 100,000.
Since there was not enough room in the city, many pilgrims
pitched tents outside the city. The paschal supper, however,
was always eaten within the city walls. This meant that many
ate the meal in the open, in courtyards, and on rooftops.

Normally, the Hebrews ate two meals a day, one around ten
o'clock and another later in the afternoon. The paschal meal,
however, was eaten at night, just at the appearance of the first
stars. Thus everyone began the meal at the same time and celebrated it as one family.

The passover ceremonies begin

As Jesus and his apostles wait for the first stars to appear,
they see passover fires blazing all over the city. Once the stars
appear, Jesus, acting as father, begins the passover ceremonies.

First, he asks for the cup of kiddush, a wine cup especially
prepared for the occasion. For the paschal meal red wine is
usually used. It reminds the Jews of blood-smeared doorposts in
Egypt and of the covenant-blood which Moses sprinkled on their
ancestors at Mt. Sinai.

After blessing the cup, Jesus drinks from it and passes it on
for the rest to drink from. Such a ritual dramatizes the close
friendship that links those gathered for the paschal meal.

When the drinking ritual is over, all go to the table. Instead of sitting, as was customary at ordinary meals, they recline on couches at this meal, after the custom of the Greeks and Romans at banquets.

Jesus gives his apostles an example

Some of the apostles complain because John, the youngest, gets the seat of honor next to Jesus. Jesus takes the occasion to teach them. "'The kings of the Gentiles lord it over them, and their princes have themselves styled benefactors. That must not be your way! No, the greatest in your group must be like the youngest, and the leader like the servant.'" Luke 22:25-26.

To drive the lesson home, Jesus takes a water basin and washes the feet of all present. This was customary at certain ancient banquets, but it was not the rule for paschal meals. When Jesus finishes, he says, ". . . if I have washed your feet--I, the Master and Rabbi--you, too, ought to wash one another's feet; for I have set you an example, so that what I have done to you, you, too, should do." John 13:14-15.

After Jesus finishes, the paschal ritual resumes; and all perform the ritual washing of the right hand.

Next, the first course is set before Jesus. It consists of a bowl of herbs and haroseth (a mixture of grated fruits and nuts with spices and vinegar). This dish is passed around for each to take as much as he wishes. It is during this passing that Jesus says, " . . . one of you will betray me--one who is eating with me." Mark 14:18. Judas dips his hand with Jesus into the bowl of herbs. As he does, Jesus says quietly, "Do quickly what you mean to do." John 13:27. At first some of the apostles are disturbed when Judas leaves, but they recall that Judas keeps the purse. Perhaps Jesus wants him to buy something for the feast or to give alms to the poor. John 13:29-30. It was customary to help the poor on this night.

Next, the diners wash their hands and prepare for the main course. It consists of roast lamb, unleavened bread, herbs and haroseth, and a second cup of wine.

Jesus gives his apostles a new commandment

When the meal is set before the father, it is customary for the youngest to ask the meaning of the special features of the paschal meal. Why, for instance, is the bowl of herbs passed before the breaking of the bread? At other meals, bread is broken first. These questions give the father an opportunity to carry out the command of Exodus 12:27, which states that he must explain the meaning of the paschal ritual to the children present. Normally, this explanation involves telling the story of the exodus from Egypt. During the story the father also explains the meaning of the various ingredients of the meal. The bitter herbs, with the clay-colored sauce, remind the Jews of their days of slavery when they made clay bricks under the broiling Egyptian sun. The lamb reminds them of how God mercifully passed over their blood-smeared doorways to save their firstborn. The unleavened bread reminds them of the unleavened bread which they ate after departing from Egypt.

Jesus follows this practice. Possibly, during his explanation, Jesus inserts the remarks about his own passing from the world. "At last the Son of Man is glorified . . . only a little while longer am I with you. . . . A new commandment I give you: love one another; as I love you, so I want you, too, to love one another. By this token all the world must know that you are my disciples --by cherishing love for one another." John 13:31-35.

Jesus announces his passage to the Father

Then Peter says to Jesus: "'Master, where are you going?' Jesus explained: 'Where I am going you cannot at present follow me. But you will follow me later.' 'And why, Master,' replied Peter, 'cannot I follow you right now? I will lay down my life for you!' Jesus answered: 'You will lay down your life for me? I must be frank with you: before cockcrow you will disown me three times.'" John 13:36-38.

Peter looks troubled. Jesus continues: "'Do not let your heart be troubled! . . . I have told you this now before it takes place, so that, when it does take place, you may revive your faith.'" John 14:28-31.

Then turning to the others, Jesus says: "'Mark well . . . you will scatter, each going back to his home, and leave me all alone! Not that I am really alone, for the Father is with me. I have forewarned you of this event, that you may find peace of soul in union with me. In the world, afflictions are in store for you. But have courage; I have overcome the world.'" John 16:31-33.

Jesus continues the usual paschal liturgy by praying the Passa-Haggadah, a Hebrew prayer. Following it all join in singing the first half of the Hallel, a hymn of praise: "When Israel came forth from Egypt . . . The sea beheld and fled; . . . The mountains skipped

212

like rams, the hills like the lambs . . . tremble, O earth, before the face of the God of Jacob . . ." Psalm 113.

Next, a second cup of wine is passed and drunk. It is now time to eat the main meal.

Jesus gives his body to be our food

The meal opens with the father saying grace over the un-leavened bread. It is at this point that Jesus inserts the words of consecration, changing the unleavened bread into his own body. When all eyes were turned toward him, he "took bread in his hands and after he had given thanks broke it and said, 'This is my body which is given up for you; do this in remembrance of me.'" 1 Corinthians 11:24.

Jesus then gives the "blessed bread" to his disciples. He does not eat any himself. The apostles wonder about this. They also wonder about the new blessing and the new interpretation that Jesus gives the unleavened bread. His words recall that day on the mountainside when he had said: "'I am the bread of life. Your fathers ate the manna in the desert, and they died. . . . the bread which I shall give is my flesh given for the life of the world.'" John 6:48-51.

Jesus is the new paschal lamb

Next, Jesus passes the paschal lamb. As he does, the words of Second Isaia probably come to mind: "Like a lamb led to the slaughter . . . smitten for the sin of his people . . . he surrendered himself to death . . . [to] win pardon for their offenses." Isaia 53: 7-12. The meal is eaten slowly and with joy. Gradually it draws to a close.

Jesus gives us his blood and announces the New Covenant

Finally, according to custom, a third cup of wine is prepared and blessed. It is at this point that Jesus inserts the words of consecration, changing the wine into his own blood. "After he had finished supper, he took the chalice in his hands and said, (1 Corinthians 11:25) 'This is my covenant-blood, which is about to be shed for the sake of many.' (Mark 14:24) 'Do this . . . in remembrance of me.'" 1 Corinthians 11:24.

Again, the apostles note that Jesus does not drink of the wine. Again, they wonder about the new blessing and the new interpre-

213

tation he has given to the cup of wine. He calls it his "covenant-blood which is about to be shed for the sake of many."

This expression is familiar to them. Jesus is clearly alluding to the covenant which God made at Sinai after Israel's deliverance from Egypt. On this occasion Moses dashed blood upon the people saying, "This is the blood of the covenant which the Lord has made with you . . ." Exodus 24:8. The apostles also recall the covenant meal which Moses and the elders ate in God's presence on the mountain, immediately after the blood ritual. Exodus 24:11. This is exactly what they are doing this very night. Is Jesus teaching them that this is a New Covenant? New Covenant blood? a New Covenant meal?

Before they can answer, Jesus begins the final phase of the paschal meal: the singing of the last half of the Hallel. They join in:

> The cup of salvation I will take up . . .
> Precious in the eyes of the Lord
> is the death of his faithful ones . . .
> The stone which the builders rejected
> has become the cornerstone. . . .
> Blessed is he who comes in the name of the Lord . . .
> Give thanks to the Lord, for he is good;
> for his kindness endures forever. Psalm 115:4-6 and 117:22-29

BIBLE MESSAGE

Christ teaches us. The Passover was Israel's greatest feast. At the time of Christ it had a double aspect. First, it looked to the past and commemorated that chain of glorious events by which God freed Israel from Egypt and made them his chosen people at Mt. Sinai. Second, it looked to the future and anticipated that glorious day when the promised Messia would come to free Israel forever from all her enemies.

Discuss: a) the time, place, and manner of celebrating the passover meal, b) why the passover meal was an ideal time for Christ to inaugurate the New Covenant, c) the example Christ gave to the complaining apostles, d) the new commandment that Christ taught, e) how and when Christ inaugurated the New Covenant, f) how and when Christ gave us his body to eat and his blood to drink, g) the thoughts that probably passed through the minds of the apostles during the Last Supper.

1 Holy Thursday and Good Friday.   The Holy Thursday Mass liturgy is a reliving of the Last Supper. On Holy Thursday Christians from all over the world gather to partake of Christ's body.

A special aspect of many Holy Thursday Masses is the liturgical enactment of the "washing of the feet." It is a symbol of the charity that Christ wished to exist between the members of the mystical body.

The Holy Thursday service ends with the procession of the body of Christ to the "repository."

On Good Friday there will be no Mass offered, but all will gather for the reading of the Passion, solemn prayers, the veneration of the cross, and Holy Communion.

Take your missal and with the help of your teacher, or by yourself, make an outline of the liturgy of Holy Thursday and Good Friday.

2 True friend.   With the cheers of Madison Square Garden still ringing in his ears, a young man marched in triumph into a New York restaurant. After fifteen rounds he was now the lightweight champion of the world.

"What'll it be, Champ?" shouted one of his admirers. "You name it and you can have it."

How good that must have sounded to the hungry fighter. Everyone waited. Then came the surprise.

Instead of placing an order the boxer pulled back the sleeve of his coat and glanced at his watch. It was just after midnight. He shook his head: "I will not take anything. It is First Friday, and I am going to Holy Communion in the morning."

That event took place September 14, 1936 before the change in the Communion fast.

The next morning, hungry and tired, the boxer happily knelt at the Communion rail to greet Christ in the Holy Eucharist. He was lightweight boxing champion of the world; but, more important, he was Christ's true friend.

Why do you think the boxer wanted to go to Holy Communion on First Friday? Why is the receiving of Holy Communion an important part of every Mass?

Draw up a column of reasons why high-school students may find it difficult to go to Holy Communion. In another column, opposite the first one, list remedies for each difficulty. Review the role of the meal in ancient covenants. See page 69.

DOCTRINAL POINTS

Holy Eucharist

In the sacrament of the Holy Eucharist, Jesus Christ is present, whole and entire, under the appearances of bread and wine. When we say Christ is present whole and entire, we mean he is there body and blood, and soul and divinity. Moreover, Christ is present whole and entire under both appearances, the bread and the wine. Because of this, it suffices to receive the Eucharist under the form of bread only.

The act of receiving Jesus Christ in the sacrament of the Holy Eucharist is called Holy Communion. This expression is very appropriate, for it sums up the most important effect of the Eucharist: union with Christ and a more fervent love of God and neighbor.

In addition to this main effect, Holy Communion has three other effects: 1) it increases sanctifying grace; 2) it preserves from mortal sin and remits venial sin; 3) it lessens our inclinations to sin and helps us to practice good works.

Some practical points

Communion may not be received more than once a day, except when one who has already received Communion falls dangerously ill and is given Viaticum.

We prepare for Holy Communion by fasting from food and alcoholic drinks for three hours and from nonalcoholic liquids for one hour before the moment at which we receive Communion. This preparation applies for all Masses, whether they are celebrated at midnight, morning, or evening.

By liquid we mean anything that is drunk rather than eaten, such as tea, coffee, soups, and malted milks. Water never breaks our fast and may be drunk up to the moment of Communion.

If we are sick, even if not confined to bed, we may take nonalcoholic beverages and medicine (whether liquid, solid, or having an alcoholic base) before Mass or Communion without any time limit. (We are, however, not exempted from the obligation of abstaining from solid food and alcoholic liquids for three hours.)

Communion may be received without fasting when one is in danger of death or when it is necessary to save the Blessed Sacrament from insult or injury.

The best way to prepare for Holy Communion is to follow the

Mass and say the same prayers as the priest. This is best done by using a missal.

The best way to spend the time immediately after Holy Communion is by making sincere acts of love, thanksgiving, and petition. When the priest is finished giving out Holy Communion, we ought again to follow the Mass. At the end of Mass we might well spend some more time in further prayer.

We are never obliged to go to confession before Communion, only when we are conscious of mortal sin. To receive Holy Communion in the state of mortal sin would be a grave sin. One who sincerely doubts whether he has committed a mortal sin is not obliged to confess before Holy Communion. If while on our way to the Communion rail, or while at it, we recall a mortal sin which has not been confessed, and if we cannot withdraw without attracting attention, we may make an act of perfect contrition and receive Holy Communion. At our next confession we must include the sin which we remembered before Communion. Venial sin should never keep us away from Holy Communion.

Study questions

"If into melted wax other wax is thrown, the two are certain to get thoroughly mixed one with the other. In the same way, he who receives the body and blood of the Lord is so united with Him, that he is to be found in Christ and Christ in him."

1 Did St. Cyril really mean this, or was he exaggerating a bit? 2 How is Christ present in the Eucharist? 3 Why is it sufficient to receive Holy Communion under one species only? Discuss: a) the effects of Holy Communion, b) the fasting regulations, c) the necessity or nonnecessity of confession before Holy Communion, e) the best way to spend the time immediately before and after Holy Communion.

4 Christ suffers and dies for us

After Jesus and his apostles finish eating the passover supper,
they leave the upper room and descend into the darkened streets
of Jerusalem. Jesus leads his apostles outside the city wall to a
garden overlooking the city. There in the moonlight Jesus begins
the opening phase of his passion. Let us read how the Gospel
records this great act of love.

After chanting the hymn of thanks,
they set out for the Mount of Olives. . . .
"Rest here," he said to his disciples, "till I finish praying."
Then, taking Peter, James, and John with him,
he gave way to terror and weariness, and said to them:
"I am plunged in sorrow, enough to break my heart!
Stay here and keep awake."
He then went a short distance forward,
threw himself on the ground, and prayed . . .
"Abba, Father, you can do all things! Spare me this cup!
No, not what I will, but what you will!"
He then came back and found them sleeping. . . .
Again he went away and prayed, using the same words.
On returning, he again found them sleeping. . . .
When he returned the third time, he said to them:
". . . Rise; let us go. Look, my betrayer is close at hand."
    There was no delay. He was still speaking
when Judas, one of the Twelve, came upon the scene,
accompanied by a numerous throng armed with swords and
clubs--emissaries of the chief priests,
and the entire Supreme Council. Mark 14:26-43

Christ's agony in the garden

The olive orchard of Gethsemani was located about a half-
hour's walk from the supper room. The word "gethsemani" means
"olive press." From Gethsemani one got a good view of the city.
Jesus and the apostles probably departed for the garden about
eleven, going by way of the Fountain Gate.
    Arriving at Gethsemani Jesus takes aside Peter, James, and
John, who had earlier witnessed his glorious transfiguration.
Mark 9:2-3. Now they will witness his agony. The apostles,
in typical oriental fashion, spread their cloaks on the ground
and soon fall asleep.

218

Just as Christ began his ministry of teaching by prolonged prayer in the desert, so Christ begins his ministry of suffering by a prolonged prayer. The spirit of his prayer is basically that of the Our Father, which he taught his apostles. "Father . . . may your will, not mine, be done." Luke 22:42.

The bloody sweat recorded by Luke, the doctor, is not unknown in medical history. Luke 22:44. It calls attention to Christ's human nature and reveals the severe mental anguish that Jesus experiences at this time.

Reason for Christ's agony

Writers have speculated on the cause of this anguish. Their conclusions are, generally, the same. Jesus saw: 1) the deep malice of sin, which was about to do him to death; 2) the inhuman suffering he is about to undergo; and 3) the base ingratitude of so many who will reject him, in spite of what he is doing out of love for them.

Jesus shows he is master of his fate

When the mob enters the garden, Jesus advances to meet them. The kiss with which Judas greets Jesus is not unusual. Oriental males customarily greet each other this way. When the mob attempts to sieze Jesus, he clearly shows they could not do so if he willed otherwise. Each time he utters the divine name "I am he," the soldiers draw back helplessly. John 18:6. When Peter slashes off the ear of one of the mob, Jesus stops him from further knife play and heals the victim. John 18:11.

Having made his point, Jesus yields to his captors. His hour has come.

Study questions

1 What great truth does Christ teach us by the way he causes the mob to fall back each time he utters the divine name? 2 Discuss: a) why Christ took aside only the apostles who had witnessed his transfiguration, b) the spirit of Christ's prayer to his Father, c) the cause of Christ's bloody sweat, d) the kiss of Judas, e) why Christ stopped Peter from knife play (Read John 18:11), f) how the above points contain important lessons for us today.

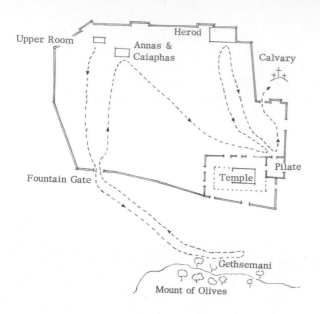

Upper Room

Herod

Annas &
Caiaphas

Calvary

Fountain Gate

Temple

Pilate

Gethsemani

Mount of Olives

△

Jerusalem, as it probably was in Christ's time
Jerusalem today, as viewed from the Mt. of Olives

▽

Jesus is taken before Annas

When the mob finally lays hold of Jesus, the apostles flee in
all directions. Jesus is quickly chained and paraded off to the
high priest by the mob. Let us read about it in the Gospel.

Then the men laid their hands on him and arrested him. . . .
all turned their backs on him and took to flight . . .
They led Jesus before the chief priest,
and all the chief priests, the elders, and the Scribes assembled.
Peter, meanwhile, had been following him at a distance
all the way into the palace of the chief priest,
where he loitered among the guards,
warming himself in the glow of the fire.
    Now the chief priests . . . were looking for testimony
unfavorable to Jesus in order to have him put to death;
but they did not find any. . . . Finally, some stood up and,
falsely testifying against him, said:
"We ourselves have heard him say:
'I can tear down this sanctuary made by the hands of men,'
and 'Within three days, I can build up another
not made by the hands of men.'"
And thus, again, their testimony did not agree!
    Then the chief priest rose in full view and asked Jesus:
. . . "Are you the Messias, the Son of the Ever Blessed?"
"I am," replied Jesus; "moreover, you are going to see
the Son of Man enthroned at the right hand of the Almighty
and coming wrapt in the clouds of the sky."
    The chief priest tore his garments . . .
"You heard the blasphemy! What is your verdict?"
They all voted him liable to the penalty of death.
And now some made free to spit on him . . .
Even the guards struck him with the open hand.
    While Peter was in the courtyard below . . .
he burst out cursing and swearing:
"I have nothing to do with this man . . ."
And he broke out into sobs and tears. Mark 14:46-72

Jesus declares he is the Messia, the Son of God

The soldiers, hirelings of the Jewish leaders, lead Jesus to
Annas, a former high priest and father-in-law of Caiaphas the
current high priest. John 18:13.

No time is lost. A group of priests is gathered and an unofficial hearing ensues. Witnesses are summoned to testify against Jesus. Jewish law required the testimony of at least two witnesses when a capital charge was made. When the witnesses can't agree, Annas challenges Jesus to testify against himself. "'Are you the Messias, the Son of the Ever Blessed?' 'I am,' replied Jesus; 'moreover, you are going to see the Son of Man enthroned at the right hand of the Almighty and coming wrapt in the clouds of the sky.'"

Instantly all recognize the messianic prophecies of Daniel. Daniel 7:13. Christ reveals his identity in an unmistakable way. But the minds of the priests are closed to truth.

Annas rejects Jesus' claim

Annas shouts, "blasphemy" and tears his robes--a ritual display of holy anger when one hears another blaspheme. The death sentence is demanded. To a man, the assembled group votes that Jesus stand official trial in the morning. Jewish law stipulated that all proceedings in which the life of a man was at stake must take place in broad daylight.

The assembly and the guards begin to manhandle Jesus, even though Jewish laws laid down penalties for judges who strike a prisoner or allow others to do so.

Peter denies Jesus

Meanwhile Peter is suspected of being a disciple of Jesus. His Galilean accent, noticeable in Jerusalem, has forced him into successive denials of Jesus. It was said that a Galilean peasant so confused certain letters of the alphabet that it was difficult to tell whether he was saying immar (lamb), camar (wool), or hamar (wine). With Peter's third denial, a cock crows. Peter remembers the Master's words. He dashes into the early morning darkness weeping bitterly. Matthew 26:75.

Study questions

1 What great truth does Christ teach us by his answer to Annas? 2 Discuss: a) why the high priests ignored Christ's answer, b) why Annas tore his robes, c) why Christ's trial was postponed until daylight, d) why it was surprising that the guards manhandled Jesus, e) why Peter was suspected, and f) how the above points contain important lessons for us today.

Jesus before Pilate

Early the next morning, Jesus is hauled up from the dark
dungeon into which he had been lowered for the night. He is led
immediately before the Sanhedrin, the Supreme Council of Jerusalem. Caiaphas, the reigning high priest, conducts a hasty trial.
It ends in a matter of minutes. Jesus is then marched off to the
praetorium: Pilate's headquarters. Let us read how the Gospel
records this.

They next led Jesus from Caiaphas to the praetorium.
It was early morning. . . .
Pilate therefore came out to face them.
"What charge," he said, "do you bring against that man?"
By way of answer they replied:
"If this man were not a criminal,
we should not have handed him over to you. . . ."
Pilate then went back into the praetorium and summoned Jesus.
"Are you the King of the Jews?" he asked him. . . .
"My kingdom," Jesus explained, "is not a worldly one."
. . . "Then you are a king after all!" Pilate said to him.
"You are right," replied Jesus; "I am a king.
For this purpose I was born, and for this purpose
I came into the world -- to give testimony to the truth.
Only he who is open to the truth gives ear to my voice."
"What is truth?" Pilate said to him,
and with that went outside again to face the Jews.
He said to them: "I find no guilt in him.
It is a custom among you that I release someone
at your request at the Passover.
Do you want me, therefore, to release as your choice
the King of the Jews?"
Back came their shout:
"No; not this man, but Barabbas." Barabbas was a robber.
    Then Pilate took Jesus in charge and had him scourged.
The soldiers also plaited a crown of thorns
and put it on his head;
besides, they threw a purple cloak round him and,
marching up, saluted him: "Long live the King of the Jews!"
They also slapped him in the face.
Pilate went outside once more . . . anxious to release him;
but the Jews kept shouting:
"If you release this man, you are not a friend of Caesar.

223

"Anyone who declares himself a king
renounces allegiance to Caesar."
    Pilate accordingly, on hearing such language,
had Jesus led out, and . . . handed him over to them
for crucifixion.   John 18:28-19:16

Jesus proclaims his kingship over all men

Next morning Caiaphas convenes the Sanhedrin, a council
of seventy Jewish leaders who act as a kind of court of hearing
for politico-religious matters. The trial is a mere formality,
a hasty repetition of the midnight hearing. Jesus is found guilty.
    The Sanhedrin, powerless to pronounce the death verdict,
decides to send Jesus to Pilate. But since it is almost certain that
Pilate will not give a death verdict on grounds of blasphemy alone,
the priests trump up three political charges. Jesus 1) incites
revolt among the people, 2) opposes paying taxes to Caesar, and
3) poses as a king. Luke 23:2.
    It is "early morning" (John 18:28) when the leaders march
Jesus over to the praetorium, Pilate's headquarters. Six o'clock
seems a strange hour to take a prisoner to the governor, until
one recalls that Romans customarily rose early, giving the
morning to business and reserving the afternoon for amusements.
    At once Pilate sizes up the situation. He sees it as a religious
squabble among the Jews. Thus, learning that Jesus is Galilean,
he sends him to Herod, the tetrarch of Galilee. Luke 23:6. But the
maneuver fails, and soon the leaders return with Jesus. Pilate
cross-examines Jesus, asking him if he is a political king and
therefore a threat to the Roman state. Jesus explains that his
kingship is of a spiritual kingdom. "For this purpose I was born,
and for this purpose I came into the world--to give testimony to
the truth." John 18:37.
    "What does religious truth mean to me?" Pilate, a man of the
world, looks upon Jesus as some sidewalk prophet who can't
possibly harm the Roman government. He is satisfied. "Not
guilty!" He proposes to release him according to the custom by
which the Roman governor released a prisoner each year on the
Passover.
    But the people demand a different prisoner. Pilate then tries
a compromise move. He orders Jesus scourged. Perhaps this
will satisfy the leaders and the mob. Roman scourgings left
their victims in terrible condition.

Jesus is scourged

The Jews were familiar with scourging. They had practiced it from ancient times, but only for certain grave offenses. Deuteronomy 25. They used only an ordinary whip, and the number of lashes was limited to forty. Romans, on the other hand, were far more cruel. They did not limit lashes, and they used whips designed to dig deeply into the victim's body. The Roman writers, Cicero and Plutarch, tell how victims of Roman scourgings sometimes collapsed to the ground spurting blood and dying before the punishment ended. This was to be Jesus' fate.

When the brutal beating ends, the soldiers, who hate Jews, decide to vent their anger still more on the "king of the Jews." They force a crown of thorns down around his head and subject Jesus to a sacrilegious mockery.

Jesus is condemned

At last Jesus is brought before the people. The sight of him is shocking, but even more shocking are the shouts of the Jews. "Crucify him." Pilate's strategy backfires. "If you release this man," the leaders cry out, "you are not a friend of Caesar. Anyone who declares himself a king renounces allegiance to Caesar." John 19:12. This kind of talk frightens Pilate.

Calling for a basin of water, Pilate washes his hands. Matthew 27:24. The Jews clearly recognize the symbolism of Pilate's act. They themselves have used it in their past. Deuteronomy 21:6-7.

Study questions

1 What great truth does Christ teach us by his reply to Pilate's question about his kingship? 2 Discuss: a) why the Sanhedrin sent Jesus to Pilate, b) why Pilate scourged Jesus, c) why Pilate handed Jesus over to the people, d) Pilate's hand-washing ritual, and e) how the above points contain important lessons for us today.

Jesus is put to death

Amid shouts and screams Jesus is handed over to be crucified. With Roman efficiency the soldiers assemble the necessary ropes, nails, hammer, and timber. When all is ready, the captain bellows the order and the procession moves off to Calvary. Let us read how the Gospel records this.

Then they led him out to be crucified. . . .
They led him to a place called Golgotha,
which means "Skull's Mound."
Here they offered him drugged wine; but he did not take it.
. . . His clothes they divided among them
by drawing lots for them, to see what each was to get.
. . . There was also the usual inscription stating his guilt:
"The King of the Jews."
Together with him they crucified two bandits,
one at his right, the other at his left.
Thus the Scripture was fulfilled which says:
"He was classed with lawless men."
    Meanwhile the passers-by kept insulting him.
They shook their heads and said:
"Bah! You are the one that can pull down the sanctuary
and build it up in three days!"
"Save yourself and come down from the cross!"
The chief priests joined the Scribes and said
in the same taunting manner to one another:
"He saved others! He cannot save himself!"
"Let the Messias, the king of the Jews,
come down from the cross this instant:
we want to see and believe!"
. . . About noon darkness fell upon the whole land
and lasted till three o'clock.
At three o'clock Jesus cried out with a strong voice:
"Eloi, Eloi, lama sabachthani," which means:
"My God, my God, why do you abandon me?"
. . . Jesus uttered a loud cry and expired.
    Then the curtain of the sanctuary
was torn in two from top to bottom.
When the centurion, who stood by facing him,
saw that he had expired under such circumstances he said:
"This man was really the Son of God."   Mark 15:20-39

Jesus offers his life in sacrifice

Plutarch, the historian, says that a criminal condemned to
crucifixion, carried the wood upon which he was to be spiked.
Jesus is no exception. John 19:17. The cross weighed about
seventy pounds. Sometimes, however, the condemned person
carried only the cross beam. For a man weakened by loss of
blood from a Roman scourging, the weight of the cross would

226

have been overwhelming. It is not surprising that the soldiers commandeer a Cyrenean, named Simon, to help Jesus with the burden. Matthew 27:32.

The distance from Pilate's headquarters to Calvary is about a quarter of a mile. The streets leading to it are narrow and paved with cobblestones, worn smooth and slippery by years of use. Moreover, they are jammed with people. Luke 23:27.

Calvarius in Latin means a bare, skull-like hill. Calvary is located just outside the city gate, near the main road, so as to be as public as possible. In no time the hill swarms with the glittering helmets of soldiers and the multicolored garments of the mob.

Jesus is victim and priest

The soldiers begin the execution by stripping Jesus. St. John, who normally omits crucifixion details, goes out of his way to point out that Jesus' tunic was woven in one piece from top to bottom like those of the high priest. John 19:23. Jesus is not only victim in the sacrifice of the Mass, but also the high priest of it.

Next Jesus is stretched on the cross and nailed. In all likelihood the nails, which the Psalmist prophesied should pierce the Savior's hands and feet (Psalm 21:17-18), were the type used by carpenters to secure heavy joists.

At the last moment Jesus is offered a drink to deaden the severe pain that begins to shoot through his body. This was common. Even today, some countries continue this practice in the case of criminals about to be executed. Jesus refuses the drink. Mark 15:23.

Jesus is proclaimed king of all nations

Next the placard reading "King of the Jews" is secured to the cross. Written in Latin, Greek, and Hebrew (John 19:20), the placard testifies to Christ's kingship over not only the Jews but all nations.

Finally, Jesus is hoisted into place. The pain is beyond endurance. As minutes lengthen, Jesus' body muscles begin to spasm and stiffen like cables. Sensing his utter helplessness and apparent defeat, the mob begins to mock him. Thus the Psalmist's words are realized. "I am a worm, not a man; the scorn of men, despised by the people. All who see me scoff at me; they mock me . . . 'He relied on the Lord; let him deliver him, let him rescue him, if he loves him.'" Psalm 21:7-9. But Jesus does not anger. He forgives the people. Luke 23:34.

Knowing the end of his earthly sojourn is near and seeing "his mother and the disciple whom he loved standing by, Jesus said to his mother: 'Mother, this is your son.' He then said to the disciple: 'This is your mother.'" John 19:26-27. Christian tradition has always looked upon St. John as a symbol of all mankind beneath the cross. Mary is from now on to act as the mother of all men.

Jesus is the new paschal lamb

As death draws perilously near, Jesus is consumed with a scorching thirst. To relieve him a sponge is soaked in wine and presented to Jesus on the end of a stalk of hyssop. This seems strange until we realize that this fern-like plant was used thirteen hundred years before to smear the blood of the first paschal lamb on Israelite doorposts on the occasion of the first Passover. Exodus 12:22. Christ is the new paschal lamb. 1 Corinthians 5:7. As God's chosen people of old were saved by the blood of the lamb of sacrifice, so God's new chosen people are saved by the blood of the "Lamb of God."

The Old Covenant gives way to the New Covenant

Finally, the moment comes. Jesus cries out in a loud voice and dies. "Then the curtain of the sanctuary was torn in two from top to bottom." Mark 15:38. For centuries the temple in Jerusalem has been the symbol of God's presence among his people. Now, the tearing of the curtain symbolizes the departure of God from the temple. The Old Testament sanctuary and the Old Testament sacrifice are at an end. The Old Covenant gives way to the New Covenant. From now on the new temple of God's presence on earth will be the Church, Christ's mystical body, which will soon be born from the side of Christ. The new sacrifice will be the sacrifice of Calvary, performed in an unbloody manner, as instituted by Christ at the Last Supper.

"When the centurion, who stood by facing him, saw that he had expired under such circumstances, he said: 'This man was really the Son of God.'" Mark 15:39.

Because it is late in the day, the soldiers are ordered to hasten the death of the two thieves by breaking their legs. They

are also ordered to pierce Jesus' side to make sure he is dead.
This is done, "and immediately there came out blood and water."
John 19:34. St. Augustine and others saw blood and water as
symbols of the Christian sacraments of baptism and the Eucharist
--indeed, the symbolic formation of the Church from the side of
Christ. The Church is the new Eve formed from the side of the
sleeping Christ, the new Adam. The Church is to be the mother
of a redeemed mankind. It will be fully constituted and manifested
to the world on Pentecost.

After his death Jesus is removed from the cross. As is the
custom of the time, he is covered by a twelve or fourteen foot
sheet and placed in a rock chamber. The tomb is then sealed.

Study questions

Discuss the symbolism and significance of: 1) Christ's seam-
less tunic, 2) the trilingual inscription "King of the Jews," 3) the
giving of Mary to John, 4) the hyssop with the sponge dipped in
wine, 5) the tearing of the temple curtain, 6) the flow of blood
from Christ's side.

Many modern artists are trying to bring out the victorious
aspects of Christ's death on the cross. How did the artist of the
crucifix shown here try to do that?

DOCTRINAL POINTS

Mass

"The mystery of the Most Holy Eucharist . . . is the culmi-
nation and center, as it were, of the Christian religion.
    "Christ . . . 'at the last supper, on the night He was betrayed,
wishing to leave His beloved Spouse, the Church, a visible sacrifice, . . . offered His Body and Blood under the species of bread
and wine to God the Father, and under the same species allowed
the Apostles, whom He at that time constituted priests . . . to
make the same offering.'" (Council of Trent)

The Mass is a true sacrifice

The Mass, then, "is no mere empty commemoration of the
passion and death of Jesus Christ, but a true and proper act of
sacrifice, whereby the High Priest by an unbloody immolation
offers Himself . . . as He did upon the Cross."

The priest is the same

"The Priest is the same, Jesus Christ, whose sacred Person
His minister represents. Now the minister by reason of the
sacerdotal consecration . . . possesses the power of performing
actions in virtue of Christ's very Person. Wherefore in his
priestly activity he in a certain manner 'lends his tongue, and
his hand' to Christ."

The victim is the same

"Likewise the Victim is the same, namely our Divine Redeemer in His human nature with His true Body and Blood. The
manner, however, in which Christ is offered is different. On
the Cross He completely offered Himself and all His sufferings
to God . . . by the bloody death, which He underwent of His
free will. But on the altar, by reason of the glorified state of
His human nature . . . the shedding of His Blood is impossible;
still according to the plan of Divine Wisdom, the Sacrifice of our
Redeemer is shown forth in an admirable manner by external
signs which are symbols of His death. For by the 'transubstan-
tiation' of bread into the Body of Christ and of wine into His
Blood are both really present: now the Eucharistic species under

230

which He is present symbolize the actual separation of His Body and Blood. Thus the commemorative representation of His death, which actually took place on Calvary, is repeated in every Sacrifice of the altar, seeing that Jesus Christ is symbolically shown by separate symbols to be in the state of victimhood."

The Mass distributes the merits of Calvary

"Now the Apostle of the Gentiles proclaims the copious plenitude and the perfection of the Sacrifice of the Cross . . . however . . . it is necessary that men should individually come into vital contact with the Sacrifice of the Cross, so that the merits, which flow from it, should be imparted to them. In a certain sense it can be said that on Calvary Christ built a font of purification and salvation which He filled with the Blood He shed; but if men do not bathe in it and there wash the stains of their iniquities, they can never be purified and saved.

"The august Sacrifice of the altar is, as it were, the supreme instrument whereby the merits won by the Divine Redeemer upon the Cross are distributed to the faithful: 'as often as the commemorative Sacrifice is offered, there is wrought the work of our Redemption.' This, however, so far from lessening the dignity of the actual Sacrifice on Calvary, rather proclaims and renders more manifest its greatness and its necessity, as the Council of Trent declares. Its daily immolation reminds us that there is no salvation except in the Cross of Our Lord Jesus Christ, and that God Himself wishes that there should be a continuation of this Sacrifice 'from the rising of the sun till the going down thereof' so that there may be no cessation of the hymn of praise and thanksgiving which man owes to God, seeing that he requires His help continually and has need of the Blood of the Redeemer to remit sin which challenges God's injustice." (Mediator Dei, Vatican Library translation)

Study questions

"All our good works put together," says St. John Vianney, "can never equal the sacrifice of the Mass, because they are the works of men, and the sacrifice of the Mass is the work of God." 1 Explain how the Mass is the work of God. 2 Why did Christ institute the Mass? 3 What is the priest's role in the Mass? 4 How is Christ's death signified in the Mass? 5 How are the Mass, the Last Supper, and Calvary related?

During the season of Lent we saw how:

CHRIST TAUGHT THE PEOPLE

1 Christ taught the people through signs
2 Christ taught about God's kingdom through parables
3 Men respond differently to Christ's teaching
4 Christ taught how to enter God's kingdom
5 Christ taught how to live in God's kingdom
6 Christ chose leaders for God's kingdom

CHRIST REDEEMED MANKIND

1 Christ foretold his death and resurrection
2 The leaders of the people plotted Christ's death
3 Christ inaugurated the New Covenant
4 Christ suffered and died for us

During Eastertime we will see how:

CHRIST RISES IN VICTORY

1 Christ is glorified
2 Christ gives his apostles new power
3 Christ fulfills his promise to Peter
4 Christ ascends to his Father

CHRIST SENDS HIS SPIRIT UPON GOD'S NEW PEOPLE

1 Christ's mystical body, the Church, is born
2 Christ's mystical body builds up

He has risen from the dead. Matthew 28:7

EASTERTIME LITURGY

Christ rises in victory

The liturgy of Eastertime begins on Holy Saturday night in darkness and deathly stillness. The first thing the priest does is to light the Easter fire from a spark, struck from a flint. The flame leaps forth from the cold stone, symbolic of Christ's resurrection from the rock tomb.

The lighted candle symbolizes the victorious Christ

Next the priest lights and prepares the Easter candle, held by the deacon. Then the deacon, carrying the lighted Easter candle, heads the procession into church. As he does, he sings three times "Lumen Christi" (Light of Christ). The lighted candle, at the head of the procession, recalls how God went before the Israelites in the form of a "fiery column" freeing them from the slavery of the Egyptians. Christ is the new "fiery column" freeing not just the Israelites but all mankind from the slavery of Satan. Immediately the whole church bursts forth into light and song.

We renew our baptismal vows

Following this action the light from the Easter candle is distributed to all present. We present our smaller candles to receive the new Easter light, which symbolizes Christ's risen life. This action reminds us of what took place when we were baptized. The light and the life of Christ were communicated to each one of us. St. Paul, in one of his letters, speaks of baptism as an "illumination."

Next follows the blessing of the baptismal water and the renewal of our baptismal vows. We do this while holding in our hands the lighted candles.

We offer and receive the risen Christ

Baptism automatically leads to the sacrament of the Eucharist. And so the baptismal service is followed by the Eucharistic sacrifice. With Christ, our risen head, we unite with the other members of the mystical body to give thanks to the Father for making us his adopted sons. The Eucharistic sacrifice climaxes in the Eucharistic banquet: Holy Communion. This solemn act is our Easter guarantee and pledge that, like Christ, we will some day rise gloriously from the dead and participate in the eternal banquet in heaven to which our Father has invited us.

From the Easter liturgy

If, then , you have risen with Christ,
seek the things that are above,
where Christ is seated at the right hand of God. . . .
When Christ, your life, appears,
then you shall appear with him in glory. Easter Mass Epistle

Study project

Bring your missals to class, and be prepared to outline from memory the Easter Vigil service. Be prepared, also, to explain the various actions that make up the liturgy.

14

CHRIST RISES IN VICTORY

1 Christ is glorified

Christ's apparent defeat on Good Friday now appears for what
it really is: a glorious victory over Satan and sin. Let us read
how the Gospel records this happy news.

After the Sabbath, at dawn on the first day of the week,
Mary Magdalen and the other Mary set out to visit the grave.
All of a sudden there was a mighty earthquake
as an angel of the Lord descended from heaven and,
alighting at the entrance, rolled away the stone
and then seated himself upon it.
His appearance was like a flash of lightning
and his garment as white as snow.
By the terror he inspired,
the guards were struck down and became like dead men.
    But the angel reassured the women.
"You have nothing to fear," he said;
"I know you are looking for Jesus the Crucified.
He is not here. He has risen as he predicted.

Come here: inspect the place
where he was laid to rest
--now go quickly, and take this message to his disciples:
'He has risen from the dead . . .'"   Matthew 28:1-7

Easter is the crown of Christ's work of redemption

The good news of Easter is announced first of all to the faithful women. In turn, they announce it to the apostles, who announce it to all men.

St. Matthew describes the moment of Christ's resurrection much as he described the moment of Christ's death. Strange phenomena take place. An earthquake occurs. An angel appears. The soldiers become as dead men. Clearly, a divine force is at work.

For many years Easter was the only feast that the Church celebrated. Moreover, it was celebrated each Sunday. Only later, under the guidance of the Holy Spirit, did the Church break up this single Easter celebration into the many feast days that make up our liturgical year.

Easter has a threefold aspect

This is important to keep in mind, especially when thinking about the three paschal feasts of Easter, Ascension, and Pentecost. Actually, these three feasts are only different aspects of one divine mystery: Christ's paschal victory. Easter calls special attention to Christ's earthly victory over death. Ascension calls special attention to Christ's heavenly enthronement in glory at the right hand of the Father. Pentecost calls special attention to Christ's special sending of the Holy Spirit on his mystical body the Church.

It would be wrong to think that for forty days after his resurrection Christ went about on the earth visiting friends at times and then hiding until the next visit. On Easter Sunday Christ rose from the dead, was enthroned in heaven, and began sending the Holy Spirit. From heaven for the next forty days Christ communicated with his disciples, confirming their faith and instructing them concerning the kingdom.

What then do we celebrate on Ascension Thursday? This is the day when Christ terminated in a formal, visible way his post-resurrection appearance to his disciples. He made this clear by visibly showing his return to the Father.

So too Pentecost Sunday is the day on which took place a visible manifestation of the formal sending of the Holy Spirit upon the whole Church. It may be thought of as a day on which the people of God were corporately baptized and confirmed, becoming Christ's mystical body.

In the light of this fuller understanding of Easter's triple dimension, we can see better why the Church correctly regards Easter as the high-point of salvation history and the key feast of the liturgical year.

BIBLE MESSAGE

Christ teaches us.   In the early days of the Church, the octave of Easter was marked by eight days of continual celebration. It was even forbidden to do servile work during this period.

1 How do the Masses during the eight days after Easter still reflect this holiday spirit of the early Church? 2 How are the three feasts of Easter, Ascension, and Pentecost merely different aspects of Christ's paschal victory over death, sin, and Satan? 3 Why is Easter: a) the high point of salvation history, and b) the key feast of the liturgical year?

LITURGY & LIFE

1 Adult's feast.   In an article entitled, "Easter Is For Adults," Father Daniel J. O'Hanlon, S.J., says, "Christmas, then, has become more of a children's feast, and it appeals to the child in us. But Easter is the feast of the adult Christian, and there is no genuinely adult Christianity which is not Resurrection-centered. Christmas is a domestic feast, symbolized by the individual family gathered together around the warm hearth -- protecting, fostering, nuturing. But Easter is a missionary feast, impelling those who have caught its meaning to go out and share the good news of Christ's victory with all the world.

"This is not said to downgrade Christmas, which has so important a place in the liturgical year that if it did not exist it would have to be invented, but rather to appeal for an understanding of its true meaning and for the restoration of the central position of Easter." America magazine

What does the author mean when he says, "there is no genuinely adult Christianity which is not Resurrection-centered"? Why do you think many people have lost sight of the "central position of Easter in Christianity"?

2 Life after death.   In the City of God, St. Augustine tells of a doctor from Carthage who questioned the soul's immortality. One night he had a dream in which he saw standing before him a youth clothed in white. The young man said, "Do you see me?" The doctor answered, "Yes, I see you." The young man said, "Do you see me with your eyes?" The doctor said, "No, for my eyes are closed in sleep." "With what do you see me, then?" asked the youth. "I don't know," replied the doctor. The youth continued, "Do you hear me?" "Yes!" said the doctor. "With your ears?" asked the youth. "No," said the doctor, "they too are closed in sleep." "Are you speaking with me?" asked the youth. "Yes," said the doctor. "With your mouth?" "No." "How then?" "I don't know," said the doctor.

Then the youth said, "See, you are sleeping and you see, hear and speak. The day will come when you will sleep in death; but you will be able to see, hear, speak and feel."

The doctor awoke and knew that God had sent him an angel to teach him of the immortality of the soul.

What is meant by the immortality of the soul? How is Christ's resurrection a pledge that we too will rise from the dead?

2 Christ gives his apostles new power

On Easter Sunday evening Jesus appears to the apostles in the upper room. Without warning, he passes through the door into their midst. Let us read how the Gospel records this.

Late in the evening that same day
--the first day of the week--
although the doors of the place
where the disciples gathered were bolted for fear of the Jews,

Jesus came and stood before them, and said:
"Peace be to you!"
With that, he let them see his hands and his side.
The disciples were delighted to see the Lord.
Then Jesus said to them again:
"Peace be to you!
As the Father has made me his ambassador,
so I am making you my ambassadors."
With this, he breathed on them and said:
"Receive the Holy Spirit.
Whenever you remit anyone's sins, they are remitted;
when you retain anyone's sins, they are retained."
    Thomas, one of the Twelve, called the Twin,
was not with the group when Jesus came.
So the other disciples said to him:
"We have seen the Master!"
But he replied: "Unless I see in his hands
the print of the nails, and put my finger into the place
where the nails were, and lay my hand into his side,
I am not going to believe!"
    Eight days later, his disciples were again in the room,
and Thomas was with them.
Jesus came, though the doors were bolted,
and, standing before them, said:
"Peace be to you!"
He then addressed Thomas:
"Let me have your finger; put it here, and look at my hands.
Now let me have your hand, and lay it into my side.
And do not be incredulous, but believe!"
Then Thomas burst out into the words:
"My Master and my God!"
"Because you have seen me," Jesus said to him,
"is that why you believe?
Blessed are those who have not seen
and yet believe!"   John 20:19-29

Christ gives his apostles power to forgive sins

Christ's Sunday evening visit to the apostles is made through
closed doors. The body which was beaten and racked with pain is
now radiantly glorious and attractive. It possesses the four qualities that our risen bodies will also possess some day: 1) impassi-
bility--freedom from pain and death; 2) brightness--the light of

glory; 3) agility--ability to pass instantly from one place to another; 4) subtility--a spirit-likeness.

On this occasion Christ gives his apostles a special Easter gift--the power to forgive sins. He breathes on them as God had breathed on Adam, when he infused into Adam the spirit of life. (St. John uses the same word used by the writer of Genesis.) The apostles are, in a sense, re-created by Christ. They are given a new power.

Christ replaces the Sabbath

Sunday now begins to receive new prominence in the life of the apostles. Christ's resurrection took place on Sunday. The power to forgive sins was given to the apostles on Sunday. A week later, on Sunday, Christ will re-appear to the assembled group. On Pentecost Sunday the Holy Spirit will visibly descend upon the Church. This new prominence, given to Sunday, is not accidental. It teaches the apostles that the Old Testament and all of its structures, including the Sabbath, are now replaced by a new order.

Christ is the God of Abraham, Isaac, and Jacob

Thomas' demand for physical proof of the resurrection is granted by Christ. What Christ would not permit Mary Magdalen to do, he now allows Thomas to do: to touch his person. (Christ is now ascended to his Father.) The expression Thomas uses to profess his faith is the same as the Psalmist used in addressing Yahweh, the God of Israel. Psalm 34:23. Thomas now realizes, as do all the other apostles, that the risen Christ is truly Yahweh, the God of Abraham, Isaac, and Jacob.

From the liturgy

Let me have your hand,
see, here is the mark of the nails. Alleluia!
Doubt no longer, but have faith.
Alleluia, alleluia! Low Sunday: Communion prayer

BIBLE MESSAGE

Christ teaches us.   In 1728 Benjamin Franklin wrote the following epitaph for himself: "The body of Benjamin Franklin (like the cover of an old book, its contents worn out and stripped of its lettering and gilding) lies here, food for worms; but the work shall not be lost, for it will appear once more in a new and elegant edition, revised and corrected by the Author."

1 In what four ways especially will our bodies be "revised and corrected" when we rise from the dead? 2 Discuss: a) the "recreation of the apostles" by Christ on Easter night, b) the way Christ taught that Sunday replaced the Sabbath, and 3) how Christ taught Thomas that he was God.

LITURGY & LIFE

1 Body beautiful.   A magazine ad read: "You can have a virile, rugged, he-man body, fast! Let me make your life thrilling, exciting and romantic . . . too! in just 15 minutes, in the privacy of your own room, and your convenience, I will prove through my triple-progression course that I can slap inches of muscles over your whole body--giving you an EXCITING NEW BODY!"

Discuss: a) the ad, b) the desire to make the body as attractive as possible, c) the exciting new body we will one day get.

2 Soul beautiful.   Regarding Christ's Easter gift of confession, Pope Pius XII said: "By it genuine self-knowledge is increased, Christian humility grows, bad habits are corrected, spiritual neglect and tepidity are conquered, the conscience is purified, the will strengthened, a salutary self-control is attained and grace is increased in virtue of the sacrament itself."

Discuss: a) how and why Christ instituted the sacrament of confession, and b) each point made by the pope.

DOCTRINAL POINTS

Easter Communion

Christ said, "Unless you eat the flesh of the Son of Man and drink his blood, you have no life in you. He who eats my flesh and drinks my blood is in possession of eternal life; and I will raise him from the dead on the last day." John 6:53-54.

To help every Catholic carry out Christ's command, the Church requires, under pain of serious sin, that every Catholic with the use of reason go to Holy Communion during the Easter time. For the United States the Easter Communion time begins with the first Sunday of Lent and ends on Trinity Sunday.

The Church sets aside the Easter for this because during this time, especially, it is fitting that we should die to sin by penance and rise to the life of grace (Christ-life) by receiving the sacrament of the Eucharist, which is a pledge of our future resurrection.

Every high-school student will want to contact Christ as often as possible during the year in Holy Communion. Pope Pius X urged daily Communion.

3 Christ fulfills his promise to Peter

During the forty days after Easter, Jesus makes other appearances to his apostles. One morning after the apostles have fished the whole night without luck, Jesus appears to them as they are about to quit. Let us read how the Gospel records this:

> But just as day was breaking, Jesus stood on the beach.
> The disciples did not know, however, that it was Jesus.
> "Well, lads," Jesus said to them,
> "you have no fish there, have you?"
> "No," they replied.
> "Cast your net to the right of the boat," he said to them,
> "and you will find something."
> So they cast it, and now they were not strong enough
> to haul it up into the boat because of the great number
> of fish in it.
> Then the disciple whom Jesus loved said to Peter:
> "It is the Master!"

. . . When they had come ashore,
they noticed hot embers on the ground,
with fish lying on the fire and bread.
Jesus said to them:
"Bring some of the fish you caught just now."
So Simon Peter boarded the boat
and hauled the net upon the beach.
It was full of fish, one hundred and fifty-three in all,
and in spite of the great number the net did not break.
"Come, now," Jesus said to them, "and have breakfast."
. . . Then Jesus approached, took the bread in his hands,
and gave them of it. He did the same with the fish.
. . . After they had breakfasted, Jesus said to Simon Peter:
"Simon, son of John, do you love me more than these others do?"
"Yes, my Master," he replied; "you know that I really love you."
"Then," Jesus said to him, "feed my lambs."
He asked him a second time:
"Simon, son of John, do you love me?" . . .
It grieved Peter that he had asked him the third time:
"Do you really love me?"
and he replied:
"Master, you know everything; you know that I really love you!"
"Then," Jesus said to him, "feed my sheep.
I tell you the plain truth: when you were young,
you used to put on your own belt and go where you wished;
but when you grow old, you will stretch out your arms
for someone else to gird you and carry you
where you have no wish to go."
He said this to signify the kind of death
by which he was to glorify God.
And having said this, he said to him: "Follow me." John 21:4-19

The apostles will be fishers of men

At the beginning of his teaching ministry in Galilee, Jesus
promised his apostles that he would one day make them fishers
of men. Mark 1:17. In this prophetic action Jesus assists the
apostles in catching a miraculous haul of fish. The number of
fish mentioned seems to be symbolic. St. Jerome notes that
Greek zoologists believed that there were 153 different kinds of
fish in the world. The apostles will, indeed, be fishers of every
kind of man the world over.

The meal on the beach has all the overtones of a "communion breakfast." Scripture scholars point out that St. John employs the same vocabulary to describe this event as he does to describe Christ's eucharistic promise in John 6.

Peter will lead the Church

Christ's threefold test of Peter recalls Peter's triple denial at the night of Christ's arrest. Peter's threefold reparation leads to his commission to shepherd the flock of Christ. The promise that Christ made earlier to Peter is now fulfilled. Matthew 16:18. Peter will also be like the Good Shepherd described in John 10:11. He will one day lay down his life for his flock.

BIBLE MESSAGE

Christ teaches us. Walking along the Sea of Galilee one day, Jesus saw Simon Peter and his brother Andrew casting for fish. Jesus said to them, "Come, follow me, and I will make you fishers of men." Mark 1:17. The two men immediately left their fishing nets and followed Christ.
Discuss: a) what it means to be fishers of men, b) the symbolism of the 153 fish, c) the significance of Peter's threefold test, d) the significance of the beach breakfast.

LITURGY & LIFE

1 Catholic action. In his role as Christ's vicar on earth, Pope Pius XI reminded Catholic laymen that they are privileged to take active part in the Church's apostolate of "fishing for men." "Catholic action," he said, "is the participation of the laity in the apostolate of the Church's hierarchy."
Discuss the meaning of: laity, hierarchy, and Catholic action. List ways that high-school students can engage in Catholic action. Name organizations existing in the school for this purpose.

2 Peter and the artists. Artists have depicted St. Peter in a variety of ways: 1) holding two (sometimes three) keys, 2) seated on a throne with his hand raised as though blessing or teaching, 3) drawing water from a rock with his staff (as Moses did in Exodus 17:6), and 4) with a rooster.

Explain what artists were trying to get across concerning Peter in each of the four ways mentioned.

DOCTRINAL POINTS

Catholic action

Catholic action is religion in action. It is the result of a living faith in God, a confident hope in the coming of God's kingdom, and the loyal love for Christ.

The high-school student who has accepted Christ and Christ's message will not rest until he has done all he can to share this message with others.

According to Pope Pius XI, the organization of Catholic action for high-school students is one of the most important duties of Catholic schools. The students' role in the great program is to learn thoroughly the principles of Christ's message, to study the application of those principles to their present and future lives, and to live and act according to those principles during their years at school. Thus it will be natural for them, when they have finished their formal education, to think and act in every arena of life according to the teaching of Christ.

Even during their school days students can carry out the work of Catholic action in their social dealings with others, in their homes, in their school studies, and in the school's extracurricular activities. Programs such as the Sodality, Apostleship of Prayer, Y.C.S., and Y.C.W. offer scope and opportunity for every alert student to engage in Catholic action.

Study questions

Discuss what is meant by: a) principles of Christ's message, and b) application of those principles to life. Give concrete examples how a high-school student can carry out the principles of Catholic action in his social dealings: a) in his home, b) in school, c) in his community, d) in his parish.

4 Christ ascends to his Father

Forty days after Easter, Jesus leads his disciples outside of the city to the Mount of Olives. There, after instructing them, he ascends to the Father. Let us see how the Bible records this.

In my former book, Theophilus,
I spoke of all that Jesus did and taught
from the beginning until the day on which he was taken up,
after giving instructions through the Holy Spirit
to the apostles whom he had chosen.
To them he showed himself alive after his passion,
giving many conclusive proofs,
appearing to them throughout forty days
and discussing matters pertaining to the kingdom of God.
Thus, for example, while eating with them,
he charged them not to depart from Jerusalem,
but to await what the Father had promised.
"This you have heard from me," he said,
"that while John baptized with water,
you shall be baptized with the Holy Spirit not many days hence."
    So, when they had come together they asked him,
"Lord, will you at this time restore the kingdom to Israel?"
    "It is not for you," he answered them, "to know the times
or the dates which the Father has fixed by his own authority;
but you shall receive power when the Holy Spirit come upon you,
and you shall be my witnesses in Jerusalem and in all Judea
and Samaria and even to the very ends of the earth."
    After he had said this, he was lifted up before their eyes,
and a cloud took him out of their sight.
While they were gazing up to the sky as he went,
at that moment two men stood beside them in white garments
and said, "Men of Galilee,
why do you stand looking up to the sky?
This Jesus who has been taken up from you
will come in the same way
as you have seen him going into the sky." Acts 1:1-11

Christ's ascension marks an end and a beginning

Christ's ascension is a visible sign. It serves two purposes: 1) it marks the end of Christ's post-resurrection teaching period on earth, and 2) it marks the beginning of Christ's glorious reign in heaven. Christ now leaves to prepare a place for his followers. "I . . . go for the very purpose of preparing a place for you." John 14:2. The preface of the Ascension Mass puts it beautifully. He was "taken up into Heaven . . . that He might make us sharers in His Godhead."

When all is ready Christ will come again. The name frequently given to Christ's final coming, the hour of which no man knows, is the Parousia. Christ himself referred to it in his reply to Annas. Quoting the Book of Daniel, he said, "You are going to see the Son of Man enthroned at the right hand of the Almighty and coming wrapt and in the clouds of the sky." Mark 14:62.

Christ is king of the universe

But while Christ's followers wait for his second coming, they are not to be idle. They are to carry the good news of Christ's death, resurrection, and ascension to all parts of the world. In the Old Testament days, Yahweh was the God of one people: Israel. Now Christ teaches his apostles by yet another sign that his Father wishes to give himself to all men. He wishes to be the God of all men.

The question about the kingdom, put by the apostles, shows that they still possess a confused concept about the nature of Christ's kingdom. After Pentecost, the Holy Spirit will clear this up. The apostles will learn that Christ no longer belongs to a single nation, nor is he identified with any political organization. The glorious Christ is the king of the universe.

BIBLE MESSAGE

Christ teaches us. The number forty is a symbolic number, frequently used to mark the end of one phase of God's plan and the beginning of another. It is also used to designate a period of preparation or waiting for an important event. Some other uses of this number are found in Genesis 7:4-12, Deuteronomy 9:7-18, and Numbers 14:33.

1 What phases of God's salvation plan begin and end with the forty-day period mentioned in Acts 1:3? 2 What name do we give to the final coming of Christ? 3 Between Christ's ascension and his final coming, what does Christ direct his apostles to do? 4 What does the question of the apostles concerning the kingdom indicate?

1 Paschal candle.   The paschal candle, symbol of Christ's visible presence on earth, is extinguished on Ascension Thursday. It marks the end of that post-resurrection period during which Christ appeared to his apostles confirming their faith and teaching them about the kingdom.

At what point in the Mass is the candle extinguished? When was the candle lit? Why do you think many Churches place this candle in the baptistry after the Ascension Mass?

2 Open sky.   On the Mount of Olives, at the place where tradition says our Lord ascended into heaven, St. Helen built a basilica. In order that the basilica might symbolize the event it honored, it was built open to the sky.

How would this symbolize the Ascension? Discuss how one might symbolize other mysteries of Christ's life by means of special architectural features or designs.

3 White garments.   After Christ had ascended, two figures appeared to the apostles. Like the men who appeared after Christ's resurrection (Luke 24:4), these men wore white garments. The color white frequently appears in the Bible as a symbol of what is heavenly. The Apocalypse describes saints "dressed in white garments." Apocalypse 3:4. The 24 elders are also "clothed in white robes." Apocalypse 4:4. In Daniel's vision, the Ancient One is dressed in "snow bright" robes. Daniel 7:9. Finally, when Christ was transfigured on the mountain, "his garments turned as white as light." Matthew 17:2.

Why does white naturally lend itself to symbolize what is heavenly? Discuss color symbolism in general. What is the liturgical symbolism of red, black, green, and violet?

4 Biblical clouds.   Jesus is described as being enveloped by a cloud as he ascends. The cloud is a classical biblical sign that both reveals and conceals the presence of God. A similar cloud appeared when Jesus was transfigured on the mountain. Luke 9:34. Some other examples occur in Exodus 19:9 (the cloud on Mt. Sinai), Exodus 33:9 (the cloud column that descended upon the desert meeting tent), and 3 Kings 8:10 (the cloud that filled the Temple of Solomon when it was dedicated).

Do you know of any other cases? Why would the cloud be a good sign of God's presence for the earth-bound Hebrews?

DOCTRINAL POINTS

Christ the King

On Christmas day in 1925, Pope Pius XI established the liturgical feast of Christ the King. At that time he pointed out that Christ's kingship over mankind is based upon a twofold right. Christ has: 1) a <u>natural</u> right because he is not only man but also God, and 2) an <u>acquired</u> right because he redeemed mankind from sin and Satan.

Natural right: God-man

Pope Pius XI says: "Christ has long been proclaimed King because of His preeminence over all creatures. Christ is said to reign in the <u>minds</u> of men because of the keenness of His intellect . . . and because He is Truth Itself and the source of all truth for all men.

"He reigns too in the <u>wills</u> of men, for His own human will was ever perfectly and completely obedient to the Will of the Father. Moreover by His grace and inspiration He so rules our free wills that they spring forward to the most noble endeavors.

"He reigns, too, in our <u>hearts</u> by His love 'which surpasses knowledge' (Eph. 3:19), while His mercy and kindness draw all men to Him; so that no one is loved so intensely and so universally as is Jesus Christ.

"To Christ as Man belong the title and power of King in strict reality. For it is only as Man that he may be said to have received from the Father 'power and glory and a kingdom' (Dan. 7: 13), since the Word is consubstantial with the Father and has all things in common with Him, and consequently has supreme and absolute dominion over all created things."

Acquired right: redeemer of mankind

Pope Pius XI continues: "Not only has He this natural right, but He has an acquired right as well, for He is our Redeemer and has purchased His subjects with His Blood. 'You were not redeemed with corruptible things, but with the precious Blood of Christ, as a lamb unspotted and undefiled' (1 Pet. 1:18-19). We are no longer our own property but Christ has bought us 'at a great price' (1 Cor. 6:20). Our very bodies are 'the members of Christ' (1 Cor. 6:15)."

Threefold power: legislative, judicial, executive

"Christ also possesses the threefold power of lordship. First we know from the testimony of Scripture that the dominion of our Redeemer is universal, and that He was not only given to us as Redeemer but also as Lawgiver, to whom obedience is due. The Gospels do not merely tell us that He made laws; they show Him to us in the very act of making them. He promises that those who keep His laws shall remain in His love (John 14:15; 15:10). When the Jews accused Him of breaking the Sabbath Law, He claimed judicial power which had been given Him by the Father. 'For neither does the Father judge any man but He has given all judgment to the Son' (John 5:22). The right of rewarding and punishing all living men is included in this power, for this right is inseparable from that of judging. He also holds executive power for all must obey His commands and none can escape the sanctions He imposes."

Christ must reign in each of us

Pope Pius XI concludes, saying: "The faithful by meditating on these truths will gain strength and courage to model their lives on the true Christian idea. If Christ has all power in heaven and on earth, if His dominion is over all men, since all have been purchased by His Blood, it is clear that all our faculties are under His sway.

"Christ must reign in our minds, which must assent firmly and submissively to all revealed truths and to all Christ's teaching. He must reign in our wills, which should bow in obedience to God's laws and precepts. He must reign in our hearts, which, turning aside from all natural desires, should love God above all things and cling to Him Alone." (Quas Primas, American Press translation)

Study questions

Discuss: 1) Christ's twofold right to kingship over all men and all nations, 2) Christ's threefold power of kingship, 3) how we ought to allow Christ to reign in our daily lives.

15

CHRIST SENDS HIS SPIRIT
UPON GOD'S NEW PEOPLE

1 Christ's mystical body, the Church, is born

After Christ visibly manifests his return to the Father, his
disciples return to Jerusalem. There they await the Holy Spirit,
whom Christ has promised to send them. For nine days they
pray and prepare. Then, on Pentecost Sunday, Christ's Holy
Spirit comes upon them. God's new people, the Church, is born.
Let us read how St. Luke records this great event in the Acts
of the Apostles.

When the day of Pentecost had come,
they were all together in one place.
Suddenly there came a sound in the sky,
as a violent wind blowing,
and it filled the whole house where they were staying.
And there appeared to them tongues like fire
which distributed themselves and settled on each of them.
They were all filled with the Holy Spirit
and began to speak in other tongues,
as the Holy Spirit prompted them to give utterance.

Now there were staying at Jerusalem devout men
of every nation under heaven.
When this sound was heard, a crowd of them
gathered and were bewildered,
because each one heard his own language spoken by the apostles.
Everybody was amazed and marveled, saying,
"Look, are not all those who are speaking Galileans?
How then does each of us hear his own native language?
Parthians and Medes, and Elamites, and inhabitants of
Mesopotamia, Judea and Cappadocia, Pontus and Asia,
Phrygia and Pamphylia, Egypt and the districts of
Lybia and Cyrene, and visitors from Rome,
Jews and Proselytes, Cretans and Arabians--
we hear them declaring in our own languages
the wonderful works of God." Acts 2:1-11

The Holy Spirit forms the disciples into Christ's body

The coming of the Holy Spirit coincides with the Jewish Feast
of Weeks, which occurs seven weeks after the Passover. The
Feast of Weeks was one of the three major Jewish feasts. The
Greek-speaking Jews called it Pentecost because it took place
on the fiftieth day after the Passover. The feast was a kind of
Jewish thanksgiving day for: 1) the yearly harvest, and 2) the
giving of the Sinai covenant. It was because of the feast that so
many foreign Jews had come to Jerusalem.

It is about nine o'clock in the morning when the sound of wind
is heard. The fire and noise recall the lightning and thunder that
accompanied the promulgation of the ten commandments at Mt.
Sinai. Now the Holy Spirit descends upon the disciples to pro-
mulgate a new law, not written on stone but on the hearts of men.
The words of the prophet Jeremia are realized. "The days are
coming . . . when I will make a new covenant with the house of
Israel and the house of Juda. . . . I will place my law within them,
and write it upon their hearts; I will be their God, and they shall
be my people." Jeremia 31:31-33.

Already in Old Testament times, the Holy Spirit had come
upon the prophets. But today the Holy Spirit comes in all his New
Testament fullness. The words of the prophet Joel are fulfilled.
"It shall happen in the last days, says God, that I will pour forth
my Spirit on all mankind." Acts 2:17.

By his coming, the Holy Spirit forms Christ's followers into
God's new chosen people. The old chosen people are baptized by

254

fire and the Holy Spirit into Christ's mystical body, the Church. The Old Pentecost, like the Old Covenant, is now crowned and fulfilled. "Today," says St. Augustine, "the Christian Church is born."

BIBLE MESSAGE

Christ teaches us.   Fire is frequently used in the Bible as a sign of God's presence. God assumed the shape of a "fiery torch" when he passed through the bleeding halves of animals at the time of his covenant with Abraham. Genesis 15:17. God spoke to Moses from "a fire flaming out of a bush." Exodus 3:2. God went before the Israelites in the form of "a column of fire" after they left Egypt. Exodus 13:21. God showed his glory through a "consuming fire" when he made his covenant with Israel at Mt. Sinai. Exodus 24:17.

1 Why is fire an apt sign of God's presence? 2 Discuss the relationship between: a) the old and new Pentecosts, b) the promulgation of the old and the new laws, and c) the coming of the Holy Spirit in the Old Testament and the New Testament.

LITURGY & LIFE

1 The New Testament crowns and fulfills the Old Testament. A famous window in the cathedral of Chartres shows four Old Testament prophets standing in a line, carrying on their shoulders the four evangelists of the New Testament. The prophet Isaia carries Matthew; Jeremia, Luke; Ezechiel, John; and Daniel, Mark. The story behind the window is that the artist wanted to show that: 1) the Old Testament is the support of the New Testament; and 2) the New Testament is the crown and fulfillment of the Old Testament.

How is the New Testament the crown and fulfillment of the Old? In what sense are the two Testaments a unified whole?

2 The Holy Spirit in art.   On the outside wall of Moreau Seminary at Notre Dame is a metal art piece by David Hayes, entitled "The Descent of the Holy Spirit." See the photograph on page 253.

Why is the design theme appropriate for a seminary? Why is each tongue of fire designed differently from every other one?

255

2 Christ's mystical body builds up

After the Holy Spirit descends to form the disciples into God's
new people, Peter and the rest of Christ's followers are filled
with light and strength. Let us read how the Bible records this.

Peter, presenting himself with the Eleven,
raised his voice and addressed them [the crowd]:
"Men of Judea and all you who reside in Jerusalem . . .
this is what was foretold by the prophet Joel:
   'It shall happen in the last days, says God,
   that I will pour forth my Spirit on all mankind;
   And your sons and daughters shall prophesy,
   and your young men shall see visions,
   and your old men shall dream dreams.
   And on my slaves too and my handmaids
   in those days will I pour forth my Spirit . . .
Men of Israel, hear these words.
Jesus of Nazareth was a man accredited to you by God
through miracles and wonders and signs,
which God did through him in your midst,
as you yourselves know.
When he was delivered up by the settled purpose
and foreknowledge of God, you crucified and slew him
by the hands of wicked men.
But God has raised him up
having put an end to the pangs of death,
because it was not possible that death should hold him. . . .
Therefore, exalted by the power of God,
and receiving from the Father the promised Holy Spirit,
he has poured forth that which you see and hear. . . .
Therefore, let all Israel know most assuredly
that God has made him both Lord and Christ--
this very Jesus whom you have crucified." Acts 2:14-36

The Holy Spirit enlightens and strengthens Christ's disciples

Before he suffered and died Christ told his disciples, "There is
still much I might say to you, but you are not strong enough to bear
it at present. But when he, the Spirit of truth, has come, he will
conduct you through the whole range of truth." John 16:12-13.
On Pentecost the Holy Spirit comes upon Christ's disciples
forming them into his mystical body, the Church. At the same time

the Holy Spirit confers upon Christ's apostles, special power to help teach and guide God's new people. The effect of the Holy Spirit's special gift of power is dramatically illustrated when Peter delivers his first sermon to the people. The Holy Spirit instructs Peter in the true meaning of Christ's words and gives to his words a special power to penetrate to the hearts of all.

Those who believe and are baptized the Holy Spirit incorporates into Christ's mystical body; and they begin to live with Christ's risen life.

The Holy Spirit dwells in Christ's disciples

But the Holy Spirit does even more. He begins to reside in each newly baptized Christian, sanctifying him and giving him special gifts and graces. And since the Father and Son are where the Holy Spirit is, each baptized Christian becomes a living temple of the most Holy Trinity. 1 Corinthians 3:16. Thus a second promise of Christ is fully realized. "Anyone who loves me will treasure my message and my Father will love him, and we shall visit him and make our home with him." John 14:23.

BIBLE MESSAGE

Christ teaches us.   When the apostles emerged from the upper room and began to preach without fear of the authorities, some of the crowd accused them of being drunk. Acts 2:13.

Discuss: a) what gave the apostles new courage, b) why the Holy Spirit conferred special graces upon the future leaders of the new Church, c) what role the Holy Spirit assumes in each person's life during and after baptism.

LITURGY & LIFE

1 Where God lives.   In a Reader's Digest article, an author tells how as a child he was captivated by the sight of a gypsy prayerfully peering into an old cistern. Curious to know what intrigued the old man, the little boy edged up to the cistern and tried to look over the ledge. With that the old gypsy scooped him up into his shovel-like hands and helped him over the edge.

"Do you know who lives down there?" he asked. The frightened boy shook his head.

"God lives there. Look!"

But the boy saw only his own reflection in the still water. "But that's me," said the boy.

"That's right," replied the old gypsy. "Now you know where God lives."

Was the gypsy right? Explain when and how God begins living in us. Explain how and when we begin living in God. How ought this to influence our daily actions?

DOCTRINAL POINTS

Gifts of the Holy Spirit

The prophet Isaia, referring to Christ, said: "The spirit of the Lord shall rest upon him: a spirit of wisdom and of understanding, a spirit of counsel and of strength, a spirit of knowledge and of fear of the Lord, and his delight shall be the fear of the Lord." Isaia 11:2-3.

We also receive these gifts

These gifts which our Lord had in a perfect way, the Holy Spirit, also, gives to us. We call them the seven gifts of the Holy Spirit.

The gift of wisdom helps us to see the world in its true light and to value more the things of heaven.

The gift of understanding helps us to grasp better the truths of our Catholic faith.

The gift of counsel helps us to see and pick what is most for God's glory and best for our salvation.

The gift of knowledge points out to us the path to follow and the dangers to avoid.

The gift of fortitude gives us courage and strength to combat obstacles and difficulties.

The gift of piety helps us to embrace all that is a part of God's service because of our confidence in him.

The gift of fear of the Lord helps us understand that to offend God is the greatest of all evils.

Study questions

One day after Pentecost, the apostles were dragged before the Sanhedrin and scourged for preaching about Christ. After the scourging was over, St. Luke says: "They departed from the presence of the Sanhedrin, rejoicing that they had been counted worthy to suffer disgrace for the name of Jesus. Nor did they for a single day cease teaching and preaching the good news about Jesus." Acts 5:41-42.

Discuss: a) what sustained the apostles and even caused them to rejoice in their suffering, b) each of the seven gifts of the Holy Spirit, showing by concrete examples how they help a high-school student.

During the Easter season we saw how:

CHRIST ROSE IN VICTORY

    1 Christ was glorified
    2 Christ gave his apostles new power
    3 Christ fulfilled his promise to Peter
    4 Christ ascended to his Father

CHRIST SENT HIS SPIRIT UPON GOD'S NEW PEOPLE

    1 Christ's mystical body, the Church, is born
    2 Christ's mystical body builds up

During the season after Pentecost we will see how:

CHRIST WILL RETURN

Christ's mystical body will share Christ's glory

We live and grow in Christ

LITURGY AFTER PENTECOST

We live and grow in Christ

Life and joy! These two themes run through the time after Pentecost and make it a wonderful time to be alive. During the Masses of this season we recall the great joy that is ours--we live and grow in Christ. We are members of Christ's mystical body and more closely united to him by our baptism than we are united to the members of our own family by birth.

It is no accident that the Church chose green as the liturgical color for this season. For green, more than any other color, gets across the idea of life and growth. Thus, the green vestments at each Sunday remind us of the life-giving presence of the Holy Spirit in the Church, God's new people. Christ's mystical body is growing and preparing for the day when it will blossom into the perfect people of God. Each Sunday and feast of the season considers one aspect of this mystery.

Trinity Sunday

Most fittingly, the first Sunday of the season after Pentecost is Trinity Sunday. This great feast commemorates the mystery of mysteries: the triune God. It recalls the further mystery: that mankind has been invited to share in the life of God. Christ prayed at the Last Supper, "All are to be one; just as you, Father, are in me and I am in you, so they, too, are to be one in us." John 17:21. Such is the dignity of our Christian calling. Such is the goal toward which the new people of God are striving.

Corpus Christi

Following Trinity Sunday is Corpus Christi. It underscores the fact that God made his invitation to us through his incarnate Son, Jesus Christ. It also reminds us that God's love and life comes to us through Christ, especially in the Mass and the Eucharist.

Sacred Heart

The third feast is that of the Sacred Heart. Its vivid imagery draws our attention to the motive of Christ's action in our life: love of his Father and of us. The feast invites us to return love to Christ and our Father by uniting ourselves more closely with Christ, our head, in the Mass and the sacraments.

Precious Blood

The fourth feast is that of the Precious Blood. It impresses upon us that Christ's love for us is a love of action, not just words. "No one can give a greater proof of his love than by laying down his life for his friends." John 15:13.

Christ the King

The final major feast is that of Christ the King. It highlights Christ our King. Christ is King because he redeemed man and because it is his Father's plan: "to gather all creation both in heaven and on earth under one head, Christ." Ephesians 1:10. The Feast of Christ the King invites us to pledge ourselves anew to follow our king and to prepare to play the role he has in mind for us to play in the spreading of his Father's kingdom.

The King's return

The last Sunday of this season brings the curtain down on the Church's liturgical year. It recalls the end of the world. At that hour, which no man knows, the kingdom will be complete. Then Christ will return gloriously to lead his kingdom to the Father.

Study questions

Discuss what aspect of God's mystery of love the following feasts highlight: Trinity Sunday, Corpus Christi, Sacred Heart, Precious Blood, Christ the King. What response does each feast invite us to make? Suggest a symbol to characterize each feast.

Christ's heroes

During the time after Pentecost the Church also reviews the lives of many hero-saints. She does this to teach us the impact of Christ's power on the lives of ordinary men and women who dared to be different for Christ. The Church urges us to model our lives after these heroes and to ask them to intercede that we, too, may be as loyal to Christ as they were.

Heading the list of these feasts is Our Lady's Assumption. On this day we recall and relive the hour of Mary's triumph: her bodily assumption into heaven, where she now reigns as queen.

Other important feasts during this time are those of the apostles, many popes, and a host of martyr-heroes.

The year closes with two special feasts: All Saints and All Souls. On All Saints we salute the Church triumphant--God's heroes in glory. On All Souls we pray for the Church suffering-- those members of Christ's mystical body still in purgatory. These friends of God have fought the good fight and are now awaiting the day when they will join the rest of the saints and Christ in heaven.

Study questions

Make a list of some of the more important saints whose feasts are celebrated during the time after Pentecost. List a few of your favorite saints, telling why you prefer them.

16

CHRIST WILL RETURN

Christ's mystical body will share Christ's glory

The last book of the Bible is called the Apocalypse. The book was written to comfort the early Christians who were being persecuted at the time. It looks ahead to the last days of the world, when Christ will return to lead his mystical body in glory to his Father in heaven. There it will share his risen glory forever. Let us read the introduction to the Apocalypse.

A revelation received from Jesus Christ
which God gave him to reveal to his servants.
These revelations deal with what must soon take place.
He made them known by sending his angel to his servant John,
who attests that whatever he perceived is the word of God
and the testimony of Jesus Christ.
Blessed is he who reads in public the words of this prophecy,
and blessed are those who hear them
and observe what is written here, for the time is near.
John to the seven congregations that are in Asia.
Grace be to you and peace from him whose name is

"He is, " "He was, " and "He is coming, " and
from the seven Spirits who are before his throne,
and from Jesus Christ, the trustworthy witness,
the first to rise from the dead,
and the sovereign of the kings of the earth.
To him who loves us and has freed us from our sins
through his own blood and has made us a kingdom,
priests for his God and Father,
belong glory and power for ever and ever. Amen.
　　Take note. He is coming amid the clouds,
and every eye will see him, even of those who pierced him.
And all the tribes of the earth will lament over him.
"Yes, Amen. I am the Alpha and the Omega, "
says the Lord God, "whose name is, 'He is, ' and 'He was'
and 'He is coming, ' the Almighty." Apocalypse 1:1-8

The Apocalypse assures Christ's members of victory

The Apocalypse describes in symbolic language how Christ's mystical body, God's kingdom on earth, will continue to grow to completion in spite of persecution and obstacles. It tells how Christ will come on the last day to lead the faithful to his Father.

The Apocalypse was written by St. John around A.D. 96 from Patmos (an island off Greece), where he was imprisoned for his faith. John addressed his letter to "seven congregations, " a symbolic name for the "whole Church" (seven is a symbolic number meaning "fullness").

John writes in heavy oriental imagery, which is meaningless to his persecutors but filled with rich significance for the persecuted Christians. Much of John's imagery is drawn from the Old Testament prophets, especially Ezechiel.

The name scholars give to the special literary form of writing used by St. John is "apocalyptic": that is, a mysterious and symbolic writing designed to comfort and encourage those in persecution and struggle. John's message is this. As Christ overcame the world by his passion and resurrection, so Christ's mystical body, the Church, will triumph in this time of persecution and struggle.

The Apocalypse is a book for our time

The Apocalypse is a book of special importance and significance for us today. Clearly, we are not suffering persecution by

the sword. Our persecution is more subtle. It is the day to day
struggle to win the world to Christ. To persevere in this struggle we need encouragement and assurance of victory. The Book of
the Apocalypse does just this. It reminds us that Christ has tri-
umphed over the forces of evil. It goes on to assure us that because we are members of Christ's mystical body, we will share
in Christ's victory. We need only keep in contact with and follow
Christ, our head and king. This is achieved, above all, by Mass,
the sacraments, prayer, and Catholic action.

By our efforts we will achieve our own salvation and help to
bring to fulfillment Christ's kingdom on earth. We will hasten the
day when Christ will come again and lead his mystical body in
triumph to his Father in heaven.

BIBLE MESSAGE

Christ teaches us.   The word apocalypse is a Greek word
meaning "revelation."

Discuss: a) the purpose, authorship, and literary form of the
Apocalypse, b) what important message the Apocalypse contains
for high-school students today.

LITURGY & LIFE

1 Our battle.   Here is part of an article from the French
Communist paper, Paix et Liberté.

"The Gospel is a much more powerful weapon for the renovation of society than our Marxist view of the world. Yet it is
we who shall conquer you in the end. . . . Of our salaries and
wages we keep only what is absolutely necessary and the rest
we give up for the propaganda purposes.

"To this same propaganda we also devote our leisure time
and part of our vacation. . . . How can anyone believe in the all-
surpassing value of this Gospel if you do not practice it, if you
do not spread it, if you sacrifice neither your time nor your
money for that purpose?"

Why is the Gospel a more powerful weapon for the renovation
of society? Explain what we mean when we pray in the Our Father,
"thy kingdom come." What can a high-school student do to help
bring about God's kingdom?

2 Our king.   A Christian general was brought prisoner before Mohamet II and given his choice between death and renouncing
his faith. His answer was swift and to the point. Baring his chest,
all covered with battle scars, he said, "What, must I receive a
thousand wounds for an earthly king and fear to die for the King
of Heaven?"

How does Christ differ from an earthly king? How does his
kingdom differ from earthly kingdoms? Why are men willing to
die for Christ the King?

STUDY INDEX

Abraham, 29, 67 ff., 89, 104,
  139, 242
Adam. See Man
Amos, 31, 115
Angels
  creation of, 169
  fall of, 169
  role of, 169-70
  in art, 170
Apostles
  call of, 198 ff.
  role of, 200-201, 245
  formation of, 199 ff., 203, 211,
    235, 240, 245, 256 ff.
  ministry of, 256, 259
Apostolate, 1, 117, 246-47, 267 ff.
Ascension, 9, 33, 238, 248 ff.

Baptism
  foreshadowed, 69, 82

preparation for, 188
incorporation into Christ,
  104, 190, 236, 262
membership in God's king-
  dom, 189-93, 257
participation in Christ's
  kingship and priesthood,
  95
substitutions for, 191-92
and faith, 75, 191
of Christ, 6, 160
in art, 6, 188
Bible, 21 ff.
  books of, 26, 27, 96
  how to read, 43 ff., 88
  reverence for, 24
  authorship, 22, 27, 45, 81
  inspiration, 22, 25 ff.
  composition and interpretation,
    22 ff., 27, 39 ff., 43-45, 49,

Prayer
  mental, 5, 42
  Christ's teaching on, 196, 219
  power of, 121
  Psalms 103, 151
Presentation. See Christ
Promised land, 90 ff.
Prophets
  vocation of, 31, 113 ff.
  of northern kingdom, 114 ff.
  of southern kingdom, 119 ff.
  See also individual names,
    e.g., Isaia
Psalms
  in liturgy, 102
  division of, 101-102
  as Wisdom literature, 27, 96
  as prayer, 15, 16, 101-102, 151
Purification, 143, 146
Public life, 156 ff.

Redemption. See Salvation
Resurrection
  key mystery of salvation, 175-76
  foretold by Christ, 202 ff.
  achieved by Christ, 235 ff.
  triple aspect of, 238
  Christian pasch, 174-76
  victory over Satan, 171
  in art, 184
Revelation
  nature of, 25-26
  private, 26
  public, 26
Roboam, 114, 118

Sacrifice. See Mass
Saints
  and miracles, 180
  feasts, 265
Sacraments
  actions of Christ, 14 ff.
  See Baptism, Confession, Eucha-
    rist

Salvation
  promise of, 63
  nature of, 66
  realized in Christ, 202 ff.
  continued in Church, 12 ff.,
    64-65
  outside the Church, 192
  in art, 64-65
  history of, 22, 24, 29 ff.,
    33-34
Samuel, 92, 94, 129
Samson, 92
Saul, 92, 94, 99
Simeon, 141 ff.
Solomon, 31, 113, 140
Salvation history. See Salvation
Satan, 57, 166-70, 178
Sin
  nature of, 107
  occasion of, 61
  actual, 62
  mortal, 62
  venial, 62
  original, 53
  effects of, 56 ff.
  Adam, 53 ff.
  Cain, 59
  Tower of Babel, 59
  David, 105-107
Synagogue service
  nature of, 150, 151
  relation to Mass, 18 ff.

Temple
  building of, 104
  destruction of, 122, 130
  rebuilding and rededication
    of, 127, 130
  foreshadows Christ's body,
    104
  Christ replaces, 148-49
  mystical body, 148

276

Temptation
  nature of, 53, 55
  relation to sin, 53, 55
  of Christ in desert, 165 ff.
Types 72-73
  See also Christ and Typology

Virtues
  infused theological, 125
  received in baptism, 195
  See also Faith, Hope, and
    Charity

Vocation
  Abraham, 67
  David, 94
  Israel, 87
  Our 95, 112, 137, 195

Worship. See Liturgy

Zacharia, 206